The ASTD Trainer's Sourcebook: SALES

The ASTD Trainer's Sourcebook: SALES

By Herbert R. Miller

McGraw-Hill, Inc.

New York San Francisco Washington D.C. Auckland Bogotá
Caracas Lisbon London Madrid Mexico City Milan
Montreal New Delhi San Juan Singapore
Sydney Tokyo Toronto

Library of Congress Catalog Card Number: 95-07644-7

ISBN 0-07-053436-5

Sourcebook Team:

Co-Publishers:	Phil Ruppel, McGraw-Hill Business & Professional Division
	Nancy Olson, American Society for Training and Development
Acquisitions Editor:	Richard Narramore, McGraw-Hill Business & Professional Division
Series Advisor:	Richard L. Roe
Managing Editor:	Anne Coyle
Editor:	Charlene Ables
Image Formatting:	Claire Condra Arias, Ellipsys International Publications, Inc.

Contents

Preface

I'd like to tell you how this series came about. As a long-time editor and resource person at University Associates/Pfeiffer & Company, I was frequently asked by trainers, facilitators, consultants, and instructors to provide them with training designs on a variety of topics. These customers wanted one-hour, half-day, and full-day programs on such topics as team-building, coaching, diversity, supervision, and sales. Along with the training designs, they required facilitator notes, participant handouts, flipchart ideas, games, activities, structured experiences, overhead transparencies, and instruments. But, that wasn't all. They wanted to be able to reproduce, customize, and adapt these materials to their particular needs—at no cost!

Later, as an independent editor, I shared these needs with Nancy Olson, the publisher at the American Society for Training and Development. Nancy mentioned that ASTD received many similar calls from facilitators who were looking for a basic library of reproducible training materials. Many of the classic training volumes, such as Jones and Pfeiffer's *Handbook of Structured Experiences* and Newstrom and Scannell's *Games Trainers Play* provided a variety of useful activities. However, they lacked training designs, handouts, overheads, and instruments—and, most importantly, they tended to be organized by method rather than by topic. You can guess the rest of the story: Welcome to *The ASTD Trainer's Sourcebook*.

This sourcebook is part of an open-ended series that covers the training topics most often found in many organizations. Instead of locking you into a prescribed "workbook mentality," this sourcebook will free you from having to buy more workbooks each time you present training. This volume contains everything you need—background information on the topic, facilitator notes, training designs, participant handouts, activities, instruments, flipcharts, overheads, and resources—and it's all reproducible! We welcome you to adapt it to your particular needs. Please photocopy . . . edit . . . add your name . . . add your client's name. Please don't tell us . . . it isn't necessary! Enjoy.

Richard L. Roe
ASTD Sourcebook Series Advisor

"KNOWLEDGE AND HUMAN POWER ARE SYNONYMOUS"

*K*nowledge generates human performance. It doesn't take a famous quote or the picture of a tree to know that. But full potential requires the proper elements. Your professional growth can thrive, as a member of the American Society for Training and Development.

As an ASTD member you will get:

Information on the forefront of practice and technology

Access to colleagues around the world for idea-sharing

Opportunity to contribute to the advancement of your profession

through...international conferences and expositions...best practices...electronic resources and networking...benchmarking publications...personalized research assistance...and much more.

Join ASTD now...and become part of a worldwide association of nearly 58,000 leaders in the field of workplace learning and performance.

**Call 703.683.8100. Or fax 703.683.1523
Mention Priority Code: MH5A
TDD: 703.683.4323**

 ASTD
AMERICAN SOCIETY
FOR TRAINING AND
DEVELOPMENT

*Delivering Performance
in a Changing World*

Chapter One:

Introduction

Welcome to *The ASTD Trainer's Sourcebook: Sales*—your one-stop reference for basic sales training materials. You can use these materials "as is" or customize them in any way you wish to meet your specific needs.

This chapter serves three purposes.
- First, it provides an opportunity to set forth a few biases about sales and sales training—biases that influenced the design of this book.
- Second, it provides a description of the contents of the book and how the various parts relate to one another.
- Third, in the process of describing the contents, we set the stage for what you need to do to get ready to conduct the sessions contained in this book.

So, what are we waiting for?

Sales Training: Our Biases

First of all, there are three ingredients in successful sales training.
- Substance
- Relevance
- Energy

Secondly, there are three broad content areas that should be covered to one degree or another in successful sales training workshops.
- Communications skills
- Sales skills
- A context within which to explore communications and sales skills—namely, a sales process

Let's explore these ingredients and the content areas in more detail.

The Ingredients for Success

By "substance," we mean the knowledge, the skills, the tools that are transferred to participants in a sales training session. Substance is the major contribution that this book will make to your success in sales training. Collected between the covers of this book you will find all sorts of content and techniques that have been gathered over the years—all of which are substance that has contributed to successful training sessions in a broad range of topic areas, in locations pretty well scattered around the globe.

"Relevance" is a straightforward concept that we will not belabor. We are all keenly aware that the more clearly we are able to show participants the relationship between what *we talk about* in our sales training sessions and what *they must do* every minute of every day on the job, the more successful and lasting the effects of the training. It is difficult to build that level of relevance into a book such as this. The things that make sales training truly relevant to a person selling computer networks are no doubt quite different to those that make such training relevant to a salesperson who sells mobile homes or small appliances. What we have done, however, is to build into these materials the *opportunity* for you to add the information, comments, emphases, and twists that you know will enhance the relevance of sales training in your environment.

Finally, we have "energy."
- The style and enthusiasm that you bring to the front of the room
- The level of involvement that you *draw out of* participants
- The level of enthusiasm you *kindle among* the participants
- The way you and the participants interact to make the most of the substance and relevance of your sales training sessions

Point-blank, this book *will not* turn you into another Jack Carew, Dale Carnegie, Tony Robbins, or Zig Ziglar. This book will, however, arm you with the confidence that comes from knowing that you have prepared yourself thoroughly for your facilitation role—allowing you to focus your "facilitator" energies on *delivering* substance and relevance, and on *creating* the "magic" of a truly successful sales training session. The sort of personal and situation-specific magic that nobody can package in a book, box, or can.

The Content for Success

In this book, we focus on key communications and sales skills, set in the context of a sales process that is as applicable to "one-call close" situations as it is to more complex multi-call sales cycles. This sales process has four phases.

- Earn the right
- Understand the need
- Make a recommendation
- Complete the sale

The basic philosophy underlying this sales process and our approach to it is quite simple.

- A salesperson is there to sell.
- Customers are there because they *really* want to and/or need to buy.
- The salesperson does *not* have a right granted by a higher-being to pursue the sale—*he or she must earn it.*

Given this philosophy and the context of our sales process, we focus on four important sales skills and five basic communications skills in this book.

- Building rapport
- Qualifying opportunities
- Describing benefits
- Handling obstacles

- Listening
- Verifying
- Observing
- Questioning
- Explaining

For basic background information on the sales process and the skills we will cover, see the participant handout titled "Effective Selling" (pages 213 through 219). Additional background on these skills is included in other parts of the chapter titled "Participant Handouts."

What's In This Book

There are three aspects involved in getting organized for sales training workshops. The first is planning—characterized by thinking and other intellectual labor. The second involves getting everything ready—facilities, materials, supplies, etc. This is a combination of manual labor and some basic, easily structured decision making. The third aspect involves ensuring yourself that you are ready—preparing yourself and rehearsing so that you don't mess up all the hard work you put in on the first two aspects.

The next two chapters of this book focus mainly on the first two aspects of getting organized—with a few words on the third.

- *Planning the Workshop*

    Tips for ensuring that the training meets the needs of your audience, customizing materials to more accurately target those needs, etc. Also, a few tips on ensuring that you are ready.

- *Getting Everything Ready*

    Checklist-driven guidance for making sure that materials and supplies are ready when and where you need them, arranging facilities, getting materials duplicated, etc.

The next three chapters cover the training activities themselves— complete facilitator's notes for the three events that constitute a complete sales-training program addressing the communications skills, sales skills, and sales process mentioned previously.

- *A One-Hour Sales Seminar*

    A complete training plan for a one-hour seminar

- *A Half-Day Communications Workshop*

    A complete training plan for a half-day workshop stressing communications skills in the context of the sales process

- *A One-Day Sales Workshop*

    A complete training plan for a one-day workshop stressing sales skills in the context of the sales process, and reinforcing the use of effective communications skills

These training plans are structured to work together to make up a comprehensive sales workshop. However, as indicated in the next chapter, they are easily separated if need be.

The final chapters contain the resources and materials on which the seminar and workshops are based.

- *Participant Handouts*

    A collection of content-focused handouts that provide the background for the topics covered in the sessions. These handouts also provide an enduring reference for workshop participants—as well as words that go with the "music" that we have provided for you in the training plan chapters.

- *Learning Activities*

    A collection of activities, including necessary instructions and activity-focused handouts that provide a foundation for the level of active participant involvement that is key to the success of your sessions.

    A special series of activities, "Targeting Your Sales Efforts," provides opportunities for participants to apply workshop lessons to their own work, thus contributing to the "relevance ingredient" in your sales workshops.

- *Assessments*

    A short collection of simple assessments. Applied and discussed properly, these assessments help set the stage for ongoing training—and, more importantly, for self-improvement activities that participants can undertake once they leave the sessions.

- *Overhead Transparencies*

    A collection of overhead transparency masters specifically designed for use within each of the three sessions. These provide a core set that you can enhance with other overheads, as required to meet your particular needs.

- *Prepared Flipcharts*

Good grief! Prepared flipcharts? This guy must be compulsive beyond belief!

    A collection of flipchart masters designed to support the three sessions. Prepared flipcharts are a great way to provide structure to your workshops and assure that key points are recorded. Plus, they save time and enhance the appearance of professionalism with which you approach your facilitation work.

That's the content of the book. Now, it's time to move on to the topic of preparing to use these materials in your own sales training sessions.

Chapter Two

Planning the Workshop

In the realm of thinking and other mainly intellectual labor, we will discuss four tasks involved in preparing for the sales seminar and workshops.

- Familiarize yourself with the content of this book.
- Define the particular needs for sales training within your organization.
- Adjust these materials to fit your needs, as required.
- Organize the sessions.

This chapter contains some general suggestions and comments to help you with those tasks. In addition, we will include a few tips on assuring that you are ready for the sessions. In the next chapter, we will turn our attention to the part of the preparation job that involves the combination of manual labor and basic structured decision making.

Familiarizing Yourself With This Book

In order to complete the remaining tasks outlined in this chapter, you need to become familiar with this book and the materials with which you will be working. Here is a suggested approach.

- Review the "Participant Handouts" chapter to familiarize yourself with the content of the workshop. This material will give you a good "feel" for our approach to sales training in these sessions. You will also begin to see some of the activities that have been incorporated in the form of short exercises.
- Review the "Learning Activities" chapter to see the range of individual and group activities that are built into the sessions. Some of these learning activities also contain additional content in the form of critique sheets.
- Review the "Assessments" chapter, mainly to see what's there.
- Review the "Overhead Transparencies" and "Prepared Flipcharts" chapters to see the kinds of support that we use to structure the flow of the workshop.

Having done that, move toward the front of the book and review the three "training plan" chapters to see how the three designs, one seminar and two workshops, are structured and how they can work together to create a truly outstanding sales training program.

Navigating the Training Plans

The training plans are the heart of each of the seminar and workshop sessions—the glue that draws and holds everything else together. These training plans are set out in detail on a module-by-module basis, with an agenda, statements of purpose, and objectives for each module. We have attempted to make these training plans as easy to use and as complete as possible. A sample is shown on the facing page, with annotations explained below—and icons "translated" on page 10.

A) Each section within a module has a heading that includes a statement of purpose for the section and suggested timing.

B) Within each section, you will find one or more major activities. Each is marked by an icon and a descriptive heading.

C) Additionally, you will find a number of supporting activities— each marked with an icon and explained with a suggested action.

D) Suggested actions are shown in conjunction with supporting activities—in *italics* with the appropriate action verb in **BOLD**.

E) Suggested comments accompany many of the suggested actions. While these comments are fully "scripted," *it is not intended that you "parrot" these remarks*—but rather paraphrase the key thoughts in a way that is meaningful to you and the participants.

F) At appropriate points, you will also find places to make notes about comments that you should make that are germane to the group with which you are working.

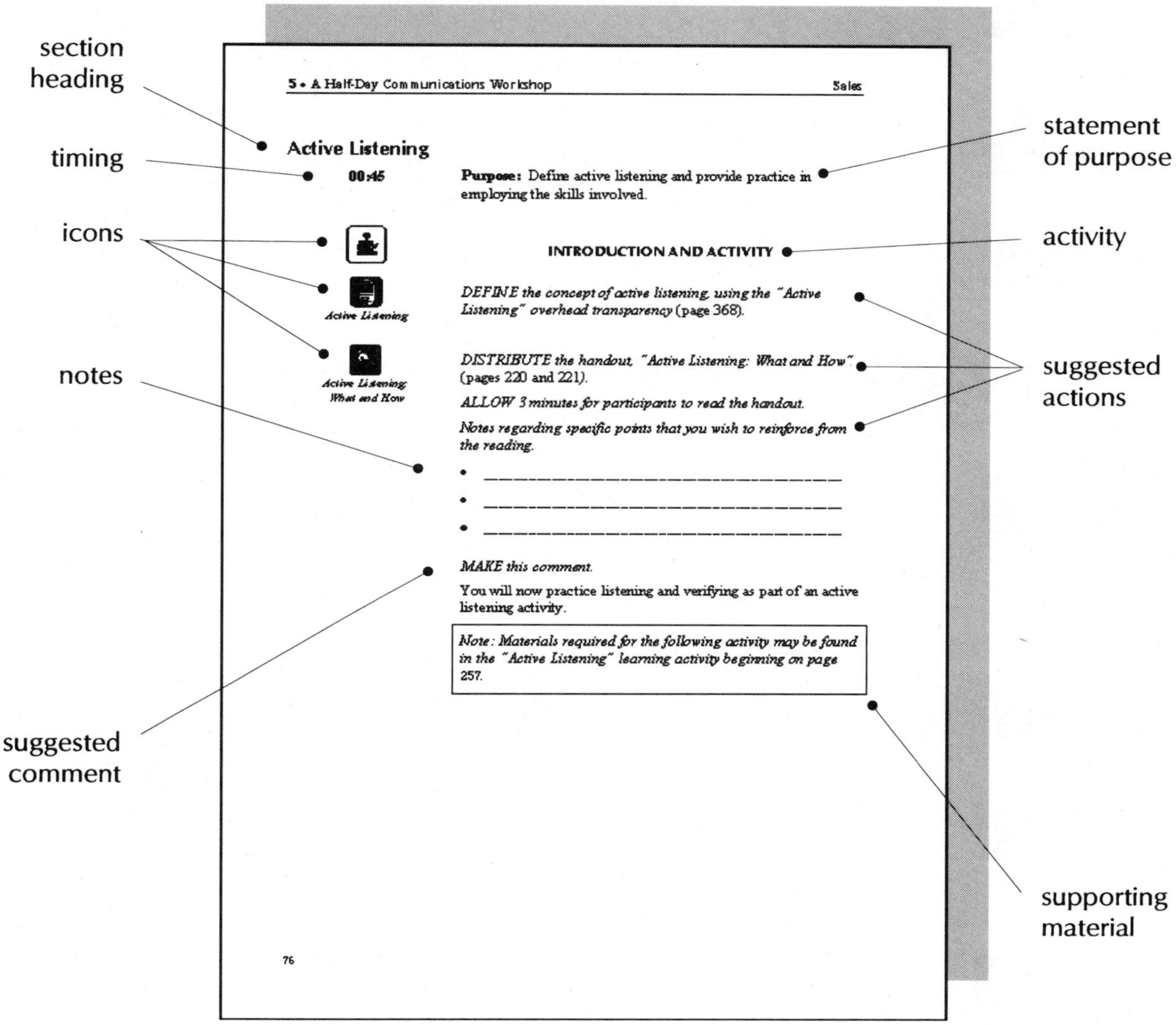
section heading
timing
icons
notes
suggested comment
statement of purpose
activity
suggested actions
supporting material
5 • A Half-Day Communications Workshop
Sales
Active Listening
00:45
Purpose: Define active listening and provide practice in employing the skills involved.
INTRODUCTION AND ACTIVITY
Active Listening
Active Listening: What and How
DEFINE the concept of active listening, using the "Active Listening" overhead transparency (page 368).
DISTRIBUTE the handout, "Active Listening: What and How" (pages 220 and 221).
ALLOW 3 minutes for participants to read the handout.
Notes regarding specific points that you wish to reinforce from the reading.
MAKE this comment.
You will now practice listening and verifying as part of an active listening activity.
Note: Materials required for the following activity may be found in the "Active Listening" learning activity beginning on page 257.
76

Understanding the Icons

These are the icons that are used to mark *major* activities.

- Activities that feature *facilitator commentary*. In these activities, you—as facilitator—present information that will be key to subsequent workshop activities.

- Activities carried out in *table groups*. You assign participants to small groups to complete the activity at hand.

- And . . . activities completed on an *individual* basis.

- Activities that revolve around *group discussion*. Such activities typically follow major exercises on which participants have worked individually or in groups.

- Finally, activities that are part of the special "Targeting Your Sales Efforts" series. As noted in the introductory chapter, these activities direct participants to develop materials that will be useful to them when they return to their jobs.

These are the icons that are used to mark *supporting* activities.

- An overhead transparency is to be shown. The title of the overhead transparency is shown beneath the icon and, additionally, is referenced in the text accompanying the icon.

- A participant handout, part or all of a learning activity, or an assessment is to be handed out. As with the previous icon, the name of the item to be handed out is shown with the icon and in the accompanying text.

- A question is to be asked. Wording for the question is provided, as are suggested answers when appropriate.

- A flipchart is to be used. If the flipchart is one of the "prepared flipcharts" recommended for the workshop, its title appears with the icon and in the accompanying text.

- And . . . a flipchart is to be posted. The name of the flipchart(s) and the area in which it is to be posted are included in the accompanying text. ("Flipchart areas" are discussed in the "Prepared Flipcharts" chapter, page 385.)

Now that we've set the stage for familiarizing you with this book, let's move on to the task of defining your sales training needs.

Defining Your Sales Training Needs

This task is essentially a needs assessment that can be either as simple and informal or as complex and formal as you wish to make it. We are not going to discuss the "ins and outs" of conducting needs assessments, but will simply observe that there are a number of sources from which you can draw to gather the "needs" information you require. These sources include:

- Your own knowledge and awareness of the sales training situation in your organization
- Sales management
- The sales training population
- The customer base with which your salespeople work

Having gathered the information you require, you are in a position to move forward and shape these sales training sessions to meet your specific needs.

Without regard to how you approach this task, there is one item that must come out of your assessment—namely, a description of the "typical sales situation" that will provide the content for the "Typical Sales Situations" flipchart (page 393), and that will be the foundation of many participant activities and discussions. Consider describing the sales situation in terms of the nature of both the sales interaction and the sales process.

The sales interaction

- Where does it occur?
- How long does it last?
- Is it formal? Informal?
- And so on . . .

The sales process

- Is it short? Long?
- How many interactions or "calls" are typically involved?
- How many people are involved?
- And so on . . .

Need to stimulate thinking about sales training needs?

✓ Select a few of the assessments, lists of tips, and critique sheets that address suspected "hot buttons" in your sales training area, and use them as guides in interviews and other data gathering activities.

✓ Use the various assessments, lists of tips, and critique sheets as a source of ideas for constructing various data gathering instruments—questionnaires, interview guides, etc.

✓ Conduct the one-hour sales briefing to familiarize management with the training sessions, focusing both on *what* skills are covered during the sessions as well as *how*.

Adjusting the Materials to Fit

Let's talk about some of the things that you can do to customize these materials to fit your own needs. Being mindful of our discussion of the ingredients in successful sales training, you need to do a minimum amount of customization to assure that you address the "relevance" issue.

- Local "color"—examples, background, etc.
- Topics to be emphasized or de-emphasized

In addition, you will need to adjust session timings to fit constraints such as participant schedules, blocks of time ordinarily allocated to training, etc. Beyond that, you can do as much or as little customization as you wish to in order to prepare for these sessions.

Adding Local "Color"

It is imperative that you prepare yourself to include local examples and other background information to assure that the sessions are as relevant as possible for participants. To that end, we have provided spaces throughout the training plans for you to make notes of such information. If you run out of space or wish to add some local color at a point where we neglected to provide a space, . . . well, aren't we glad someone invented margins. ☺

Activities are another good place to add local color. There are two places where it is very easy to do, and well worth some thought.

- The "importance of communications" demonstration—where you can substitute a customer statement that might be more familiar to your participants. (See pages 56 and 57.)
- The "active listening" activity—where you have the option of defining the discussion topic for the exercise, rather than using the default. (See page 76 or 257.)

> Want to put in some more effort into local color? The two communications demonstrations and two role plays that we use are based on a common situation—the sale of a coffee maker.
>
> ✓ Devise a new sales situation featuring a product that is directly relevant to your situation.
>
> ✓ Then rewrite the various salesperson and customer handouts in those activities to fit this new situation.
>
> This is a lot more work—but the effort could be worthwhile if it significantly enhances the relevance and effectiveness of your sessions.

Adjusting Emphasis

As a part of assessing sales training needs in your organization, you will probably discover that the skills covered in the workshop fall into one or another of these categories.

- Participants need some work, perhaps at the level of skill enhancement.
- Participants are very strong and need little, if any, work.
- Participants are very weak, and need a great deal of work.
- The skill itself is not especially important in the participants' typical sales situation.

Such information provides the basis for looking at and adjusting the emphasis on various topics in the workshops—leave well enough alone, add emphasis here, reduce it there, perhaps eliminate a topic altogether.

Integrating Your Own Materials

An excellent way to adjust emphasis and ensure a high level of relevance in this sales training is to select specific training materials that you currently use and then integrate them into these sessions where appropriate.

- Use your materials in addition to those provided here.
- Substitute your materials for certain of the items included here.
- Blend your materials with those in this book, creating a more detailed handout, an enhanced learning activity, etc.

Selecting From These Materials

A little quick arithmetic performed on the half-day and one-day agendas[1] in this book will reveal that there is more than can be accommodated comfortably in your traditional half-day and one-day training sessions. Unless you have flexibility in your training schedules, this means pruning a bit here and a tad there.

As luck would have it, we intentionally built in a few extras here and there—under the assumption that it's always easier to cut a few things rather than add things or do a quick soft-shoe to get you through to five o'clock. Our suggestions:

- Be selective about the assessments that you use. They're important, but you don't wish to assess the daylights out of people—and they run about ten minutes each.
- Eliminate a couple of the "Targeting Your Sales Efforts" activities that you think are of marginal value. Don't get carried away here, though. These activities are important to the relevance issue.

While all the workshops were designed to work together, it is possible to run only one or two of them. For example, if you have reason to be more selective, there are alternatives open to you. Here are two examples.

- Perhaps you'd like to combine the one-hour seminar and the half-day communications workshop into a single event.
  - Use the training plan for the one-hour seminar (ending just before page 61) in place of pages 66 through 68.
  - Then complete the "Targeting Your Sales Efforts" section and continue with the remaining modules.
- Suppose your salespeople are known to be strong in communications skills. You'd like to omit the half-day communications workshop, and run the one-hour seminar followed a few days later by the one-day workshop.
  - Use the training plan for the one-hour seminar. However, replace the discussion of the communications workshop and agenda on page 61 with a discussion of the logistics and agenda for the sales workshop.
  - Complete the one-hour seminar with the "Targeting Your Sales Efforts" material from pages 72 and 73 of the half-day training plan.
  - Carry out the training plan for the one-day workshop essentially "as is"—and make the various start-of-module

---

[1] Miss Hess, my high school Latin teacher, is probably turning over in her grave. Alas, modern usage seems to favor this corrupt usage of the venerable Latin noun *agendum*.

reviews of communications skills general, rather than tying them specifically to events in the half-day workshop.

What to do with "leftovers" . . . always a problem! With a little assistance, the people who manage the sales activities of your participants could make good use of some of the materials that you leave out of the sales training sessions.

✓ Assessments (leftover and otherwise) might be useful in coaching situations.

✓ "Targeting Your Sales Efforts" activities, packaged with an appropriate handout or two, can form the basis for mini-training sessions incorporated into sales meetings.

Once you have thought through the way you will customize your sessions, you can focus on . . .

Establishing Your Agenda

You are now in a position to establish the agenda for your sales training sessions. You know what you are keeping, what you're emphasizing, what you might be adding or deleting. In combination with the time constraints within which you must work, you have all the information you need to finalize the agenda—a task for which we have provided a worksheet in the next chapter. (See page 23.)

Organizing the Sessions

At this point, you are beginning a transition into the logistics of getting ready—which is the business of the next chapter. However, there are a few tasks that qualify as intellectual labor and that need to be addressed before you can set the "getting ready" machinery into motion. Here are some of those tasks, not all of which might be relevant in your situation.

- Negotiating number of participants, number of sessions, time to be allocated for training, etc.
- Determining which people will be considered as potential participants in the sessions
- Establishing a procedure for announcing the sessions, enrolling participants, and following up on enrollment
- Identifying activities to ensure pre-workshop preparation and post-workshop follow-up for participants
- Preparing materials such as announcements, pre-workshop preparation packages, invitation letters, enrollment acknowledgments, etc.

If you have well-established processes for activities such as these, they will be fairly straightforward. If not, they will require more effort on your part. You will find a basic level of help for these tasks in the next chapter.

Thoughts About Participant Preparation and Follow-Up

There is little doubt that pre-workshop preparation activities and post-workshop follow-up activities can enhance the value of workshop experiences for participants. Orchestrating these activities and making them happen is quite another issue, however.

The training plans in this book have some built-in features that can provide the basis for basic preparation and follow-up—if you are in an environment where the required mechanics can be put into place. Here are a few suggestions.

- "Sales: A Quick Skills Assessment" (page 333) can be the basis for a simple pre-workshop preparation activity. Rather than having participants complete it during the one-hour seminar (as indicated on page 54), provide the assessment to participants' managers. Ask participants to complete the assessment and then discuss it with their managers, resulting in a preliminary identification of workshop expectations.
- As a simple follow-up activity after the workshops, then, have participants meet with their managers and discuss the workshop in the context of that assessment and the expectations identified—focusing on "what's next" for the participants' post-workshop professional development.

Here are two additional follow-up suggestions—in addition to our earlier suggestions for using "leftovers" (page 15).

- Have participants review with their managers the "Targeting Your Sales Efforts" activities that were completed. Then establish a plan to ensure that the results of those learning activities are put to direct use in day-to-day work—and that both participants and managers monitor performance and identify areas for improvement.
- Have participants review with their managers the "action plans" created as a result of completing various assessments during the workshops. Then identify specific actions (self-improvement and otherwise) that participants can take, and establish a plan to turn these actions into improved performance.

Now, before moving on to the next chapter, let's talk briefly about being sure that *you* are ready for the sessions.

Ensuring Your Own Preparation

Once you have completed the tasks described in this chapter and the next, you should be quite well prepared to conduct each of the sessions described in this book. Here are a few tips that facilitators generally find helpful.

- Review your notes and the other information that you gathered during your planning for the sessions to ensure that sessions will adequately address the needs that you uncovered.

- Using your checklists, double-check with the people responsible for helping you to be sure everything is ready.

- Be sure you are familiar with the facility in which you will conduct the sessions. Know how you will organize the room, how you will organize your flipchart areas (see page 385)— and know whom to contact if a problem should develop with equipment, ventilation, etc.

- Be sure you know where you will put all of your materials, so you can put your hands on them effortlessly during the sessions.

- Be sure you are completely familiar with what you will do as facilitator from the beginning of a session to the end—your execution of the training plans in this book.

- Consider preparing your own "high-level" outline that is keyed to major activities, use of overhead transparencies and prepared flipcharts, and other landmark events. This is an excellent way to "personalize" the sessions and ensure that you are completely familiar with your role as a facilitator— and to avoid the unbecoming need to stand in front of your group and thrash furiously through the training plan to find your place.

Bottom line . . .

- Prepare thoroughly.
- Project a positive attitude.
- Stay aware of the content and flow of the session.
- Stay on topic.
- Stay on schedule.
- Maintain a high energy level.

Chapter Three:

Getting Everything Ready

Now for the "basic decision making and manual labor" activities. Here are the tasks that we have identified for this part of your preparation activity.

Put on the java . . . crunch time!! Work on those check lists! Check off those boxes!

- Finalize the agenda.
- Arrange for facilities.
- Initiate and monitor enrollment activities.
- Duplicate materials—participant handouts, learning activities, and assessments.
- Produce overhead transparencies.
- Produce prepared flipcharts.
- Ensure the availability of other supplies during the session.
- Organize catering and other support, as required.

To help with this work, we have created a series of tools and checklists.

- There is a master checklist that covers each of the tasks listed above. Use this to organize the "getting ready" effort and to monitor progress.
- There are specific tools and checklists for each of the tasks. If you are fortunate enough to be able to delegate some of these tasks, the tools become "work orders" for the lucky ones— giving you some reason to believe that all will be ready at the right place, at the right time. If you must do all these tasks yourself, . . . well, the tools and checklists should help you keep your sanity and maintain a semblance of organization.

About now, perhaps some of you are thinking "Isn't this checklist business getting just a bit carried away?" We don't think so— especially if you don't have permanent training facilities. Experience tells us that doing everything you can *at this point in time* to ensure that all will be organized and ready to go at "curtain time" makes a significant contribution to

Jeez! Is this guy . . .? Oh well . . . I suppose I can play along with him just this once.

- Your appearance of being "in control" and totally professional as a facilitator
- The smooth, hassle-free flow of your sessions
- Your ability to focus 99 percent of your concentration on the "energy" ingredient of successful workshops

If you are moving into the "getting ready" phase at this point, copy the remaining pages in the chapter, staple multi-page tools and checklists together so they don't get all mixed up, and then begin.

Getting Ready: Master Checklist

Use this checklist to finalize the specific tools and checklists that follow.

- If you are delegating the task, enter the name of the person responsible in the "By Whom?" column.
- Enter the date the task should be completed in the "By When?" column.

Then, use this list to track progress, as appropriate.

Note that certain of these checklists are "worst case," designed to optimize success when everything—facilities, supplies, etc.—must be organized from scratch. If you have permanent training facilities, some of these checklists may be unnecessary.

Task		By Whom?	By When?
Finalize the Agenda		*Me !*	*ASAP*
Enter session dates and times on the agendas.	❑		
Delete events that you will exclude.	❑		
Add new events.	❑		
Adjust elapsed times.	❑		
Identify times and duration for breaks, lunch.	❑		
Add "start" and "stop" times.	❑		
Arrange for Facilities			
Enter date by which arrangements must be complete on the checklist.	❑		
Enter "requirements" information.	❑		
• Day/date, times			
• Number of people (participants, observers, etc.)			
• Number of breakout rooms, if needed			
• Other requirements you may have			
Receive feedback regarding arrangements that have been made and key information about the facilities.	❑		

Task	By Whom?	By When?

Initiate and Monitor Enrollment

> *Note*: The way in which these activities are carried out is dependent on procedures that are in place in your organization. Therefore, these steps are presented at a general level.

Enter key dates for enrollment activities on the checklist. ❑

Draft session announcement. ❑

Draft enrollment acknowledgment. ❑

Duplicate Materials

Enter date by which duplicated materials are required. ❑

Enter any special duplication requirements (three-hole punched paper, two-sided copying, etc.). ❑

Delete items you will not use from the list. ❑

Add materials to be used that are not listed. ❑

Estimate the total number of participants and table groups for each session. ❑
- We suggest three participants per table group.

Based on those estimates, enter numbers on the lines provided in the "All" and "TG" (table groups) columns. (See pages 33 through 35.) ❑
- Consider increasing those numbers by 10 to 15 percent so you have spares.
- If others will attend the sessions (observers, etc.), increase numbers to accommodate them.

Produce Overhead Transparencies

Enter date by which transparencies are required. ❑

Enter any special packaging requirements (mounted, in sleeves, etc.). ❑

Delete transparencies you will not use from the list. ❑

Add transparencies to be used that are not listed. ❑

Task	By Whom?	By When?

Produce Prepared Flipcharts

Enter date by which flipcharts are required. ❑

Indicate production method to be used. ❑

Provide additional guidelines for preparing flipcharts, as appropriate. ❑

Provide "local" copy for flipcharts, as needed (for example, session logistics, etc.). ❑

Delete flipcharts you will not use from the list. ❑

Add flipcharts to be used that are not listed. ❑

Ensure Availability of Other Supplies

Enter number of people for each session. ❑

Enter dates of sessions. ❑

Delete items not required; add others if necessary. ❑

Enter information regarding when and where items ❑
are to be delivered.
- You may need to delay completing this checklist until facilities arrangements are complete.

Provide a list of names for place cards (if used). ❑
- Allow adequate time to complete place cards.

Organize Catering and Other Support

Enter date by which catering and other support is to ❑
be organized.

Enter the type of catering desired for each session. ❑

Enter the nature of other support required. ❑

Finalize the Agenda

In this section, you find module-by-module agendas for the seminar and the two workshops—based on the timings included in the training plan chapters. Use these agendas as a basis for finalizing the specific agendas you will use.

One-Hour Sales Seminar

Session day/date _____   *Begin at* _____   *End at* _____

                                        Break time _____

	Page	Timing[1]	Start	Stop
Introduction to Effective Selling		**01:05[2]**		
General Orientation	47	00:10		
Setting the Stage	49	00:15		
Establishing Expectations	54	00:10		
The Importance of Communications	56	00:15		
Summary	59	00:15		

---

[1] Suggested elapsed time.
[2] This is a facilitator's hour—similar to the well-known baker's dozen.

Half-Day Communications Workshop

Session day/date _____   *Begin at* _____ *End at* _____

Break times _____

		Page	Timing	Start	Stop
1	**Introduction to the Communications Workshop**		**00:35**		
	Review of the Seminar	66	00:10		
	Orientation to This Workshop	69	00:10		
	Targeting Your Sales Efforts	72	00:15		
2	**Listening and Verifying**		**00:55**		
	Introduction	75	00:05		
	Active Listening	76			
	• Introduction and Activity		00:35		
	• Individual Assessment		00:10		
	Summary	81	00:05		
3	**Observing and Questioning**		**01:05**		
	Introduction	83	00:05		
	The Observing Skill	84			
	• Commentary and Exercise		00:20		
	• Individual Assessment		00:10		
	Introduction to Questioning	87			
	• Group Discussion		00:10		
	• Individual "Target" Activity		00:15		
	Summary	91	00:05		

		Page	Timing	Start	Stop
4	**More on Questioning**		**01:45**		
	Introduction	93	00:05		
	Buying Objectives and Influences	94			
	• Group Discussion		00:15		
	• Individual "Target" Activity		00:15		
	More on Questioning	99			
	• Group Discussion		00:15		
	• Demonstration Role Play		00:25		
	• Individual "Target" Activity		00:15		
	• Individual Assessment		00:10		
	Summary	107	00:05		
5	**Explaining**		**01:00**		
	Introduction	110	00:05		
	The Explaining Skill	111			
	• Group Discussion		00:10		
	• Demonstration Role Play		00:25		
	• Individual Assessment		00:10		
	Summary	116	00:10		

One-Day Sales Workshop

Session day/date _____   *Begin at* _____   *End at* _____

                                      Break times _____   *Lunch* _____

		Page	Timing[3]	Start	Stop
1	**Introduction to the Sales Workshop**		**00:20**		
	Review of the Seminar	122	00:10		
	Orientation to This Workshop	126	00:10		
2	**Earn the Right**		**01:10**		
	Introduction	130	00:10		
	Building Rapport	133			
	• Group Discussion		00:20		
	• Individual "Target" Activity		00:15		
	• Individual Assessment		00:10		
	"Earn the Right" Assessment	141	00:10		
	Summary	142	00:05		
3	**Understand the Need**		**02:05**		
	Introduction	145	00:10		
	Qualifying Opportunities	148			
	• Commentary and Discussion		00:15		
	• Individual "Target" Activity		00:15		
	• Individual Assessment		00:10		
	The First Two Phases: A Role Play	154	01:00		
	"Understand the Need" Assessment	159	00:10		
	Summary	160	00:05		

---

[3] Suggested elapsed time.

Arrange for Facilities

Date facilities arrangements to be completed _____

There are two aspects to this task.
- Selecting and reserving appropriate facilities. Specifications for the seminar and workshop rooms are on page 31.
- Obtaining key information about the facilities.

Once you have facilities organized, do the following.
- Record particulars about the facilities in the spaces provided.
- Communicate that information to the facilitator.
- Leave a copy of the specifications with the facility person—so he or she has a record of what you expect.

One-Hour Sales Seminar

Requirements: Day/date _____ From _____ To _____

Number of participants _____   Observers _____

Other requirements: _____

The facility: Location _____

Comments: _____

Information Required	Notes
Name, location, and phone number of person responsible for the facility	
Emergency procedures	
Location of restrooms and other facilities	
Operation of built-in equipment (screens, etc.)	
Location and operation of ventilation controls	
Location of light switches and electrical outlets	

Half-Day Communications Workshop

Requirements: Day/date _____   From _____   To _____

Number of   Observers
participants   _____   _____

Number of breakout rooms   _____

Other requirements: _____

The facility: Location   _____

Comments: _____

Information Required	**Notes**
Name, location, and phone number of person responsible for the facility	_____
Emergency procedures	_____
Location of restrooms and other facilities	_____
Operation of built-in equipment (screens, etc.)	_____
Location and operation of ventilation controls	_____
Location of light switches and electrical outlets	_____

One-Day Sales Workshop

Requirements: Day/date _____   From _____   To _____

Number of   Observers
participants   _____   _____

Number of breakout rooms   _____

Other requirements: _____

The facility: Location   _____

Comments: _____

Information Required	**Notes**
Name, location, and phone number of person responsible for the facility	_____
Emergency procedures	_____
Location of restrooms and other facilities	_____
Operation of built-in equipment (screens, etc.)	_____
Location and operation of ventilation controls	_____
Location of light switches and electrical outlets	_____

Room Specifications

These are specifications for the seminar and workshop rooms.

Room dimensions

- Up to 12 people—800 ft^2 (80 m^2)
- 12 to 24 people—1000 ft^2 (100 m^2)

Wall space for posting flipcharts—
30 linear feet (10 m). Note that the space will
be divided into "areas" for the various
sessions, as noted in the training plans.

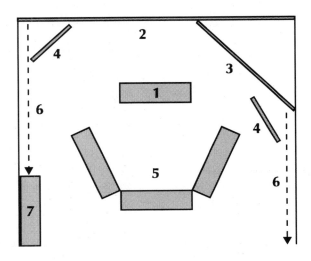

Participant seating

- U-shaped arrangement
- Equal or similar number of seats on each side of U
- Minimum table width—24 inches (60 cm)
- Minimum table length, per participant—32 inches (80 cm)

Front of room

- Table for overhead projector and facilitator materials—8 ft long (2.5 m)
- One projection screen
- One overhead projector (with spare lamp)
- One whiteboard
- Two flipchart stands
- Two or more electrical outlets, with extension cords as required

Legend

- 1—Facilitator table
- 2—Whiteboard
- 3—Projection screen
- 4—Flipchart stands
- 5—Participant tables and seating
- 6—Wall space for flipcharts
- 7—Supplies table

Other

- Seating for observers should be in the back of the room, if required.
- Facilities for breaks (and lunch) should be nearby.
- Breakout rooms (if used) should hold 3 to 4 people, be nearby, and be easily accessible.
- A table for supplies should be near the facilitator and be easily accessible.

Initiate and Monitor Enrollment

There are three phases in this task.
- Announce
- Monitor
- Follow up

Announce

Date by which announcement is to be distributed _____

Task	
Duplicate announcements	❑
Distribute announcements	❑

Monitor

Date by which enrollment is to be completed _____

Task	
Track replies	❑
Record enrollments	❑
Acknowledge enrollments	❑
Follow up on late/missing enrollments, as required	❑

Follow Up

Date on which follow-up is to be completed _____

Task	
Contact participants to confirm attendance, answer questions	❑
Attempt to fill seats vacated by last-minute cancellations	❑

Duplicate Materials

Materials to be duplicated by _____

Special requirements _____

Use the lists in this section as follows.
- Duplicate the quantities indicated in the "Quantity" column.
- Clip copies of each item together.
- For items shown as a bulleted list under a main item (for example, the three under "Active Listening"), clip those items together as a set.

One-Hour Sales Seminar

Item	Pages Begin	End	All	Table Group	Facilitator
Your Sales Experiences	212		____		❑
Effective Selling	213	219	____		❑
(Optional) Sales: A Quick Skills Assessment	335		____		❑
					❑
					❑

Half-Day Communications Workshop

Item	Pages Begin	End	All	Table Group	Facilitator
Typical Sales Situations and Customers	256		____		❑
Active Listening: What and How	220	221	____		❑
Active Listening					
• The Speaker Role	260		____		❑
• The Listener Role	261	262	____		❑
• The Observer Role	263	264			❑
Active Listening Assessment	337		____		❑
Observing: What You Can Learn	223	227	____		❑
What Impressions Do You Make?	339		____		❑
Questions for "Earn the Right"	266				❑
Why Customers Buy	228	229	____		❑

Item	Begin	End	All	Table Group	Facilitator	
Buying Objectives and Buying Influences	269					❑
Types of Questions	230	232	___			❑
A Questioning Demonstration						
• Observer's Critique Sheet	273		___			❑
• Instructions for the Salesperson	274					❑
• Instructions for the Customer	275				2	❑
Questions for "Understand the Need"	278	279	___			❑
Questioning Assessment	341		___			❑
Explaining	233	234	___			❑
An Explaining Demonstration						
• Observer's Critique Sheet	283		___			❑
• Instructions for the Salesperson	284				2	❑
• Instructions for the Customer	285				2	❑
Explaining Assessment	343		___			❑
_____						❑
_____						❑
_____						❑

One-Day Sales Workshop

Item	Begin	End	All	Table Group	Facilitator	
Building Rapport	235	236	___			❑
Beginning a Sale	288	289	___			❑
Building Rapport Assessment	345		___			❑
"Earn the Right" Assessment	347		___			❑
Qualifying Opportunities	237	238	___			❑
Approaches to Qualifying	291	292	___			❑
Qualifying Skills Assessment	349		___			❑
The First Two Phases: A Role Play	319	330	___			❑

Item	Pages			Quantity	
	Begin	End	All	Table Group	Facilitator
• Observer's Critique Sheet	297		_____		❑
• Instructions for the Salesperson	298		_____		❑
• Instructions for the Customer 1	299			_____	❑
• Instructions for the Customer 2	300			_____	❑
• Instructions for the Customer 3	301			_____	❑
"Understand the Need" Assessment	351		_____		❑
Testing for Readiness	239		_____		❑
Approaches to Testing for Readiness	303		_____		❑
Describing Benefits	240	241	_____		❑
Benefit Statements	306		_____		❑
Describing Benefits Assessment	353		_____		❑
Presenting a Recommendation	242	245	_____		❑
Making a Recommendation	309	310	_____		❑
"Make a Recommendation" Assessment	355		_____		❑
Asking for the Order	246	247	_____		❑
Approaches to Asking for the Order	313	314	_____		❑
Handling Obstacles	248	249	_____		❑
Approaches to Handling Obstacles	317	318	_____		❑
Handling Obstacles Assessment	357		_____		❑
The First Two Phases: A Role Play					
• Observer's Critique Sheet	324		_____		❑
• Instructions for the Salesperson 1	325			_____	❑
• Instructions for the Customer 1	326			_____	❑
• Instructions for the Salesperson 2	327			_____	❑
• Instructions for the Customer 2	328			_____	❑
• Instructions for the Salesperson 3	329			_____	❑
• Instructions for the Customer 3	330				❑
"Complete the Sale" Assessment	359				❑
					❑
_____					❑
_____					❑
_____					❑

Produce Overhead Transparencies

Overhead transparencies to be prepared by _____

Package completed overhead transparencies as follows.
- ❏ Blank sheets interleaved between transparencies
- ❏ Masters interleaved between transparencies
- ❏ In frames
- ❏ In sleeves
- ❏ In a binder

One-Hour Sales Seminar

Item	Page	
Our Purpose	362	❏
Key Assumptions	363	❏
Effective Selling	364	❏
Workshop Roles	365	❏
Workshop Guidelines	366	❏
_____		❏
_____		❏

Half-Day Communications Workshop

Item	Page	
Key Assumptions	363	❏
Effective Selling	364	❏
Workshop Roles	365	❏
Workshop Guidelines	366	❏
Listening and Verifying: Overview	367	❏
Active Listening	368	❏
Observing and Questioning: Overview	369	❏
Observing	370	❏
Early Questions	371	❏
More on Questions: Overview	372	❏
Types of Questions	373	❏

Item	Page	
Explaining: Overview	374	☐
Explaining	375	☐
		☐
		☐
		☐
		☐

One-Day Sales Workshop

Item	Page	
Key Assumptions	363	☐
Effective Selling	364	☐
Workshop Roles	365	☐
Workshop Guidelines	366	☐
Earn the Right: Overview	376	☐
Building Rapport	377	☐
Understand the Need: Overview	378	☐
Qualifying Opportunities	379	☐
Make a Recommendation: Overview	380	☐
Describing Benefits	381	☐
Complete the Sale: Overview	382	☐
Obstacles	383	☐
		☐
		☐
		☐
		☐

Produce Prepared Flipcharts

Prepared flipcharts to be completed by _____

Method by which flipcharts are to be produced:
- ❑ Hand printed, using pages referenced below as the source of text
- ❑ Flipchart or poster maker, using pages referenced below as masters
- ❑ Other _____

Tips for Assembly

✓ Assemble the completed flipcharts into two pads, as shown in the lists below.

✓ Leave a blank page between each prepared flipchart.

✓ Be certain that the flipcharts are legible.

Tips for Preparing Hand-Made Flipcharts

✓ Use the writing style to which you are accustomed—script, printing, all caps, whatever—as long as it is legible.

✓ Write large enough and bold enough for all to see.

✓ Use dark-colored, broad-tipped markers.

✓ Use different colored markers for emphasis.

✓ Check readability from various locations in the room—using the actual room or one that is similar.

One-Hour Sales Seminar

Item	Page	Pad 1	Pad 2	
Sales Experiences	386	✓		❑
Effective Selling	387	✓		❑
Communications Workshop Agenda (optional)	388	✓		❑
Sales Workshop Agenda (optional)	389		✓	❑
Workshop Expectations (optional)	390	✓		❑
What You Believe the Customer Said	391	✓		❑
What the Customer Really Said	392		✓	❑

Typical Sales Situations	393	✓		❑
Communications Workshop Logistics	394		✓	❑
				❑
				❑

_____

_____

Half-Day Communications Workshop

Item	Page	Pad 1	Pad 2	
Communications Workshop Agenda	388	✓		❑
Communications Workshop: Purpose and Goals	395		✓	❑
Workshop Expectations	390	✓		❑
Questions for "Earn the Right"	398	✓		❑
Buying Objectives	399	✓		❑
Buying Influences	400		✓	❑
Why Customers Buy	401	✓		❑
Specific/Closed Questions	402	✓		❑
Leading Questions	403		✓	❑
Questions for "Understand the Need"	404	✓		❑
Sales Workshop Agenda (Optional)	389	✓		❑
Explaining Skill	405	✓		❑
Sales Workshop: Logistics	406		✓	❑
				❑
				❑
				❑

_____

_____

_____

One-Day Sales Workshop

Item	Page	Pad 1	Pad 2	
Sales Workshop: Purpose and Goals	407	✓		❑
Sales Workshop Agenda	389		✓	❑
Targeting Your Sales Efforts	396		✓	❑
Observing	397	✓		❑
Questions for "Earn the Right"	398	✓		❑
What Do You Want to Accomplish?	408	✓		❑
Effective Selling	387	✓		❑
Building Rapport	409	✓		❑
Beginning a Sale	410		✓	❑
Approaches to Qualifying	411	✓		❑
Role Play Questions	412	✓		❑
Role Play Questions, continued	413		✓	❑
Approaches to Testing for Readiness	414	✓		❑
Features and Benefits	415	✓		❑
Benefit Statements	416		✓	❑
Recommendations	417	✓		❑
Competitive Edge	418		✓	❑
Making a Recommendation	419	✓		❑
Buying Signals	420	✓		❑
Asking for the Order	421		✓	❑
Approaches to Asking for the Order	422	✓		❑
Common Obstacles	423	✓		❑
Handling Obstacles	424		✓	❑
Approaches to Handling Obstacles	425	✓		❑
Role Play Questions	426	✓		❑
Role Play Questions, continued	427		✓	❑
				❑
				❑

Ensure Availability of Other Supplies

Number of participants and observers _____

Deliver supplies to:

	Attention	*Address*	*By date*
One-Hour Seminar	_____	_____	_____
Half-Day Workshop	_____	_____	_____
One-Day Workshop	_____	_____	_____

Participant and Observer Supplies

Item	Quantity	
Place card, with name imprinted	1	❏
Pencil	1	❏
Binder (one inch spine, with 20 sheets of writing paper)	1	❏
Mints or other small candies to keep people sweet	Enough	❏
Copy of this list showing what is packed	1	❏

Room Supplies

Item	Quantity	
Box of whiteboard markers (chisel point, dark colors)	1	❏
Box of flipchart markers (dark colors)	1	❏
Packet of overhead transparency markers	1	❏
Box of blank overhead transparencies	1	❏
Spare flipchart pads	2	❏
Whiteboard cleaning fluid	1	❏
Packet of cleaning cloths	1	❏
Scissors	1	❏
Roll of clear tape	1	❏
Material to post flipcharts, appropriate to wall surface		❏
• Roll of masking tape	2	
• Push-pins	200	

Item	Quantity	
Elastic bands	20	❑
Three-hole punch	1	❑
Roll of packing tape (reinforced, wide)	1	❑
Copy of this list showing what is packed	1	❑

Organize Catering and Other Support

Date catering and other support arrangements to be completed _____

Catering

The following are general guidelines for refreshments.
- Coffee and tea on arrival for sessions; additionally, other beverages and/or snacks as appropriate
- Coffee, tea, and a light snack at an appropriate mid-morning and/or mid-afternoon time
- Optionally, coffee and tea available on a continuous basis throughout the sessions

The following are general guidelines for lunch.
- Allocate maximum of one hour, including time for a short walk or other occasion to get a breath of fresh air.
- Consider sandwiches and fruit, light buffets, or similar alternatives that focus on light food and speedy service; heavy meals will be regretted by all as the afternoon wears on.

Also, all catering should be provided at locations close to the rooms in order to minimize "travel" and other unproductive time.

One-Hour Seminar	Half-Day Workshop	
Arrival	**Arrival**	**Break**
Date _____	Date _____	Date _____
Time and place _____	Time and place _____	Time and place _____
Beverages	Beverages	Beverages
❑ Coffee	❑ Coffee	❑ Coffee
❑ Tea	❑ Tea	❑ Tea
❑ _____	❑ _____	❑ _____
Food items	Food items	Food items
❑ _____	❑ _____	❑ _____
❑ _____	❑ _____	❑ _____
❑ _____	❑ _____	❑ _____
❑ _____	❑ _____	❑ _____

One-Day Workshop

Arrival	Break 1	Break 2
Date _____	Date _____	Date _____
Time and place _____	Time and place _____	Time and place _____
Beverages	Beverages	Beverages
❏ Coffee	❏ Coffee	❏ Coffee
❏ Tea	❏ Tea	❏ Tea
❏ _____	❏ _____	❏ _____
Food items	Food items	Food items
❏ _____	❏ _____	❏ _____
❏ _____	❏ _____	❏ _____
❏ _____	❏ _____	❏ _____

Lunch

Date _____	Food items
Time and place _____	❏ _____
	❏ _____
Beverages	❏ _____
❏ Coffee	❏ _____
❏ Tea	❏ _____
❏ _____	

Other Support

Item		Comments
Availability of spare equipment (overhead projector, etc.)	❏	
Availability of duplicating service nearby	❏	
_____	❏	
_____	❏	
_____	❏	

Chapter Four

A One-Hour Sales Seminar

This chapter contains the training plan for your one-hour sales seminar—ready to go "as is" or to be tailored to meet your needs. In its current form it is intended to be used in conjunction with one or both of the training designs that follow. If you wish, you can easily modify it to assess participant perceptions of their sales training needs and the priority of those needs.

The chapter is divided into three parts:
- Purpose and objectives of the seminar
- The seminar agenda
- The training plan for the seminar

You will find information on preparing for this seminar in the chapters titled "Planning the Workshop" and "Getting Everything Ready" (pages 7 and 19, respectively).

Purpose and Goals

Purpose

Orient participants to our concept of effective selling, describe the training events that are planned, and establish participant expectations for the training.

Goals

Participants will be able to:
- Describe key assumptions that are a part of the *mindset* required for successful selling efforts.
- List the phases of an "effective selling" sales process.
- List the key communications skills and sales skills that are a part of the *skill set* to be covered in the workshops.
- Describe the relationship of communications and sales skills to the sales process—and to effective selling.

The following objectives may be generalized to apply to skills in general or apply specifically to the communications and sales workshops:
- Describe their expectations in the areas of communications and sales.
- Indicate ways in which they can meet expectations that will not be addressed in sales training or the communications and sales workshops.
- Demonstrate to themselves the importance of—and difficulties involved in—applying effective communications skills.
- (Optional) Describe the purpose of the communications and sales workshops, and the general approach to be taken.

Seminar Agenda

	Page	Timing[1]	Start	Stop
Introduction to Effective Selling		**01:05**[2]		
General Orientation	47	00:10		
Setting the Stage	49	00:15		
Establishing Expectations (or Training Priorities)	54	00:10		
The Importance of Communications	56	00:15		
Summary	59	00:15		

---

[1] Suggested elapsed time.

[2] As noted previously, this is a facilitator's hour—similar to the well-known baker's dozen.

Introduction to Effective Selling

General Orientation

00:10

Purpose: Orient participants to the purpose and goals of this seminar and (optionally) the communications and sales workshops.

Note: This introduction is based on the recommended approach for offering the communications and sales workshops. If you are tailoring this approach—to conduct a less directed discussion of needs or to meet other needs—you will need to tailor this introduction to match your approach.

FACILITATOR COMMENTARY

WELCOME participants to the one-hour sales seminar, being certain to make these points during your introductory comments.

- With your active involvement, this seminar will be interesting and profitable for everyone.

- Thank you for allocating an hour of your time to this important activity.

If you are following this one-hour seminar with the half-day and/or the full-day workshop, do the following:

Our Purpose

DESCRIBE the purpose of this seminar. If appropriate, show the "Our Purpose" overhead transparency. (See page 362.)

MAKE points about the purpose of this seminar that you believe are important for <u>this</u> workshop.

- _____
- _____
- _____

INTRODUCE yourself, covering points that—in the minds of the participants—will establish your credibility in sales and/or sales training.

REQUEST participants to introduce themselves, providing name, responsibility, experience, and/or other information that would be of interest to the group.

DESCRIBE important logistical details.

- Timing for the seminar

- Safety procedures to be followed in the event of an emergency

Setting the Stage

00:15

Purpose: Establish the importance to successful sales efforts of of communication skills and sales skills.

INDIVIDUAL EXERCISE

INTRODUCE the exercise.

- At this point, you will take a few minutes to reflect on sales experiences in which you have been involved.

Your Sales Experiences

DISTRIBUTE the exercise handout, "Your Sales Experiences" (page 212).

REVIEW the instructions on the handout with participants.

ALLOW 2 minutes to complete the written exercise.

Procedural note: During the following brief discussion of participant comments on sales experiences, attempt to draw out responses that will allow you to reinforce these points about "mindset" and "skill set" during your summary and the subsequent discussion of keys to effective selling.

- *The messages on the overhead transparency "Key Assumptions," used during the summary discussion*
- *The importance of each of the three broad sales training topic areas—the sales process, communications skills, and sales skills*

Mentally organize the responses to facilitate your summary and the subsequent discussion.

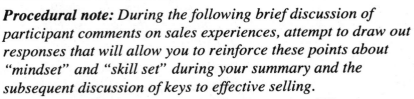

GROUP DISCUSSION

ASK participants to offer comments on their sales experiences, based on the work just completed.

Sales Experiences

RECORD comments on the "Sales Experiences" flipchart (page 386).

> *Procedural note:* The points in the "Key Assumptions" overhead transparency are a key part of the "mindset" on which this—and any other—sales training approach is based. The discussion points that follow need to be made in a way that
> - *Is natural and comfortable for you.*
> - *Make it absolutely clear that these points are the premise on which participant success depends.*
> - *Don't raise participant anxiety or blood pressure any more than necessary.*

Key Assumptions

MAKE this point about sales, using the "Key Assumptions" overhead transparency (page 363).

- From the point of view of a salesperson, the sale begins as *an opportunity*.

- The challenge is to move from the opportunity to success— *completing the sale*.

DESCRIBE key assumptions about the roles of the customer and salesperson as the salesperson moves from <u>an opportunity</u> to <u>completing the sale</u>, using the "Key Assumptions" overhead transparency.

REFER to participant responses from the "Sales Experience" flipchart as you discuss the overhead transparency, thus allowing you to reinforce key points using the participants' own experiences in sales situations.

KEY POINTS   *MAKE these key points.*

- Customers are there because they have a problem to solve or a need to satisfy—and, therefore, they want to buy and need help with the buying decision.

- Salespeople need to—and are expected to—sell.

- As a consequence, in a sales situation your job is to *learn about the customer's need* and then *complete the sale*.

- This is the first part of the *mindset* with which you approach selling—a mindset that provides *motivation* and *direction* for your work.

ASK this question.

- Are there any questions about this topic?

ANSWER the questions, as appropriate.

FACILITATOR COMMENTARY

MAKE a statement such as the following as a transition to a brief discussion of the key topic areas.

- Your responses to the "sales situation" exercise also point to three areas that are important in effective selling.
    - The flow of the *sales process*—whether it is confined to a single meeting or covers multiple calls
    - The use of effective *communications skills* throughout the sales effort
    - The use of certain key *sales skills* at appropriate points in the sales process

Effective Selling

DESCRIBE briefly the phases of the sales process shown on the "Effective Selling" overhead transparency.

MAKE this point about the sales process.

- The sales process is the second part of the *mindset* with which you approach selling—providing *direction* for your work.

DESCRIBE briefly the communications and sales skills shown on the "Effective Selling" overhead transparency.

MAKE these points during your description.

- Communications skills and sales skills are part of the *skill set* with which you approach selling.

- Each of the communications skills is important—to one degree or another—*in each phase* of the selling process.

- Unlike communications skills, however, the sales skills tend to be important *in specific phases* of the sales process.

RELATE responses from the "Sales Experiences" flipchart to these areas and their individual components.

KEY POINTS   *MAKE these key points.*

- Positive sales experiences can generally be traced to a salesperson's *mindset* and *skill set*—his or her mastery of each of the areas that are important to effective selling.

- By contrast, unsatisfactory experiences can often be traced to a salesperson's deficiencies in those areas—lack of understanding, lack of skill, etc.

Effective Selling

DISTRIBUTE the handout, "Effective Selling" (pages 213 through 219).

ALLOW 5 minutes for participants to read the handout.

Effective Selling

REINFORCE the following, using the "Effective Selling" flipchart (page 387) and participant experiences recorded on the "Sales Experiences" flipchart (page 386).

- The importance of communication skills across all phases of the sales process.

- The importance of sales skills during particular phases of the sales process.

Notes regarding additional points that you wish to reinforce from the reading:

- _____

- _____

- _____

POST the "Sales Experiences" and "Effective Selling" flipcharts in the "Workshop Overview" area.

*Communications
Workshop Agenda;
Sales Workshop Agenda*

If you will be following this one-hour seminar with the half-day and/or the one-day workshop, do the following:
DESCRIBE the half-day and one-day workshop agenda, using the "Communications Workshop Agenda" and "Sales Workshop Agenda" flipcharts (pages 388 and 389).

PROVIDE a rationale for the specific topics you are emphasizing and/or including in the agenda—referring to the "Effective Selling" flipchart as appropriate.

Notes regarding design rationale for your workshop:

- _____

- _____

- _____

POST the "Communications Workshop Agenda" and "Sales Workshop Agenda" flipcharts in the "Workshop Overview" area.

?

ASK this question.

- Are there any questions about the discussion or the agenda for the forthcoming workshops?

ANSWER the questions, as appropriate.

Establishing Expectations

(Optional) If you are following this one-hour seminar with the half-day and/or the one-day workshop, do the following:

00:10

Purpose: Determine participant expectations for the communications and sales workshops, and reconcile those expectations with the purpose and goals of the workshops.

Procedural note: If "Sales: A Quick Skills Assessment" has been used as part of participant preparation for the communications and sales workshops, allow 1 minute for participants to review the assessment. Then, skip ahead to the group discussion.

INDIVIDUAL ASSESSMENT

INTRODUCE the assessment.

- You will now take a few minutes to complete a simple assessment of your skills in sales—an assessment based on three of the topic areas important to effective selling.

- You will then use the desired areas of improvement that you identify in this assessment to stimulate thinking about your expectations for the communications and sales workshops.

*Sales: A Quick
Skills Assessment*

DISTRIBUTE the "Sales: A Quick Skills Assessment" (page 335).

REVIEW the instructions on the assessment with participants.

ALLOW 3 minutes to complete the assessment.

Procedural note: During the discussion that follows, you will ask participants to volunteer desired improvements <u>with the highest priority</u>.

- *You should note these on the flipchart, and attempt to group similar expectations together.*

- *However, do not concern yourself with separating communications- and sales-related expectations.*

Indicate the following at the conclusion of the discussion:

- *Those expectations that <u>will</u> be met during the workshops, with reference to the "Communications Workshop Agenda" and "Sales Workshop Agenda" flipcharts*

- *Those that <u>will not</u> be met—along with an indication of ways in which participants will be able to satisfy those expectations through other workshops, personal growth activities, independent study, etc.*

To facilitate this discussion, consider writing expectations that <u>will</u> be met on the left side of the flipchart, and those that <u>will not</u> be met on the right side.

Workshop Expectations

GROUP DISCUSSION

ASK participants to volunteer the highest priority improvements to be made as a result of these workshops.

RECORD expectations on the "Workshop Expectations" flipchart, grouping similar expectations together.

INDICATE the following at the conclusion of the discussion.

- Those expectations that <u>will</u> be met during the two workshops

- Those that <u>will not</u> be met—along with an indication of ways in which participants will be able to satisfy them

POST the "Workshop Expectations" flipchart in the "Workshop Overview" area.

The Importance of Communications[3]

00:15

Purpose: Stress the importance of effective communication skills by illustrating how easily communication can break down or be distorted.

TABLE GROUP ACTIVITY

BREAK the workshop into table groups of four to six people.

PRESENT the instructions for the activity "What Did the Customer Say?" (See pages 252 through 254.)

1. I will ask one volunteer from each table group to go into the hall with me.

2. I will read to these volunteers a statement made by a customer. *They will not be allowed to take notes.*

3. Each volunteer will return to his or her table group and select one individual as a "listener." The volunteer will repeat the customer statement to the listener—out of hearing range of other team members or other teams. *The listener is not allowed to ask questions—just listen.*

4. That person, in turn, will select another listener and repeat what he or she heard. Once again—*no questions.*

5. That procedure will be repeated until there are no more listeners available in a table group.

6. The last listener in each group should make notes of what he or she heard.

ASK this question.

- Are there any questions about what you will be doing?

ANSWER the questions, as appropriate.

ASK participants to move into table groups and volunteers to come with you into the hall.

---

[3] Reprinted with permission of HRD Press, Inc., 22 Amherst Rd., Amherst, MA 01002, 1-800-822-2801 (U.S. and Canada) or (413) 253-3488.

READ the customer statement to the volunteers—either the one here or your own.

- We have a major problem with your company. We're launching a new product next month and our production schedule is in jeopardy because of the key component that you provide. We awarded you a contract a month ago for 10,000 components—the first shipment of which arrived on schedule two days ago. However, ten of the first 100 "out of the box" failed to meet our specifications. Our production manager, Fred Flemming, said "With a failure rate that high, it's pointless to test the rest—and another shipment's due in two days!" We need the components—on time and to specifications. You're in trouble! Your major competitor says they can have 5,000 up-to-spec components here in three days, and the rest within a week. So . . . can you replace that first shipment — and how fast? What confidence do we have that the remaining components will meet specifications?

Notes about your "customized" customer statement, if you elect to substitute your own:

ASK volunteers to return to their table groups.

GROUP DISCUSSION

RECONVENE the full group.

What You Believe the
Customer Said

ASK one of the final listeners to report what he or she heard—making notes on the "What You Believe the Customer Said" flipchart (page 391).

ASK other final listeners to report on what they heard—making notes on the flipchart and noting additional points or differences, as well.

What the Customer
Really Said

REVEAL the "What the Customer Really Said" flipchart (page 392).

COMPARE briefly the content of that flipchart with what the listeners reported hearing.

ASK this question.

- What was there about this exercise that interfered with successful communication?

LOOK FOR answers that allow you to lead the group to a conclusion such as this about the exercise.

- The exercise was somewhat artificial; people couldn't make notes, ask questions, or verify.

- Nonetheless, under the best of circumstances, it is difficult to concentrate and be a good listener.

- Effective communication is two-way and requires use of multiple skills—listening, questioning, verifying, observing, and explaining.

POST the "What You Believe the Customer Said" and "What the Customer Really Said" flipcharts in the "Communications Skills" area.

ASK this question.

- Are there any questions before we move on?

ANSWER the questions, as appropriate.

Summary

00:15   **Purpose:** Review key points from the module, and (optional) prepare participants for the subsequent workshops.

FACILITATOR COMMENTARY

MAKE this comment.

- At this point, we have concluded the seminar, in preparation for the communications and sales workshops.

REVIEW key points made during the seminar, using the flipcharts that have been posted.

- Sales Experiences

- Effective Selling

- Communications Workshop Agenda

- Sales Workshop Agenda

- Workshop Expectations

- What You Believe the Customer Said

- What the Customer Really Said

ASK this question.

- Are there any questions about what we have covered during this seminar?

ANSWER the questions, as appropriate.

GROUP DISCUSSION

MAKE this comment.

- Before concluding this seminar, there is one more topic to discuss—namely, a description of the nature of the sales interactions and sales process in which you are typically involved.

- (Optional) We will use this description as the basis for discussion and activities during the communications and sales workshops.

- The purpose of this discussion is to be sure that we all have a common understanding of the environment in which you will be applying the lessons of any training that follows.

Typical Sales Situations

USE the "Typical Sales Situations" flipchart (page 393) to describe the nature of the sales interactions and sales process in which workshop participants are typically involved.

ASK this question.

- Are there any differences of opinion between this description of typical sales situations and what you face on a day-to-day basis?

DISCUSS any differences with the group.

AGREE on the resolution of any differences that exist.

ADJUST the description on the flipchart to reflect group agreement.

POST the "Typical Sales Situations" flipchart in the "Workshop Overview" area.

FACILITATOR COMMENTARY

Option: If you intend to follow this one-hour seminar with the half-day and/or the one-day workshop, do the following:

MAKE these comments.

- At this point we will review quickly the forthcoming workshops—roles, "ground rules," agenda, and logistics.

Workshop Roles

KEY POINTS

DESCRIBE workshop roles for both the participants and facilitator, using the "Workshop Roles" overhead transparency (page 365).

MAKE these key points.

- The key to success for this workshop is *your active involvement* throughout the day.

- *My main responsibility* is to assure that we "stay on track," achieve the goals of the workshop, and meet your expectations.

Workshop Guidelines

KEY POINTS

DESCRIBE workshop "ground rules," using the "Workshop Guidelines" overhead transparency (page 366).

MAKE these key points.

- The purpose of these of these ground rules *is not* to restrict you or inhibit you.

- Rather, the purpose is to assure that each of you can fully participate in and benefit from the workshop.

Communications Workshop Agenda

REVIEW quickly the agenda for the communications workshop, using the "Communications Workshop Agenda" flipchart (page 388)

Communications Workshop: Logistics

REVIEW quickly the logistics for the communications workshop, using the "Communications Workshop Logistics" flipchart (page 394).

- Day and Date
- Time
- Location
- Recommended dress

KEY POINT   *MAKE* this key point.

- Please be sure to bring your materials from this seminar—handouts, notes, etc.—to the communications workshop.

?   *ASK* this question.

- Are there any questions about the communications workshop?

ANSWER the questions, as appropriate.

MAKE these concluding comments.

- Thank you for your time and involvement in today's seminar.

- (Optional) I am looking forward to working with you in our forthcoming workshops.

- (Optional) Remember . . . bring the materials you have gathered so far to the communications workshop.

Procedural note: *If you are running the half-day and/or the full-day workshops, be sure to save the flipcharts used and/or developed during this seminar. Most of them will be used for reference during the forthcoming workshops.*

Chapter Five:

A Half-Day Communications Workshop

This chapter contains the training plan for your half-day communications workshop—ready to go "as is" or to be tailored to meet your needs. The chapter is divided into six parts.

- Purpose and goals of the workshop
- One part for each of the five modules that comprise the half-day workshop, containing the purpose, objectives, and training plan for that module

You will find information on preparing for this workshop in the chapters titled "Planning the Workshop" and "Getting Everything Ready" (pages 7 and 19, respectively).

Purpose and Goals

Here are statements of the purpose and goals for the half-day workshop.

Purpose

Provide knowledge and practice on communications skills that are important to effective selling.

Goals

The participant will:

- (if they have attended the one-hour seminar) relate the information covered there to the content and structure of this communications workshop.
- Describe the concept of active listening, and effectively apply listening and verifying skills throughout the sales process.
- Describe the skills of observing and questioning as applied in the "Earn the Right" phase, and effectively apply those skills in the sales process.
- Describe the concept of buying objectives and buying influences; describe questioning skills that are important in the "Understand the Need" phase, and effectively apply those skills in the sales process.
- Describe the skill of explaining, and effectively apply that skill throughout the sales process.

Each module in the half-day communications workshop has its own statement of purpose and objectives, providing an additional level of detail about the module.

> **Procedural note:** *If participants attended the one-hour seminar, be sure the following flipcharts from it are posted in the "Workshop Overview" area prior to the beginning of Module One.*
>
> - *Effective Selling* (page 387)
>
> - *Workshop Expectations* (page 390)
>
> - *Communications Workshop Agenda* (page 388)
>
> - *Typical Sales Situations* (page 393)
>
> If participants did not attend the one-hour seminar, post the "Effective Selling" and "Communications Workshop Agenda" flipcharts in the "Workshop Overview" area. The other two flipcharts will be developed during this workshop.

1. Introduction to the Communications Workshop

Purpose   Review the topics covered in the one-hour seminar. (Optional) Orient participants to this workshop, and introduce the "Targeting Your Sales Efforts" exercises.

Objectives The participant will:
- Describe key assumptions that are a part of the *mindset* required for successful selling efforts.
- List the phases of an "effective selling" sales process.
- List the communications skills to be covered in this workshop.
- Describe the relationship of communications to sales skills and the sales process—and to effective selling.
- Describe the purpose of the communications workshop, and the general approach to be taken in this workshop.
- Define typical sales situations and customers, as a basis for the "Targeting Your Sales Efforts" activities.

Agenda

		Page	Timing[1]	Start	Stop
1	**Introduction to the Communications Workshop**		**00:35**		
	Review of the Seminar (optional)	66	00:10		
	Orientation to This Workshop	69	00:10		
	Targeting Your Sales Efforts	72	00:15		

---

[1] Suggested elapsed time.

Introduction and Optional Review of the Seminar

00:10   **Purpose:** Introduce yourself and (optional) review the results of the one-hour effective selling seminar.

Procedural note: The tempo of this overview should be fast—faster yet if the one-hour seminar was held recently. Be sure not to belabor this overview.

FACILITATOR COMMENTARY

WELCOME participants to the half-day communications workshop, being certain to make these points during your introductory comments.

- With your active involvement, this workshop will be interesting and profitable for everyone.

- Thank you for allocating a half day of your time to this important activity.

Procedural note: The following introductions should either be brief or briefer—depending on how well participants know you and one another, whether they attended the seminar, etc.

INTRODUCE yourself quickly, reviewing points that will establish your credibility in sales and/or sales training.

REQUEST participants to reintroduce themselves quickly, providing name, responsibility, experience, and/or other information that would be of interest to the group.

MAKE this comment.

- (Optional) Before we begin today's topics, we will review quickly some key information originally covered during the one-hour effective selling seminar held on _____ [indicate day/date].

Key Assumptions

REVIEW quickly these points about sales, using the "Key Assumptions" overhead transparency (page 363).

- From the point of view of a salesperson, the sale begins as *an opportunity.*

- The challenge is to move from the opportunity to success— *completing the sale.*

REVIEW key assumptions about the roles of the customer and salesperson as the salesperson moves from <u>an opportunity</u> to <u>completing the sale</u>, using the "Key Assumptions" overhead transparency.

KEY POINTS

MAKE these key points.

- Customers are there because they have a problem to solve or a need to satisfy—they want to buy and need help with the buying decision.

- Salespeople need to—and are expected to—sell.

- Therefore, in a sales situation, your job is to *learn about the customer's need* and then *complete the sale.*

- This is the first part of the *mindset* with which you approach selling—a mindset that provides *motivation* and *direction* for your work.

Effective Selling

REVIEW briefly the phases of the sales process shown on the "Effective Selling" overhead transparency (page 364).

MAKE this point about the sales process.

- The sales process is the second of the *mindset* with which you approach selling—providing *direction* for your work.

REVIEW briefly the communications and sales skills shown on the "Effective Selling" overhead transparency.

MAKE this point about communications and sales skills.

- Communications skills and sales skills are part of the *skill set* with which you approach selling.

- Today, we will work with the communications skills that are important to effective selling.

KEY POINTS   *MAKE these key points.*

- Positive sales experiences can generally be traced to a salesperson's *mindset* and *skill set*—his or her mastery of each of the areas that are important to effective selling.

- By contrast, unsatisfactory experiences can often be traced to a salesperson's deficiencies in those areas—lack of understanding, lack of skill, etc.

ASK this question.

- Are there any questions about this quick review of the information on effective selling introduced during the one-hour seminar?

ANSWER the questions, as appropriate.

Orientation to This Workshop

00:10

Purpose: Orient participants to today's workshop, including purpose and goals, the approach to conducting it, and logistics.

GROUP DISCUSSION

ASK participants to volunteer the highest priority improvements to be made as a result of these workshops.

Workshop Expectations

RECORD expectations on the "Workshop Expectations" flipchart, grouping similar expectations together (page 390).

INDICATE the following at the conclusion of the discussion.

- Those expectations that <u>will</u> be met during the two workshops

- Those that <u>will not</u> be met—along with an indication of ways in which participants will be able to satisfy them

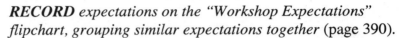

POST the "Workshop Expectations" flipchart in the "Workshop Overview" area.

Procedural note: *If participants attended the one-hour seminar, follow Option 1, below. If they did not attend the one-hour seminar, follow Option 2.*

FACILITATOR COMMENTARY

Option 1

MAKE this comment.

- During the one-hour seminar, you established your expectations for the communications and sales workshops.

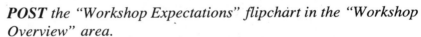

Workshop Expectations

REVIEW quickly the expectations established for the communications and sales workshops, using the "Workshop Expectations" flipchart (page 390).
[end option]

Option 2

GROUP DISCUSSION

ASK participants to volunteer the highest priority improvements to be made as a result of these workshops.

Workshop Expectations

RECORD *expectations on the "Workshop Expectations" flipchart, grouping similar expectations together.*

INDICATE *the following at the conclusion of the discussion.*

- Those expectations that <u>will</u> be met during the two workshops

- Those that <u>will not</u> be met—along with an indication of ways in which participants will be able to satisfy them

POST *the "Workshop Expectations" flipchart in the "Workshop Overview" area.*

Communications Workshop: Purpose and Goals

DESCRIBE *the purpose and goals of this workshop, using the "Communications Workshop: Purpose and Goals" flipchart (page 395).*

RELATE *participant expectations to the purpose and goals of this workshop—as well as to the forthcoming sales workshop, if applicable.*

[end option]

MAKE *these points about particular goals that you will stress in* <u>this</u> *workshop.*

- _____

- _____

- _____

POST *the "Communications Workshop: Purpose and Goals" flipchart in the "Workshop Overview" area.*

Communications Workshop Agenda

REVIEW *the agenda for the communications workshop, using the "Communications Workshop Agenda" flipchart (page 388).*

> **Procedural note:** *The tempo of the overview of workshop roles and guidelines should be fast—faster yet if the participants attended the one-hour seminar.* <u>*Be sure not to belabor this overview.*</u>

Workshop Roles

KEY POINTS

REVIEW workshop roles for both the participants and facilitator, using the "Workshop Roles" overhead transparency (page 365).

MAKE these key points.

- The key to success for this workshop is *your active involvement* throughout the day.

- *My main responsibility* is to assure that we "stay on track," achieve the goals of the workshop, and meet your expectations.

Workshop Guidelines

KEY POINTS

REVIEW "ground rules" for the workshop, using the "Workshop Guidelines" overhead transparency (page 366).

MAKE these key points.

- The purpose of these "ground rules" *is not* to restrict you or inhibit you.

- Rather, the purpose is to assure that each of you can fully participate in and benefit from the workshop.

DESCRIBE important logistical details.

- Timing of and facilities for breaks and lunch (if applicable)

- Location of telephones, restrooms, and other important facilities

- Safety procedures to be followed in the event of an emergency

ASK this question.

- Are there any questions before we discuss a series of special activities that are important to success in the communications and sales workshops—and in your selling efforts?

ANSWER the questions, as appropriate.

Targeting Your Sales Efforts

00:15

Purpose: Introduce a special series of workshop activities, "Targeting Your Sales Efforts."

COMMENTARY AND INITIAL ACTIVITY

MAKE these comments.

- During this workshop, you will complete a number of activities to which we will refer as "Targeting Your Sales Efforts."

- Each of these activities provides an opportunity for you to apply the lessons of the workshops to your own sales situation—resulting in a "tool kit" to take back, use in your day-to-day work, and ultimately provide more focus and efficiency in your sales efforts.

Targeting Your Sales Efforts

DESCRIBE the "Targeting Your Sales Efforts" activities, using the "Targeting Your Sales Efforts" flipchart (page 396).

POST the "Targeting Your Sales Efforts" flipchart in the "Target" area.

> **Procedural note:** *If participants attended the one-hour seminar, they will have discussed typical sales situations, and you will have developed the "Typical Sales Situations" flipchart. If participants did not attend the seminar, you will need to spend a few minutes developing it with the participants before distributing the "Typical Sales Situations and Customers" handout.*

INITIAL "TARGET" ACTIVITY

INTRODUCE an initial activity that is the foundation for the remaining "Targeting Your Sales Efforts" activities.

- In order to provide a basis for completing the various "Targeting Your Sales Efforts" activities in this workshop, you will now spend a short time identifying typical sales situations and typical customers whom you meet in those situations.

- (Optional) Before you do that, let's review the typical sales situations that we discussed and to which we agreed during the one-hour seminar.

Typical Sales Situations

USE the "Typical Sales Situations" flipchart (page 393) to review the nature of the sales interactions and sales process in which participants are typically involved.

Typical Sales Situations and Customers

DISTRIBUTE the learning activity, "Typical Sales Situations and Customers" (page 256).

REVIEW the instructions for the learning activity with participants.

ALLOW 5 minutes to complete the activity.

ASK this question.

- Are there any questions about the work you have just completed in this initial "Targeting Your Sales Efforts" activity?

ANSWER the questions, as appropriate.

Communications Workshop Agenda

MARK OFF the topics that have been covered on the "Communications Workshop Agenda" flipchart.

MAKE this comment.

- Now let's move on to the "business" of the workshop.

2. Listening and Verifying

Purpose   Introduce the concept of active listening, and provide practice in listening and verifying skills through application of that concept.

Objectives   The participant will:
- Describe the general role and importance of listening and verifying skills in the sales process.
- Define the concept of active listening.
- List tips that are key to success in active listening.
- Apply listening, verifying, and active listening skills throughout his or her sales efforts.

Agenda

		Page	Timing[1]	Start	Stop
2	**Listening and Verifying**		**00:55**		
	Introduction	75	00:05		
	Active Listening	76			
	• Introduction and Activity		00:35		
	• Individual Assessment		00:10		
	Summary	81	00:05		

---

[1] Suggested elapsed time.

Introduction

00:05

*Listening and Verifying:
Overview*

Purpose: Introduce the content of the module; position the importance of listening and verifying in the sales process.

FACILITATOR COMMENTARY

USE the "Listening and Verifying: Overview" overhead transparency (page 367) to describe the topics to be covered in the module.

MAKE these points about the importance of listening and verifying skills.

- Listening is key to your success from the beginning of the sales process to its successful end—a point that scarcely needs to be belabored.

- Verifying is equally important, and goes hand in hand with effective listening.

  – Often, what we think we hear is not, in fact, what we should have heard.

  – (Optional)This point undoubtedly "came home" to you in the communications activity during our one-hour seminar.

- In this module, we will discuss and practice these skills in a context referred to as "active listening."

ASK this question.

- Are there any questions about this before we start?

ANSWER questions, as appropriate.

Active Listening

00:45

Purpose: Define active listening and provide practice in employing the skills involved.

Active Listening

INTRODUCTION AND ACTIVITY

DEFINE *the concept of active listening, using the "Active Listening" overhead transparency (page 368).*

*Active Listening:
What and How*

DISTRIBUTE *the handout, "Active Listening: What and How" (pages 220 and 221).*

ALLOW *3 minutes for participants to read the handout.*

Notes regarding specific points that you wish to reinforce from the reading.

- _____

- _____

- _____

MAKE *this comment.*

You will now practice listening and verifying as part of an active listening activity.

Note: Materials required for the following activity may be found in the "Active Listening" learning activity beginning on page 257.

TABLE GROUP ACTIVITY

BREAK the workshop into table groups of three people each.

DESCRIBE briefly the three roles and the topic of discussion for the "Active Listening" activity.

- The *speaker* will talk about this topic.

  _____

  _____

  _____

- The *listener* will listen actively to what the speaker says, and employ verification techniques to ensure accurate understanding.

- The *observer* will critique the role play, using a simple form to record his or her observations.

- There will be three rounds to the role play, so each of you will—in turn—play each of the three roles.

The Speaker Role;
The Listener Role;
The Observer Role

DISTRIBUTE "The Speaker Role," "The Listener Role," and "The Observer Role" from the "Active Listening" learning activity (pages 260, 261 and 262, and 263 and 264 respectively).

PRESENT the basic instructions for the activity.

1. Before the role plays begin, you will have 3 to 5 minutes to review your instructions and make notes about your topic on the handout called "The Speaker Role."

2. Once the role plays begin, the participant playing "observer" in each round will keep track of time.

3. Each role play discussion will be 3 minutes in length.

4. About 30 seconds before the end of the time period, the observer will ask the listener to summarize his or her understanding of the discussion.

5. At the end of each round, 3 minutes will be allowed for discussion within the table group.

6. This procedure will be repeated until each participant in the table group has played "speaker."

7. Finally, the full group will reconvene for a discussion of the active listening experiences.

ASK this question.

- Are there any questions about the instructions, thus far?

ANSWER the questions, as appropriate.

REVIEW *the instructions in each of the three handouts, either paraphrasing them or reading them aloud.*

ASK this question.

- Are there any questions about the instructions before beginning?

ANSWER the questions, as appropriate.

ASK participants to move to their table groups.

MONITOR *progress as the exercise moves forward, making sure that the groups stay on schedule.*

GROUP DISCUSSION

RECONVENE the full group.

ASK this question.

- As listeners, how did it feel to deliberately verify for understanding during the role play?

LOOK FOR answers such as these.

- Listening and verifying is work—it's not easy.

- Clearly, there is room for improvement in everyone's listening and verifying skills.

ASK this question.

- What verification techniques did you use? Which seemed most successful? Comfortable?

REINFORCE verification techniques covered in "Listener's Tips" and "Observer's Critique Sheet" during the discussion of techniques that were used, as appropriate.

- Confirms as a part of verification

- Seeks clarification when needed

- Assumes responsibility for misunderstanding

- Maintains eye contact

- Exhibits attentive body posture

ASK these questions.

- As speakers, how did it feel to have someone making a concerted effort to be sure they were understanding you?

- What effect do you think this type of listening has on your customers?

LOOK FOR answers such as these.

- It feels good to know the other person is really listening.

- It is surprising how often people don't understand what the other person really meant.

Active Listening

SUMMARIZE key points about active listening, using the "Active Listening" overhead transparency.

INDIVIDUAL ASSESSMENT

INTRODUCE the assessment.

- You will now take a few minutes to complete a simple assessment of your skills in active listening:

Active Listening Assessment

DISTRIBUTE the "Active Listening Assessment" (page 337).

REVIEW the instructions on the assessment with participants.

ALLOW 3 minutes to complete the assessment.

GROUP DISCUSSION

ASK participants to volunteer steps in their personal action plans for improving active listening skills.

MAKE notes on a blank flipchart.

REINFORCE the value of the steps identified, referring to the "Active Listening Assessment" as appropriate.

KEY POINTS   *MAKE these key points as a summary.*

- Listening is an excellent technique for building a good relationship with your customers.

- It is a way to express a genuine interest in the other person and what he or she has to say.

Summary

00:05

Purpose: Review key points from the module, and provide a transition to the next module in the workshop.

FACILITATOR COMMENTARY

MAKE this comment.

- At this point, we have discussed and practiced two skills that are key to your success throughout the sales process—listening and verifying.

- In particular, you have seen how these skills can work together as "active listening"—an approach to listening that will contribute to success in your selling efforts.

REVIEW flipcharts that have been posted during the module, as appropriate.

ASK this question.

- Are there any questions about this module?

ANSWER the questions, as appropriate.

Communications
Workshop Agenda

MARK OFF the topic that has been covered on the "Communications Workshop Agenda" flipchart.

INDICATE the topics to be covered in the next module, using the "Communications Workshop Agenda" flipchart.

3. Observing and Questioning

Purpose   Introduce the skills of observing and questioning and establish their use early in the sales process.

Objectives The participant will:
- Describe the general role and importance of observing and questioning skills in the sales process.
- Identify the types of information that can be gathered about customers through use of the observing skill.
- Determine what others see when they observe him or her.
- Define general questions and describe their use.
- Identify questions that are useful early in the sales process.

Agenda

		Page	Timing[1]	Start	Stop
3	**Observing and Questioning**		**01:05**		
	Introduction	83	00:05		
	The Observing Skill	84			
	• Commentary and Exercise		00:20		
	• Individual Assessment		00:10		
	Introduction to Questioning	87			
	• Group Discussion		00:10		
	• Individual "Target" Activity		00:15		
	Summary	91	00:05		

---

[1] Suggested elapsed time.

Introduction

00:05

*Observing and Questioning:
Overview*

Purpose: Introduce the content of the module; position the importance of observing and questioning in the sales process.

FACILITATOR COMMENTARY

USE the "Observing and Questioning: Overview" overhead transparency (page 369) to describe the topics to be covered in the module.

MAKE these points about the importance of observing and questioning skills.

- As with listening and verifying, observing and questioning are key to your success from the beginning of the sales process to its successful end.

- However, these skills are especially important early in the sales process—during the "Earn the Right" phase.

  - Observing is a valuable way to pick up clues about your customer—especially when you've not met the customer before, and your observations are about all you "know" about the individual.

  - Properly phrased questions are also important— questions that assure that you will get your customer to open up and talk to you.

- In this module, we will first discuss the use of the observing skill.

- Then, we will discuss the questioning skill—focusing on its use during the "Earn the Right" phase.

ASK this question.

- Are there any questions about this before we start?

ANSWER questions, as appropriate.

The Observing Skill

00:30

Purpose: Define the observing skill and establish its value in sales interactions.

COMMENTARY AND EXERCISE

MAKE this comment.

Observing

- Although the observing skill is valuable *throughout* the sales process, there are certain times when it is especially valuable—for example, at the beginning when you are attempting to build rapport.

USE the "Observing" overhead transparency (page 370) to define observing.

REVIEW the four steps involved in observing, as listed on the overhead transparency.

- Look for a clue (or clues) that might suggest certain characteristics or traits in your customer.

- Interpret the clues—a particularly important step when you are drawing conclusions about the customer's longer term behavior patterns.

- Verify the accuracy of your interpretation—and the presence of the characteristic that you think you detected.

- Use the clues and your interpretation of them—verified, of course—to help you relate to your customer and determine your next steps.

Procedural note: If participants in your workshop ordinarily do not meet customers in the customer's environment, omit pages 226 and 227 of the handout for the next exercise. It is relevant only when participants have the opportunity to be in the customer's work setting.

To expedite the debriefing of the exercise, select three to five of the customer characteristics or traits listed in the exercise that are the most important or relevant for your participants. Then, focus the debriefing on those characteristics.

INDIVIDUAL EXERCISE

INTRODUCE the exercise.

- You will now take a few minutes to identify clues that will make you a more effective observer, and approaches that you might take to verify your observations.

Observing: What You Can Learn

DISTRIBUTE the exercise handout, "Observing: What You Can Learn" (pages 223 through 227 or pages 223 through 225, per the comment on the previous page).

REVIEW briefly the summary of the observing skill and the instructions on the handout with participants.

ALLOW 5 minutes to complete the written exercise (3 minutes if participants are only completing the first of the two exercises).

GROUP DISCUSSION

ASK participants to describe clues they might look for, their interpretations of the clues, ways in which they might verify conclusions based on the clues, and how they might adjust their approaches based on the clues.

FOCUS the discussion on those few behavior characteristics that you identified as most important or relevant.

RECORD responses on the "Observing" flipchart (page 397).

Observing

KEY POINTS

MAKE these key points.

- Observing the customer can tell you a great deal about his or her current state of mind—and his or her reaction to you.

- Your observations of the customer and his or her environment can also tell you a great deal about long-term behavior patterns—information that is especially important in the longer-term sales process and relationships.

INDIVIDUAL ASSESSMENT

INTRODUCE the assessment.

- In any situation, including sales, observing is a two-way street.

- Now that you've thought about the clues you can get about your customers, it's time to think about the clues you reveal to them—*the impressions you make* on your customers.

What Impressions Do You Make?

DISTRIBUTE the assessment, "What Impressions Do You Make?" (page 339).

REVIEW the instructions on the assessment with participants.

ALLOW 3 minutes to complete the assessment.

GROUP DISCUSSION

ASK participants to volunteer steps in their personal action plans for improving the impressions they make on others.

MAKE notes on a blank flipchart.

REINFORCE the value of the steps identified, referring to key points such as these.

- Awareness of nonverbal behaviors
    - Facing customer
    - Eye contact
    - Friendly posture
    - Receptiveness
- Positive image, including grooming and environment

KEY POINTS

MAKE these key points as a summary.

- Properly used, observing is a very powerful skill.

- By observing, you are able to learn a great deal about your customers—*and they learn about you, too.*

Introduction to Questioning

00:25   **Purpose:** Explore the use of general questions early in the sales process—in particular, in building rapport.

GROUP DISCUSSION

MAKE this comment.

- In the introduction to this module, we agreed that the questioning skill is important to success in the "Earn the Right" phase.

- Let's assume that you've gotten beyond the very early "small talk" part of a sales effort—and it's time to "get down to business."

ASK this question.

- What is your purpose in asking questions early in a sales effort?

LOOK FOR answers that suggest this idea.

- You want to make people "open up" and talk—in particular, to begin to give you clues about why the two of you are involved in a sales interaction.

ASK this question.

- What are some examples of such questions?

RECORD responses on a blank flipchart.

LOOK FOR suggested questions that begin with <u>what, how, who, why, and where</u>.

Notes regarding typical questions for the participants' environment.

- _____

- _____

- _____

MAKE this comment.

- Questions such as these are typically referred to as "general" questions.

KEY POINTS

MAKE these key points.

- Early in a sales interaction, it is important to avoid asking questions that can be answered with a single word—especially "No!"

- Think about how many times you have said "No" to a salesperson who asked if you wished help—even when you *really* wanted some help.

Early Questions

USE the "Early Questions" overhead transparency (page 371) to review key points on general questions.

MAKE this comment with reference to the information on the flipchart.

- The typical questions that you have identified all have one purpose—to open the conversation and cause the customer to speak.

ASK this question.

- Are there any questions about general questions?

ANSWER the questions, as appropriate.

INDIVIDUAL "TARGET" ACTIVITY

INTRODUCE a "Targeting Your Sales Efforts" activity focused on general questions.

- In this "Targeting Your Sales Efforts" activity, you will identify questions to use early in the "Earn the Right" phase, in two different situations.

Questions for "Earn the Right"

DISTRIBUTE the learning activity, "Questions for 'Earn the Right'" (page 266).

REVIEW the instructions for the learning activity with participants.

SUGGEST that participants use the same situations as in the previous "Targeting Your Sales Effort" activity, if appropriate.

ALLOW 5 minutes to complete the activity.

GROUP DISCUSSION

ASK a volunteer to describe one of his or her selling situations, the question(s) to be used, and the hoped-for result.

Questions for "Earn the Right"

MAKE notes on the "Questions for 'Earn the Right'" flipchart (page 398).

ASK one or two other volunteers with different situations to describe their question(s) and hoped-for results.

MAKE additional notes on the "Questions for 'Earn the Right'" flipchart.

REINFORCE the use of general questions to open up discussion and get the customer talking.

ASK other participants for comments and suggestions on the questions—particularly those who were working with similar situations.

NOTE on the flipchart changes <u>to which the "owner" of the question(s) agrees</u>.

ALLOW 2 or 3 minutes at the conclusion of the discussion for participants to make notes and changes to their own work.

POST the "Questions for 'Earn the Right'" flipchart in the "Target" area, while participants update their work.

 ASK this question.

- Are there any questions about the activity just completed?

ANSWER the questions, as appropriate.

Summary

00:05

Purpose: Review key points from the module, and provide a transition to the next module in the workshop.

FACILITATOR COMMENTARY

MAKE this comment.

- At this point, we have concluded Module 3 of our communications workshop.

- We have discussed the "observing" skill, and have begun our discussion of questioning.

REVIEW the flipchart that has been posted in the "Communications Skills" area.

- Observing

REVIEW other flipcharts that have been posted during the module, as appropriate.

Targeting Your Sales Efforts

REVIEW the flipchart that has been posted in the "Target" area.

- Questions for "Earn the Right"

MARK OFF the activity that has been completed on the "Targeting Your Sales Efforts" flipchart.

ASK this question.

- Are there any questions about this module?

ANSWER the questions, as appropriate.

Communications Workshop Agenda

MARK OFF the topics that have been covered on the "Communications Workshop Agenda" flipchart.

INDICATE the topics to be covered in the next module, using the "Communications Workshop Agenda" flipchart.

4. More on Questioning

Purpose Introduce the concepts of buying objectives and buying influences; introduce additional techniques in questioning and establish their use—particularly in the "Understand the Need" phase.

Objectives The participant will:
- Define the concepts of buying objectives and buying influences.
- Identify typical buying objectives and buying influences in his or her sales environment.
- Define specific/closed questions and leading questions.
- Describe the role of question types in understanding a customer's need.
- Identify questions that are useful in understanding a customer's need.

Agenda

		Page	Timing[1]	Start	Stop
4	**More on Questioning**		**01:45**		
	Introduction	93	00:05		
	Buying Objectives and Influences	94			
	• Group Discussion		00:15		
	• Individual "Target" Activity		00:15		
	More on Questioning	99			
	• Group Discussion		00:15		
	• Demonstration Role Play		00:25		
	• Individual "Target" Activity		00:15		
	• Individual Assessment		00:10		
	Summary	107	00:05		

---

[1] Suggested elapsed time.

Introduction

00:05

Purpose: Introduce the content of the module; position the importance of questioning skills in understanding a customer's needs.

More on Questions:
Overview

FACILITATOR COMMENTARY

USE the "More on Questions: Overview" overhead transparency (page 372) to describe the topics to be covered in the module.

MAKE these points about the importance of the topics in this module.

- Although questioning is important throughout the sales process, skillful use of questioning is especially important when you are in the "Understand the Need" phase.

- Learning about a customer's buying objectives and buying influences is your main task during this phase, and questioning—accompanied by listening and verifying—is the main tool you use.

- In this module, we will first discuss buying objectives and buying influences.

- Then, we will discuss additional questioning skills.

  - Our primary focus will be on their use during the "Understand the Need" phase.

  - As indicated in the discussion of general questions, however, these additional questioning skills are of value throughout the sales process.

ASK this question.

- Are there any questions about this module before we start?

ANSWER the questions, as appropriate.

Buying Objectives and Influences

00:30

Purpose: Define buying objectives and influences, and identify typical buying objectives and influences in the participants' selling environment.

GROUP DISCUSSION

MAKE a brief statement that summarizes one of the typical sales situations in which participants find themselves.

The situation _____

Typical Sales Situations

REFER to the previously-posted "Typical Sales Situations" flipchart during the summary statement, as needed (posted in the "Workshop Overview" area).

ASK this question.

• In the situation just described, why is your customer there?

RECORD responses on a blank flipchart.

LOOK FOR situation-specific answers that describe problems to be solved or needs to be satisfied—in addition to the obvious answer, "They want to buy."

Notes regarding typical problems and needs that should be identified during the discussion.

• _____

• _____

• _____

REINFORCE these points, referring to answers on the flipchart as appropriate.

• Customers are there because they have a *problem* to solve.

• Customers are there because they have a *need* to satisfy.

KEY POINTS   ***MAKE*** *these key points to reinforce key assumptions about effective selling.*

- Customers want help with their buying decision—and you are there to provide that help.

- *Customers are there to buy*—and *you are there to sell.*

- Therefore, it is imperative that you *understand* the problem that must be solved or the need that must be satisfied— before you can make a sound recommendation and then complete the sale.

Buying Objectives;
Buying Influences

REFER *to the "Buying Objectives" and "Buying Influences" flipcharts (pages 399 and 400, respectively) to define the terms "buying objectives" and "buying influences."*

ASK *these questions.*

- What are some typical buying objectives in your sales situations?

- What are some of the buying influences associated with those buying objectives?

RECORD *2 or 3 buying objectives and 2 or 3 buying influences associated with each buying objective on the respective flipcharts—keeping the discussion brief.*

Notes regarding typical buying objectives and buying influences for participant situations.

- _____

- _____

- _____

- _____

- _____

MAKE SURE *that answers clearly distinguish between buying objectives and buying influences—and that they accurately reflect the participants' sales situations.*

- Buying objectives—what the customer wishes to accomplish.

- Buying influences—factors that will influence the customer's buying decision.

Why Customers Buy

DISTRIBUTE *the handout, "Why Customers Buy" (pages 228 and 229).*

ALLOW *3 minutes for participants to read the handout.*

Notes regarding specific points that you wish to reinforce from the reading.

- _____

- _____

- _____

POST *the "Buying Objectives" and "Buying Influences" flipcharts in the "Sales Process" area.*

ASK *this question.*

- Are there any questions about buying objectives and buying influences before we move on to an activity?

ANSWER *the questions, as appropriate.*

INDIVIDUAL "TARGET" ACTIVITY

INTRODUCE a "Targeting Your Sales Efforts" activity focused on buying objectives and buying influences.

- In this "Targeting Your Sales Efforts" activity, you will identify buying objectives and buying influences for two of your typical customers.

**Buying Objectives and
Buying Influences**

DISTRIBUTE the learning activity, "Buying Objectives and Buying Influences" (page 269).

REVIEW the instructions for the learning activity with participants.

SUGGEST that participants use the same customers as those involved in the situations used in the previous "Targeting Your Sales Efforts" activity.

ALLOW 5 minutes to complete the activity.

GROUP DISCUSSION

ASK a volunteer to first describe one of his or her customers, and then buying objectives and buying influences for that customer.

Why Customers Buy

MAKE notes on the "Why Customers Buy" flipchart (page 401).

ASK one or two other volunteers to describe one of their customers, and then buying objectives and buying influences for that customer.

REINFORCE responses, based on the distinction between "buying objectives" and "buying influences."

- Buying objectives—what the customer wishes to accomplish.

- Buying influences—factors that will influence the customer's buying decision.

MAKE additional notes on the "Why Customers Buy" flipchart.

ASK other participants for comments and suggestions on the buying objectives and buying influences identified—particularly those who were working with similar customers.

NOTE on the flipchart changes <u>to which the "owner" of the approach agrees.</u>

ALLOW 2 or 3 minutes at the conclusion of the discussion for participants to make notes and changes to their own work.

POST the "Why Customers Buy" flipchart in the "Target" area, while participants update their work.

ASK this question.

- Are there any questions about the activity just completed?

ANSWER the questions, as appropriate.

More on Questioning

01:05

Purpose: Define specific/closed and leading questions, and explore the use of these question types.

GROUP DISCUSSION

MAKE these comments.

- Questioning is an important tool as you work toward understanding the customer's need—the buying objectives and buying influences.

- In addition to general questions, there are other types that are especially useful during the "Understand the Need" phase of the sales process—specific, closed, and leading.

REFER to the "Buying Objectives" flipchart, posted previously.

SELECT one of the buying objectives as the basis for the following question.

ASK this question.

- What are some examples of questions that you might use as you try to understand the customer's need associated with this buying objective?

RECORD responses on a blank flipchart.

LOOK FOR suggested questions that can be categorized as specific/closed or leading.

Notes regarding typical questions for the participants' environment:

- _____

- _____

- _____

Types of Questions

DEFINE question types, using the "Types of Questions" overhead (page 373)—first reviewing "general" and then emphasizing "specific/closed" and "leading" (in that order).

EMPHASIZE the role of general questions in broadening discussion, specific/direct questions in focusing it, and leading questions in broadening <u>or</u> focusing, depending on the question.

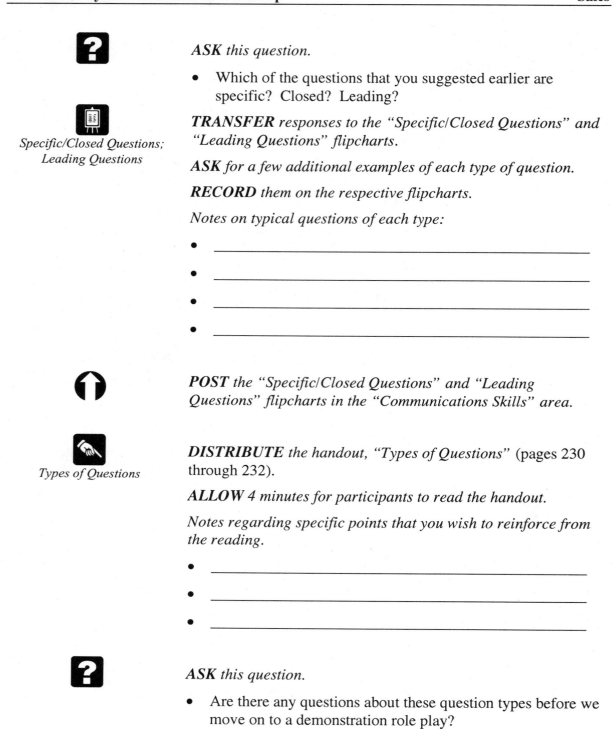

ASK *this question.*

- Which of the questions that you suggested earlier are specific? Closed? Leading?

Specific/Closed Questions; Leading Questions

TRANSFER *responses to the "Specific/Closed Questions" and "Leading Questions" flipcharts.*

ASK *for a few additional examples of each type of question.*

RECORD *them on the respective flipcharts.*

Notes on typical questions of each type:

- _____

- _____

- _____

- _____

POST *the "Specific/Closed Questions" and "Leading Questions" flipcharts in the "Communications Skills" area.*

Types of Questions

DISTRIBUTE *the handout, "Types of Questions" (pages 230 through 232).*

ALLOW *4 minutes for participants to read the handout.*

Notes regarding specific points that you wish to reinforce from the reading.

- _____

- _____

- _____

ASK *this question.*

- Are there any questions about these question types before we move on to a demonstration role play?

ANSWER *the questions, as appropriate.*

> *Note: Materials required for the following activity may be found in the "A Questioning Demonstration" learning activity beginning on page 270.*

DEMONSTRATION ROLE PLAY

MAKE this comment.

- The purpose of this demonstration role play is to illustrate the use of questions in understanding a customer's need.

ASK for two volunteers—one to role play the "customer" and the other the "salesperson."

INDICATE that the remaining participants will function as observers during the role play.

Observer's Critique Sheet

DISTRIBUTE the "Observer's Critique Sheet" from the "A Questioning Demonstration" learning activity (page 273).

REVIEW the critique sheet with participants.

STRESS the points about using each of the question types and organizing the questions into a logical, productive sequence.

- Use general, specific/closed, and leading questions to open up and then focus the discussion, as needed.

- Structure questioning logically so that your discussion produces the information that you need.

DISTRIBUTE the instruction sheets to the salesperson and customer (pages 274 and 275, respectively).

PRESENT the basic instructions for the activity.

1. We will take a short break during which the salesperson and customer will review their instructions and prepare themselves for the role play.

2. Following that, they will role play a sales situation for approximately 5 minutes.

3. I will signal the volunteers about 30 seconds before the role play is over, at which time the salesperson will summarize his or her understanding of the customer at that point in time.

4. The rest of you will then have 1 or 2 minutes to complete your critique sheets.

5. Then we will discuss the questioning demonstration as a group.

ALLOW 3 minutes for a break, during which the volunteers will prepare for their roles.

RECONVENE the group.

BEGIN the role play.

ANNOUNCE that it is time for the salesperson to summarize after about 4½ minutes.

ALLOW 30 seconds for the salesperson's summary.

GROUP DISCUSSION

MAKE this comment.

- Let's discuss the effectiveness of the questioning technique used in this demonstration role play.

ASK these questions of the salesperson.

- How did you make use of various question types during the demonstration?

- Why did you use that particular questioning approach?

- How effective was it from your point of view?

RECORD responses on a blank flipchart.

ASK this question.

- What general reactions do the observers have about what was done well? Suggestions for improvement?

REFER to each of the major categories on the critique sheet as you gather comments, in order to assure completeness of the discussion.

RECORD responses on another blank flipchart.

ASK these questions of the customer.

- What was your perception of the overall sales effort?

- How effective was the questioning technique from your point of view?

RECORD responses on a third blank flipchart.

ENCOURAGE observers to make additional constructive comments regarding their impressions, alternatives, etc.

Types of Questions

USE the "Types of Questions" overhead transparency (page 373) as a vehicle to summarize the demonstration and the discussion of question types.

ASK this question.

- Are there any questions about this demonstration?

ANSWER the questions, as appropriate.

INDIVIDUAL "TARGET" ACTIVITY

INTRODUCE a "Targeting Your Sales Efforts" activity focused on the use of questions in understanding the customer's need.

- In this "Targeting Your Sales Efforts" activity, you will think about two of your typical customers and their buying objectives, and then develop questions for each that could be used to understand their needs.

Questions for "Understand the Need"

DISTRIBUTE the learning activity, "Questions for 'Understand the Need'" (pages 278 and 279).

REVIEW the instructions for the learning activity with participants.

SUGGEST that participants use the same customers and buying objectives as in the previous "Targeting Your Sales Efforts" activity, if appropriate.

ALLOW 5 minutes to complete the activity.

GROUP DISCUSSION

ASK a volunteer to describe one of his or her customers, the typical buying objective, and then the questions of each type that could be used with the customer.

Questions for "Understand the Need"

MAKE notes on the "Questions for 'Understand the Need'" flipchart (page 404).

ASK one or two other volunteers to describe one of their customers and the buying objectives, and the questions that they developed.

MAKE additional notes on the "Questions for 'Understand the Need'" flipchart.

REINFORCE responses, based on the tips in the "Types of Questions" handout.

- Ask questions that gather the types of information you need.

- Use a deliberate line of questioning to take you and your customer where you want to go.

ASK other participants for comments and suggestions on the questions developed—particularly those who were working with similar customers.

NOTE on the flipchart changes <u>to which the "owner" of the approach agrees.</u>

ALLOW 2 or 3 minutes at the conclusion of the discussion for participants to make notes and changes to their own work.

POST the "Questions for 'Understand the Need'" flipchart in the "Target" area, while participants update their work.

ASK this question.

- Are there any questions about the activity just completed—or about the discussion of questioning?

ANSWER the questions, as appropriate.

INDIVIDUAL ASSESSMENT

INTRODUCE the assessment.

- You will now take a few minutes to complete a simple assessment of your skills in questioning.

Questioning Assessment

DISTRIBUTE the "Questioning Assessment" (page 341).

REVIEW the instructions on the assessment with participants.

ALLOW 3 minutes to complete the assessment.

GROUP DISCUSSION

ASK participants to volunteer steps in their personal action plans for improving questioning skills.

MAKE notes on a blank flipchart.

REINFORCE the value of the steps identified, referring to the "Questioning Assessment," as appropriate.

KEY POINTS

MAKE these key points as a summary.

- The skillful use of logically organized general, specific, and leading questions is important to success in the "Understand the Need" phase of the sales process—and throughout the sales process.

- Key to your success in questioning, of course, is careful use of the listening and verifying skills.

Summary

00:05

Purpose: Review key points from the module, and provide a transition to the next module in the workshop.

FACILITATOR COMMENTARY

MAKE this comment.

- At this point, we have concluded Module 4 of our communications workshop.

- We have discussed buying objectives and buying influences, and the role of three question types in learning about these during the "Understand the Need" phase of the sales process.

REVIEW the flipcharts that have been posted in the "Sales Process" area.

- Buying Objectives

- Buying Influences

REVIEW the flipcharts that have been posted in the "Communications Skills" area.

- Specific/Closed Questions

- Leading Questions

REVIEW other flipcharts that have been posted during the module, as appropriate.

*Targeting Your
Sales Efforts*

REVIEW the flipcharts that have been posted in the "Target" area.

- Why Customers Buy

- Questions for "Understand the Need"

MARK OFF the activity that has been completed on the "Targeting Your Sales Efforts" flipchart.

ASK this question.

- Are there any questions about this module?

ANSWER the questions, as appropriate.

*Communications
Workshop Agenda*

MARK OFF *the topics that have been covered on the "Communications Workshop Agenda" flipchart.*

INDICATE *the topics to be covered in the next module, using the "Communications Workshop Agenda" flipchart.*

- ***Procedural note: Option:*** *If you will be following this workshop with the one-day workshop be sure the following flipchart is posted in the "Workshop Overview" area prior to the beginning of Module 5:*

- ***Sales Workshop Agenda***

  If you ran the one-hour seminar, this flipchart was also used during that seminar.

---

5. Explaining

Purpose   Introduce the skill of explaining and establish its use in the sales process.

Objectives   The participant will:
- Describe the general role and importance of the explaining skill in the sales process.
- Describe the characteristics of a good explanation.
- Apply the explaining skill in a sales situation.

Agenda

		Page	Timing[1]	Start	Stop
5	**Explaining**		**01:00**		
	Introduction	110	00:05		
	The Explaining Skill	111			
	• Group Discussion		00:10		
	• Demonstration Role Play		00:25		
	• Individual Assessment		00:10		
	Summary	116	00:10		

---

[1] Suggested elapsed time.

Introduction

00:05

Purpose: Introduce the content of the module; position the importance of explaining in the sales process.

Explaining: Overview

FACILITATOR COMMENTARY

USE the "Explaining: Overview" overhead transparency (page 374) to describe the topics to be covered in the module, and their interrelationships.

MAKE these points about the importance of observing and questioning skills.

- Although the explaining skill can be useful throughout the sales process, it is particularly useful during the last two phases.

    – When you are presenting a recommendation in the "Make a Recommendation" phase

    – When you are handling obstacles, typically in the "Complete the Sale" phase

    – And . . . anytime you need to answer a question

- In this module, we will discuss the use of this skill.

ASK this question.

- Are there any questions about this module before we start?

ANSWER the questions, as appropriate.

The Explaining Skill

00:45

Purpose: Define the explaining skill, and establish the characteristics of a good explanation.

GROUP DISCUSSION

MAKE this comment.

- When you make a recommendation to your customer—or handle the obstacles that come up from time to time—you must make skillful use of the explaining skill.

Explaining

REVIEW the definition of explaining, using the "Explaining" overhead transparency (page 375).

ASK this question.

- If you were a customer, how would you characterize a good explanation? What would you look for?

Explaining Skill

RECORD responses on the "Explaining Skill" flipchart (page 405).

LOOK FOR answers that will allow you to reinforce characteristics of a good explanation.

- Simple language, no technical jargon
- Short, to the point
- Logical, clear transitions from one point to the next
- Credible—yet dynamic, vivid, exciting for the customer
- Focused on customer objectives

KEY POINTS

MAKE these key points.

- When your explanation is in response to a question and you don't know the answer, *don't "fake it."*
- Defer the question until you can get the information required—and then provide the necessary explanation.

Explaining

DISTRIBUTE *the handout, "Explaining" (pages 233 and 234).*

ALLOW *3 minutes for participants to read the handout.*

Notes regarding specific points that you wish to reinforce from the reading.

- _____

- _____

- _____

ASK *this question.*

- Are there any questions about the explaining skill?

ANSWER *the questions, as appropriate.*

POST *the "Explaining Skill" flipchart in the "Communications Skills" area.*

Note: Materials required for the following activity may be found in the "An Explaining Demonstration" activity guide beginning on page 280.

DEMONSTRATION ROLE PLAY

MAKE this comment.

- The purpose of this demonstration role play is to illustrate the skill of explaining.

ASK for two volunteers—one to role play the "customer" and the other the "salesperson."

INDICATE that the remaining participants will function as observers during the role play.

Observer's Critique Sheet

DISTRIBUTE the "Observer's Critique Sheet" from the "An Explaining Demonstration" learning activity (page 283).

REVIEW the critique sheet with participants.

DISTRIBUTE the instruction sheets to the salesperson and customer (pages 284 and 285, respectively).

PRESENT the basic instructions for the activity.

1. We will take a short break during which the salesperson and customer will review their instructions and prepare themselves for the role play.

2. Following that, they will role play a sales situation for approximately 5 minutes.

3. I will signal the volunteers about 30 seconds before the role play is over, at which time the salesperson will bring his or her explanation to a close.

4. The rest of you will then have 1 or 2 minutes to complete your critique sheets.

5. Then, we will discuss the demonstration as a group.

ALLOW 3 minutes for a break, during which volunteers will prepare for their roles.

RECONVENE the group.

BEGIN the role play.

ANNOUNCE that it is time for the salesperson to bring the explanation to a close after about 4½ minutes.

ALLOW 30 seconds for the salesperson to bring the explanation to a close.

GROUP DISCUSSION

MAKE this comment.

- Let's discuss the effectiveness of the explaining technique that was used in this demonstration role play.

ASK these questions of the salesperson.

- How did you organize the content of your explanation?

- Why did you use that particular approach to explaining?

- How effective was it from your point of view?

RECORD responses on a blank flipchart.

ENCOURAGE observers to make additional constructive comments regarding their impressions, alternatives, etc.

ASK these questions of the customer—using the first question to probe into each of the major categories on the critique sheet.

- What was your perception of the explanation? Content organized? Clear transitions? Credible? Etc.?

- How effective was the overall approach from your point of view?

RECORD responses on another blank flipchart.

ENCOURAGE observers to make additional constructive comments regarding their impressions, alternatives, etc.

ASK this question.

- What general reactions do the observers have about what was done well? Suggestions for improvement?

RECORD responses on a third blank flipchart.

SUMMARIZE the discussion, referring to the flipcharts.

ASK this question.

- Are there any questions about this demonstration?

ANSWER the questions, as appropriate.

INDIVIDUAL ASSESSMENT

INTRODUCE the assessment.

- You will now take a few minutes to complete a simple assessment of your skills in explaining.

Explaining Assessment

DISTRIBUTE the "Explaining Assessment" (page 343).

REVIEW the instructions on the assessment with participants.

ALLOW 3 minutes to complete the assessment.

GROUP DISCUSSION

ASK participants to volunteer steps in their personal action plans for improving explaining skills.

MAKE notes on a blank flipchart.

REINFORCE the value of the steps identified, referring to the "Explaining Assessment," as appropriate.

KEY POINTS

MAKE these key points as a summary.

- The explaining skill is key to your success in making recommendations and handling obstacles.

- In addition, it is important at any time you have to answer a question.

Summary

00:10

Purpose: Review key points from the module, and conclude the workshop.

FACILITATOR COMMENTARY

MAKE this comment.

- At this point, we have concluded the last module of our communications workshop.

- We have covered the last of the communications skills involved in effective selling—explaining.

REVIEW the flipchart that has been posted in the "Communications Skills" area.

- Explaining Skill

REVIEW other flipcharts that have been posted during the module, as appropriate.

ASK this question.

- Are there any questions about this module?

ANSWER the questions, as appropriate.

Communications Workshop Agenda

MARK OFF the topic that has been covered on the "Communications Workshop Agenda" flipchart.

[Start option]

Option: If you will be following this workshop with the one-day workshop, do the following:

MAKE *these comments.*

At this point we will review quickly the forthcoming sales workshop.

Sales Workshop Agenda

Sales Workshop: Logistics

REVIEW *quickly the agenda for the sales workshop, using the "Sales Workshop Agenda" flipchart (page 389).*

REVIEW *quickly the logistics for the sales workshop, using the "Sales Workshop: Logistics" flipchart (page 406).*

- Day and Date

- Time

- Location

- Recommended dress

KEY POINT

MAKE *this key point.*

- Please be sure to bring your materials from this workshop and the seminar (if applicable)—handouts, notes, etc.—to the sales workshop.

ASK *this question.*

- Are there any questions about the sales workshop?

ANSWER *the questions, as appropriate.*

[end option]

MAKE *these concluding comments.*

- Thank you for your time and involvement in today's workshop.

- I am looking forward to working with you in the forthcoming sales workshop.

- Remember . . . bring the materials you have gathered so far to the sales workshop.

Procedural note: *Be sure to save the flipcharts used and/or developed during this workshop. Many of them will be used for reference during the sales workshop.*

Chapter Six:

A One-Day Sales Workshop

This chapter contains the training plan for your one-day sales workshop—ready to go "as is" or to be tailored to meet your needs. The chapter is divided into six parts.

- Purpose and goals of the workshop
- One part for each of the five modules that comprise the one-day workshop, containing the purpose, objectives, and training plan for that module

You will find information on preparing for this workshop in the chapters titled "Planning the Workshop" and "Getting Everything Ready" (pages 7 and 19, respectively).

Purpose and Goals

Here are statements of the purpose and goals for the one-day workshop.

Purpose

Provide knowledge and practice on the sales process and key sales skills involved in effective selling; also, reinforce the role of communications skills in the context of the sales process.

Goals

The participant will:

- Relate the information covered during the one-hour seminar and the communications workshop (if they have attended one or both of these) to the content and structure of this sales workshop.
- Describe the "Earn the Right" phase of the sales process, effectively apply key communications skills during this phase, and successfully begin to build rapport with the customer.
- Describe the "Understand the Need" phase of the sales process, effectively apply key communications skills during this phase, and successfully qualify sales opportunities.
- Describe the "Make a Recommendation" phase of the sales process and effectively apply key communications skills during this phase; successfully test for readiness for recommendations; present effective recommendations that include clearly described benefits for the customer.

- Describe the "Complete the Sale" phase of the sales process and effectively apply key communications skills during this phase; successfully ask for the order and handle obstacles that might arise.
- Integrate all of the knowledge and skills regarding the sales process, communications, and sales into selling approaches that will be successful in his or her environment.

Each module in the one-day sales workshop has its own statement of purpose and objectives, providing an additional level of detail about the module.

Procedural note: If participants attended the one-hour seminar and/or the half-day communications workshop prior to beginning Module 1, be sure the following flipcharts from the one-hour seminar are posted in the "Workshop Overview" area:

- *Effective Selling* (page 387)
- *Workshop Expectations* (page 390)
- *Sales Workshop Agenda* (page 389)
- *Typical Sales Situations* (page 393)

If participants did not attend the one-hour seminar or the half-day communications workshop, post the "Effective Selling" and "Sales Workshop Agenda" flipcharts in the "Workshop Overview" area. The other two flipcharts will be developed during this workshop.

---

1. Introduction to the Sales Workshop

Purpose Review the topics covered in the (optional) one-hour seminar, and orient participants to this workshop.

Objectives The participant will:
- Describe key assumptions that are a part of the *mindset* required for successful selling efforts.
- List the phases of an "effective selling" sales process.
- List the key sales skills to be covered in this workshop.
- Describe the relationship of sales skills to communications and the sales process—and to effective selling.
- Describe the purpose of the sales workshop, and the general approach to be taken in this workshop.

Agenda

		Page	Timing[1]	Start	Stop
1	**Introduction to the Sales Workshop**		**00:20**		
	Review of the Seminar (Optional)	122	00:10		
	Orientation to This Workshop	126	00:10		

[1] Suggested elapsed time.

Introduction and Optional Review of the Seminar

00:10   **Purpose:** Introduce yourself and (optional) review the results of the one-hour effective selling seminar.

> *Procedural note: The tempo of this review should be fast—faster yet if the one-hour seminar and communications workshop were held recently.* <u>*Be sure not to belabor this review.*</u>

FACILITATOR COMMENTARY

WELCOME participants to the one-day sales workshop, being certain to make these points during your introductory comments.

- With your active involvement, this workshop will be interesting and profitable for everyone.

- Thank you for allocating a day of your time to this important activity.

> *Procedural note: The following introductions should either be brief or briefer—depending on how well participants know you and one another, whether they attended the one-hour seminar and/or the communications workshop, etc.*

INTRODUCE yourself <u>quickly</u>, reviewing points that will establish your credibility in sales and/or sales training.

REQUEST participants to introduce themselves <u>quickly</u>, providing name, responsibility, experience, and/or other information that would be of interest to the group.

MAKE this comment.

- (Optional) Before we begin today's topics, we will review quickly some key information originally covered during the one-hour effective selling seminar held on _____ [indicate day/date].

Key Assumptions

REVIEW quickly these points about sales, using the "Key Assumptions" overhead transparency (page 363).

- From the point of view of a salesperson, the sale begins as *an opportunity.*

- The challenge is to move from the opportunity to success—*completing the sale.*

REVIEW key assumptions about the roles of the customer and salesperson as the salesperson moves from <u>an opportunity</u> to <u>completing the sale</u>, using the "Key Assumptions" overhead transparency (page 363).

KEY POINTS

MAKE these key points.

- Customers are there because they have a problem to solve or a need to satisfy—they want to buy and need help with the buying decision.

- Salespeople need to—and are expected to—sell.

- Therefore, in a sales situation, your job is to *learn about the customer's need* and then *complete the sale.*

- This is the first part of the *mindset* with which you approach selling—a mindset that provides *motivation* and *direction* for your work.

Effective Selling

REVIEW briefly the phases of the sales process shown on the "Effective Selling" overhead transparency (page 364).

MAKE this point about the sales process.

- The sales process is the second part of the *mindset* with which you approach selling—providing *direction* for your work.

REVIEW briefly the communications and sales skills shown on the "Effective Selling" overhead transparency (page 364).

MAKE this point about communications and sales skills.

- Communications skills and sales skills are part of the *skill set* with which you approach selling.

- Today, we will see clearly the relationship between the communications skills and sales skills that are important to effective selling.

KEY POINTS

MAKE these key points.

- Positive sales experiences can generally be traced to a salesperson's *mindset* and *skill set*—his or her mastery of each of the areas that are important to effective selling.

- By contrast, unsatisfactory experiences can often be traced to a salesperson's deficiencies in those areas—lack of understanding, lack of skill, etc.

ASK this question.

- Are there any questions about this quick review of effective selling?

ANSWER the questions, as appropriate.

MAKE these comments.

- Before introducing this workshop, let's discuss quickly the description of the nature of your "typical" sales interactions and sales process.

- We will use this description as the basis for discussion and activities during this workshop.

- The purpose of this discussion is to be sure that we all have a common understanding of the environment in which you will be applying the lessons of the workshop.

Typical Sales Situations

USE the "Typical Sales Situations" flipchart (page 393) to describe the nature of the sales interactions and sales process in which workshop participants are typically involved.

ASK this question.

- Are there any differences of opinion between this description of typical sales situations and what you face on a day-to-day basis?

DISCUSS any differences with the group.

AGREE on the resolution of any differences that exist.

ADJUST the description on the flipchart to reflect group agreement.

POST *the "Typical Sales Situations" flipchart in the "Workshop Overview" area.*

[Start option]

Option: *If participants have already been through the one-hour seminar, do the following:*

MAKE *these comments.*

- Before introducing this workshop, let's review quickly the description of the nature of your "typical" sales interactions and sales process—a topic that we discussed near the end of the one-hour seminar.

- Recall that we use this description as the basis for discussion and activities during this workshop

Typical Sales Situations

USE *the "Typical Sales Situations" flipchart (page 393) to review the nature of the sales interactions and sales process in which workshop participants are typically involved.*

[end option]

ASK *this question.*

- Are there any questions about this description, before we move on?

ANSWER *questions, as appropriate.*

Orientation to This Workshop

00:10
Purpose: Orient participants to today's workshop, including purpose and goals, the approach to conducting it, and logistics.

FACILITATOR COMMENTARY

> *Procedural note: If the participants attended the one-hour seminar, follow Option 1, below. If they did not attend the one-hour seminar, follow Option 2.*

Option 1

MAKE this comment.

- During the one-hour seminar, you established your expectations for the communications and sales workshops.

Workshop Expectations

REVIEW quickly the expectations established for the communications and sales workshops, using the "Workshop Expectations" flipchart (page 390).

[end option]

GROUP DISCUSSION

ASK participants to volunteer the highest priority improvements to be made as a result of this workshop.

Workshop Expectations

RECORD expectations on the "Workshop Expectations" flipchart, grouping similar expectations together.

INDICATE the following at the conclusion of the discussion.

- Those expectations that <u>will</u> be met during the workshop

- Those that <u>will not</u> be met—along with an indication of ways in which participants will be able to satisfy them

POST the "Workshop Expectations" flipchart in the "Workshop Overview" area.

*Sales Workshop
Purpose and Goals*

DESCRIBE the purpose and goals of this workshop, using the "Sales Workshop: Purpose and Goals" flipchart (page 407).

RELATE participant expectations to the purpose and goals of this workshop—as well as to the previous communications workshop.

MAKE these points about particular goals that you will stress in <u>this</u> workshop.

- _____
- _____
- _____

POST *the "Sales Workshop: Purpose and Goals" flipchart (page 407) in the "Workshop Overview" area.*

Sales Workshop Agenda

REVIEW *the agenda for the sales workshop, using the "Sales Workshop Agenda" flipchart (page 389).*

MARK OFF *the topics that have been covered on the "Sales Workshop Agenda" flipchart.*

Procedural note: *The tempo of the overview of workshop roles and guidelines should be fast—faster yet if the participants attended the one-hour seminar and communications workshop.* <u>*Be sure not to belabor this review.*</u>

Workshop Roles

REVIEW *workshop roles for both the participants and facilitator, using the "Workshop Roles" overhead transparency (page 365).*

KEY POINTS

MAKE *these key points.*

- The key to success for this workshop is *your active involvement* throughout the day.

- *My main responsibility* is to assure that we "stay on track," achieve the goals of the workshop, and meet your expectations.

Workshop Guidelines

REVIEW *"ground rules" for the workshop, using the "Workshop Guidelines" overhead transparency (page 366).*

KEY POINTS

MAKE *these key points.*

- The purpose of these "ground rules" *is not* to restrict you or inhibit you.

- Rather, the purpose is to make sure that each of you can fully participate in and benefit from the workshop.

DESCRIBE important logistical details.

- Timing of and facilities for breaks and lunch

- Location of telephones, restrooms, and other important facilities

- Safety procedures to be followed in the event of an emergency

?

ASK this question.

- Are there any questions before we move on to the "business" of the workshop?

ANSWER the questions, as appropriate.

Procedural note: If you preceded this workshop with the half-day communications workshop, do the following. Prior to beginning Module 2, be sure the following flipcharts from the half-day communications workshop are posted in the "Communications Skills" area.

- *Observing (page 397)*

- *Questions for "Earn the Right" (page 398)*

- *Targeting Your Sales Efforts (page 396)*

If participants did not attend the half-day communications workshop, post the "Targeting Your Sales Efforts" flipchart in the "Workshop Overview" area. The other two flipcharts will be developed during this workshop .

---

2. Earn the Right

Purpose   Stress the importance of the "Earn the Right" phase of the sales process; reinforce the role of communications skills in the "Earn the Right" phase of the sales process; introduce the skill of building rapport and establish its significance in the sales process.

Objectives   The participant will:
- Describe the role and importance of the "Earn the Right" phase of the sales process.
- Describe the role of key communications skills in this phase.
- Define the concept of building rapport.
- Describe techniques for building rapport during this phase of the sales process.
- Identify approaches for beginning sales efforts with his or her customers.

Agenda

		Page	Timing[1]	Start	Stop
2	**Earn the Right**		**01:10**		
	Introduction	130	00:10		
	Building Rapport	133			
	• Group Discussion		00:20		
	• Individual "Target" Activity		00:15		
	• Individual Assessment		00:10		
	"Earn the Right" Assessment	141	00:10		
	Summary	142	00:05		

---

[1] Suggested elapsed time.

Introduction

00:10

Purpose: Introduce the content of the module; overview key communications topics; position the importance of this phase in the sales process.

Earn the Right:
Overview

FACILITATOR COMMENTARY

USE the "Earn the Right: Overview" overhead transparency (page 376) to describe the topics to be covered in the module.

- The "Earn the Right" phase itself

- Building rapport

- The role of communications skills—particularly observing, questioning, listening, and verifying.

KEY POINTS

MAKE these key points about the "Earn the Right" phase, (optionally, as a review of information covered during the one-hour seminar).

- You have your initial interaction with the customer during this phase of the sales effort; if it is a first meeting, this is the time at which first impressions are formed.

- During this phase, you must *earn the right to proceed.*

    - You must *build* that basic level of trust and confidence that encourages your customer to stay with you and, essentially, grant you the right to move forward with the sales effort.

    - Such a level of trust and confidence is *not* something you can take for granted. *You must earn it.*

The skill of building rapport is particularly important during this phase.

KEY POINTS

MAKE these key points about the four steps involved in observing:

- Look for a clue (or clues) that might suggest certain characteristics or traits in your customer.

- Interpret the clues—a particularly important step when you are drawing conclusions about the customer's longer-term behavior patterns.

- Verify the accuracy of your interpretation—and the presence of the characteristic that you think you detected.

- Use the clue and your interpretation of it—verified, of course—to help you relate to your customer and determine your next steps.

> ***Procedural note:*** *If participants went through the half-day communications workshop, do the following review of the workshop's activities. If participants did not go through the half-day workshop, simply make the following key points that summarize each topic.*

Observing

REVIEW the results of the observing activity, as recorded on the "Observing" flipchart (page 397) during the communications workshop—making these points as you summarize the results.

- Observing the customer's behavior can tell you a great deal about his or her current state of mind—and his or her reaction to you.

- Your observations of the customer and his or her environment can also tell you a great deal about long-term behavior patterns—information that is especially important in longer-term sales process and relationships.

- Having verified and interpreted your observations, you then use that information to make sure that your interaction with the customer remains "on track."

KEY POINTS

MAKE these key points about "questioning" in the "Earn the Right" phase, as a review of information covered during the communications workshop.

- General questions—beginning with *what, who, how, why,* and *where*—are especially useful in this phase.

- These questions tend to cause people to open up and talk.

Questions for "Earn the Right"

REVIEW the results of the questioning activity, as recorded on the "Questions for 'Earn the Right'" flipchart (page 398) during the communications workshop—reinforcing the use of general questions in causing people to open up and talk.

KEY POINTS

MAKE these key points about "listening," as a review of information covered during the communications workshop.

- By definition, listening means "making a conscious effort to hear."

    - *Do* concentrate on what the other person is saying.

    - *Don't* focus all of your attention on what you're going to say next.

- Listening—and more particularly, active listening—is as important in the "Earn the Right" phase as it is throughout the sales process.

KEY POINT

MAKE this key point.

- Success in the "Earn the Right" phase is key to your success in getting the sales effort off to an effective and efficient start.

ASK this question.

- Are there any questions before we turn to "building rapport"?

ANSWER questions, as appropriate.

Building Rapport

00:20

Purpose: Define "building rapport" and identify common approaches to building rapport with customers.

Procedural note: In the discussion that follows, you will be identifying short-range and longer-range objectives for building rapport.

Establish a context for "longer-range" by referring to the description of typical participant sales situations. Depending on their situation, longer-range could be minutes, hours, months—or anything in between.

GROUP DISCUSSION

MAKE an appropriate statement to set up the discussion, similar to the following.

- You and a customer have just met for the first time.

ASK this question.

- What do you want to accomplish at the start of a sales effort?

What Do You Want to Accomplish?

RECORD responses on the "What Do You Want to Accomplish?" flipchart, (page 408) under the heading "Short range."

LOOK FOR answers such as these.

- Make the customer comfortable in the sales situation.

- Gain the attention of the customer and find out why he or she is there—getting a sense of the customer's need and how you can go about learning more about the need.

- Make sure that you will be able to continue the sales effort beyond its opening moments.

KEY POINT

MAKE this key point.

- These are short-range objectives for building rapport.

ASK this question.

- What are some longer-range objectives for building rapport?

RECORD responses on the "What Do You Want to Accomplish?" flipchart, under the heading "Longer range."

LOOK FOR answers such as these.

- You wish to *earn the right* to proceed—ensuring that the customer will stay with you (and return if necessary), thus positioning yourself to learn about the customer's need and complete the sale.

- Having gained the customer's attention, you wish to begin a dialogue with the customer.

- Also, you wish to *continue* building a sense of "relationship, agreement, and harmony" that is key to your success and to a foundation of rapport between yourself and the customer.

KEY POINT

MAKE this key point as a summary to the discussion.

- Building rapport is an ongoing process that is *only beginning* early in the sales effort.

Building Rapport

USE the "Building Rapport" overhead transparency (page 377) to define the concept of building rapport and to reinforce the points made previously.

- In contemporary use, building rapport refers to achieving a sense of relationship, agreement, and harmony.

- The word "rapport" actually derives from Old French and means "to bring back."

KEY POINTS

MAKE these key points.

- In sales, the notion of relationship, agreement, and harmony is only part of our interpretation of rapport.

- The concept of "bringing back" is *key* to what we mean by building rapport.

ASK this question.

- What do you do when you meet a customer in order to begin building rapport? How do you act? Behave?

Building Rapport

RECORD responses on the "Building Rapport" flipchart (page 409).

LOOK FOR answers that fit into these categories.

- Act relaxed and at ease.

- Make the other person feel comfortable—a little "small talk" or other non-business conversation.

- Take some time before moving into the "business" aspect of the discussion.

- Listen to the other person.

- Pay attention to my own nonverbal behaviors—ensure they are positive.

- Make sure that my appearance and surroundings project a positive image.

Building Rapport

DISTRIBUTE the handout, "Building Rapport" (pages 235 and 236).

ALLOW 2 minutes for participants to look through the handout.

Notes regarding specific points that you wish to reinforce from the reading:

- _____

- _____

- _____

ASK this question.

- Are there any questions about this topic?

ANSWER the questions, as appropriate.

Effective Selling

REFER *to the "Effective Selling" flipchart* (page 387) *to remind participants of key communications skills and then the "Building Rapport" flipchart* (page 409) *to quickly review ways in which participants indicated they build rapport.*

ASK *this question.*

- Which of the communications skills are important to "building rapport" ?

LOOK FOR *these answers.*

- Questioning

- Listening

- Observing

POST *the "What Do You Want to Accomplish?" flipchart in the "Sales Process" area.*

POST *the "Building Rapport" flipchart in the "Sales Skills" area.*

INDIVIDUAL "TARGET" ACTIVITY

> ***Procedural note:*** *If the participants attended the half-day workshop, do the following. If participants did not attend the workshop, use the option below.*

INTRODUCE *a "Targeting Your Sales Efforts" activity focused on beginning the sales effort.*

* As your first "Targeting Your Sales Efforts" activity in this workshop, you will identify approaches for beginning sales efforts with your customers in two different situations.

* Before you complete that activity, take a minute to review the typical sales situations and customers that you identified for these activities—during a short activity at the beginning of the communications workshop.

ALLOW *one minute for participants to review the "Typical Sales Situations and Customers" activity.*

Option

INITIAL TARGET ACTIVITY

INTRODUCE *an initial activity that is the foundation for the remaining "Targeting Your Sales Efforts" activites.*

* In order to provide a basis for completing the various "Targeting Your Sales Efforts" activities in this workshop, you will now spend a short time identifying typical sales situations and typical customers whom you meet in those situations.

Typical Sales Situations

USE *the "Typical Sales Situations" flipchart (page 393) to review the nature of the sales interactions and sales process in which participants are typically involved.*

Typical Sales Situations and Customers

DISTRIBUTE *the learning activity, "Typical Sales Situations and Customers" (page 256).*

REVIEW *the instructions for the learning activity with participants.*

ALLOW *5 minutes to complete the activity.*

ASK *this question.*

- Are there any questions about the work you have just completed in this initial "Targeting Your Sales Efforts" activity?

ANSWER the questions, as appropriate.

[end option]

Beginning a Sale

DISTRIBUTE the learning activity, "Beginning a Sale" (pages 288 and 289).

REVIEW the instructions for the learning activity with participants.

ALLOW 5 minutes to complete the activity.

GROUP DISCUSSION

ASK a volunteer to describe one of his or her selling situations, the approach to be used, and the reason for the approach—with an emphasis on his or her proposed use of key skills.

- Questioning

- Observing

- Listening

- Building rapport

Beginning a Sale

MAKE notes on the "Beginning a Sale" flipchart (page 410).

ASK one or two other volunteers with different situations to describe their selling situations, the approach to be used, and the reason for the approach.

MAKE additional notes on the "Beginning a Sale" flipchart.

REINFORCE responses, paying particular attention to the effective use of the skills listed above.

ASK other participants for comments and suggestions on the approaches—particularly those who were working with similar situations.

NOTE on the flipchart changes <u>to which the "owner" of the approach agrees</u>.

ALLOW 2 or 3 minutes at the conclusion of the discussion for participants to make notes and changes to their own work.

POST the "Beginning a Sale" flipchart in the "Target" area, while participants update their work.

ASK this question.

- Are there any questions about the activity just completed?

ANSWER the questions, as appropriate.

INDIVIDUAL ASSESSMENT

INTRODUCE *the assessment.*

- You will now take a few minutes to complete a simple assessment of your skills in building rapport.

Building Rapport Assessment

DISTRIBUTE *the "Building Rapport Assessment" (page 345).*

REVIEW *the instructions on the assessment with participants.*

ALLOW *3 minutes to complete the assessment.*

GROUP DISCUSSION

ASK *participants to volunteer steps in their personal action plans for improving skills in building rapport.*

MAKE *notes on a blank flipchart.*

REINFORCE *the value of the steps identified, referring to the "Building Rapport Assessment," as appropriate.*

KEY POINTS

MAKE *these key points as a summary.*

- Building rapport is an ongoing process, with short- and longer-range objectives.

- In the short range, your focus is on making the customer comfortable, getting a sense of why the customer is there, and ensuring that your interaction with the customer will continue beyond its opening moments.

- In the longer range, your focus is beginning a dialogue with the customer, building a solid foundation of rapport, and ensuring that you earn—and maintain—the right to proceed.

"Earn the Right" Assessment

00:10   **Purpose:** Provide an opportunity for participants to assess skills relevant to the "Earn the Right" phase.

INDIVIDUAL ASSESSMENT

INTRODUCE the assessment.

- You will now take a few minutes to complete a simple assessment of skills relevant to the "Earn the Right" phase of the sales process.

"Earn the Right"
Assessment

DISTRIBUTE the "'Earn the Right' Assessment" (page 347*).*

REVIEW the instructions on the assessment with participants.

ALLOW 3 minutes to complete the assessment.

GROUP DISCUSSION

ASK participants to volunteer steps in their personal action plans for improving skills relevant to the "Earn the Right" phase.

MAKE notes on a blank flipchart.

REINFORCE the value of the steps identified, referring to the "'Earn the Right' Assessment," as appropriate.

KEY POINTS   *MAKE these key points as a summary.*

- The importance of making the customer feel comfortable

- The importance of observing to begin to learn about the customer

- The use of general questions to "open up" the customer

- The importance of listening

Summary

00:05

Purpose: Review key points from the module, and provide a transition to the next module in the workshop.

FACILITATOR COMMENTARY

MAKE this comment.

- At this point, we have concluded Module 2 of our sales workshop.

- Let's review the key points that have been covered.

REVIEW the flipchart that has been posted in the "Sales Process" area.

- What Do You Want to Accomplish?

REVIEW the flipchart that has been posted in the "Sales Skills" area.

- Building Rapport

REVIEW other flipcharts that have been posted during the module, as appropriate.

Targeting Your Sales Efforts

REVIEW the flipchart that has been posted in the "Target" area.

- Beginning a Sale

MARK OFF the activity that has been completed on the "Targeting Your Sales Efforts" flipchart.

ASK this question.

- Are there any questions about this module?

ANSWER the questions, as appropriate.

Sales Workshop Agenda

MARK OFF the topics that have been covered on the "Sales Workshop Agenda" flipchart.

INDICATE the topics to be covered in the next module, using the "Sales Workshop Agenda" flipchart.

> **Procedural note:** *If you preceded this workshop with the half-day communications workshop, do the following. Prior to beginning Module 3, be sure the following flipcharts from the half-day communications workshop are posted in the "Communications Skills" area.*
>
> - *Why Customers Buy (page 401)*
> - *Questions for "Understand the Need" (page 404)*

3. Understand the Need

Purpose   Stress the importance of the "Understand the Need" phase of the sales process; reinforce the role of communications skills in the "Understand the Need" phase of the sales process; introduce the skill of qualifying opportunities and establish its significance in the sales process.

Objectives   The participant will:
- Describe the role and importance of the "Understand the Need" phase of the sales process.
- Describe the role of key communications skills in this phase.
- Define the concept of qualifying opportunities.
- Describe techniques for qualifying opportunities during this phase of the sales process.
- Identify approaches for qualifying opportunities with his/her customers.
- Apply appropriate skills to successfully completing the first two phases of the sales process.

Agenda

		Page	Timing[1]	Start	Stop
3	**Understand the Need**		**02:05**		
	Introduction	145	00:10		
	Qualifying Opportunities	148			
	• Commentary and Discussion		00:15		
	• Individual "Target" Activity		00:15		
	• Individual Assessment		00:10		
	The First Two Phases: A Role Play	154	01:00		
	"Understand the Need" Assessment	159	00:10		
	Summary	160	00:05		

---

[1] Suggested elapsed time.

144

Introduction

00:10

Purpose: Introduce the content of the module; overview key communications topics; position the importance of this phase in the sales process.

Understand the Need:
Overview

KEY POINTS

FACILITATOR COMMENTARY

USE the "Understand the Need: Overview" overhead transparency (page 378) to describe the topics to be covered in the module.

- The "Understand the Need" phase itself

- Qualifying Opportunities

- The primary role of questioning—and the secondary roles of listening, verifying, and observing

MAKE these key points about the "Understand the Need" phase.

- During this phase of the sales process, you learn a number of things about your customer.

   - You find out what is on your customer's mind— problems to be solved, needs to be satisfied, etc.

   - You also find out many other things—what he or she can afford, what will influence the buying decision, who will make the buying decision, etc.

- This phase can be viewed as the heart of the sales process; what you learn here clearly influences what you do in the "Making a Recommendation" and "Completing the Sale" phases.

- The skill of qualifying opportunities is particularly important in this phase.

- Of course, you continue to build rapport and make sure you retain the right to proceed during this phase.

MAKE these key points about the importance of buying objectives and buying influences in the "Understand the Need" phase.

- Buying objectives are what your customer wants to accomplish—solve a problem, satisfy a need, etc.

- Buying influences are factors that will influence your customer's buying decision—availability of a product or service, suitability to needs, price, etc.

- Learning about these is a key task during this phase of the sales process.

Why Customers Buy

Option

REVIEW the results of the buying objectives/influences activity, as recorded on the "Why Customers Buy" flipchart (page 401) during the communications workshop—reinforcing buying objectives and buying influences and the distinction between them.

[end option]

KEY POINTS

MAKE these key points about the role of questioning in the "Understand the Need" phase.

- Clearly, questioning is an important tool as you work toward a full understanding of your customer's need.

- You can use *general* questions to cause people to open up and talk.

- *Specific* questions are useful when you need to focus or narrow the conversation—that is, you need a specific piece of information in order to proceed.

- When you want to stimulate thinking in new directions or force a particular reply or choice, you can use *leading* questions—which, depending on the question, can either open up or focus a conversation.

Questions for "Understand the Need"

Option

REVIEW the results of the questioning activity, as recorded on the "Questions for 'Understand the Need'" flipchart (page 404) during the communications workshop—reinforcing the use of each type of question in learning about buying objectives.

[end option]

KEY POINT   *MAKE* *this key point.*

- Success in the "Understand the Need" phase is key to your success in making the *right* recommendation and completing the sale.

ASK *this question.*

- Are there any questions before we turn to "qualifying opportunities" ?

ANSWER *the questions, as appropriate.*

Qualifying Opportunities

00:30

Purpose: Define the concept of qualifying opportunities and explore its use in participant sales efforts.

Qualifying Opportunities

COMMENTARY AND DISCUSSION

DEFINE the concept of qualifying opportunities, using the "Qualifying Opportunities" overhead transparency (page 379).

MAKE these points about qualifying opportunities.

- The first four questions qualify the *customer;* does the customer have a need and, if so, is he or she ready, willing, and able to buy?

- The fifth question qualifies the *opportunity;* given that you have a qualified customer, are you able to satisfy that customer's need with your product or service?

GROUP DISCUSSION

ASK this question.

- As a salesperson, what is the value to you of qualifying your sales opportunities?

LOOK FOR answers that allow you to make this point.

- By qualifying opportunities, you increase the likelihood that you are investing your valuable time and energy in sales efforts that will be successful.

ASK this question.

- What are the risks involved in qualifying your sales opportunities?

LOOK FOR answers that allow you to make this point.

- If you don't qualify carefully or if you conclude incorrectly that an opportunity is not qualified, failing to pursue the opportunity could result in lost business.

LEAD a short discussion regarding the value of qualifying opportunities in the participants' particular sales situations.

Notes regarding the value of qualifying opportunities in the participants' environment:

- _____

- _____

- _____

ASK one or two participants to reply to these questions.

- When you qualify your sales opportunities, what information do you need?

- How do you gather the information?

- How do you evaluate the information to determine if the opportunity is qualified?

RECORD responses on a blank flipchart.

LOOK FOR answers that meet these general criteria, as well as answers that are specific to the participants' selling situations.

- Draw on listening, questioning, verifying, and observing skills.

Notes regarding specific approaches to qualifying opportunities in the participants' environment:

- _____

- _____

- _____

Qualifying Opportunities

DISTRIBUTE the handout, "Qualifying Opportunities" (pages 237 and 238).

ALLOW 3 minutes for participants to read the handout.

Notes regarding specific points that you wish to reinforce from the reading:

- _____

- _____

- _____

ASK this question.

- Are there any questions about the discussion of qualifying?

ANSWER the questions, as appropriate.

INDIVIDUAL "TARGET" ACTIVITY

INTRODUCE a "Targeting Your Sales Efforts" activity focused on qualifying opportunities.

- In this "Targeting Your Sales Efforts" activity, you will identify approaches for qualifying opportunities for two of your typical customers.

Approaches to Qualifying

DISTRIBUTE the learning activity, "Approaches to Qualifying" (pages 291 and 292).

REVIEW the instructions for the learning activity with participants.

SUGGEST that participants use the same customers and buying objectives as in the previous "Targeting Your Sales Efforts" activity, if appropriate.
ALLOW 5 minutes to complete the activity.

GROUP DISCUSSION

ASK a volunteer to describe one of his or her customers, and then the approach to qualifying that customer.

Approaches to Qualifying

MAKE notes on the "Approaches to Qualifying" flipchart (page 411).

ASK one or two other volunteers to describe one of their customers, and then the approach to qualifying for that customer.

MAKE additional notes on the "Approaches to Qualifying" flipchart.

REINFORCE responses that will allow participants to gather and evaluate the information needed to qualify an opportunity.

ASK other participants for comments and suggestions on the approaches to qualifying opportunities that have been identified—particularly those who were working with similar customers.

NOTE on the flipchart changes <u>to which the "owner" of the approach agrees</u>.

ALLOW 2 or 3 minutes at the conclusion of the discussion for participants to make notes and changes to their own work.

POST the "Approaches to Qualifying" flipchart in the "Target" area, while participants update their work.

ASK this question.

- Are there any questions about the activity just completed?

ANSWER the questions, as appropriate.

INDIVIDUAL ASSESSMENT

INTRODUCE the assessment.

- You will now take a few minutes to complete a simple assessment of your skills in qualifying opportunities.

Qualifying Skills Assessment

DISTRIBUTE the assessment, "Qualifying Skills Assessment" (page 349).

REVIEW the instructions on the assessment with participants.

ALLOW 3 minutes to complete the assessment.

GROUP DISCUSSION

ASK participants to volunteer steps in their personal action plans for improving qualifying skills.

MAKE notes on a blank flipchart.

REINFORCE the value of the steps identified, referring to the "Qualifying Skills Assessment," as appropriate.

KEY POINTS   *MAKE these key points as a summary.*

- By qualifying opportunities, you increase the likelihood that you are investing your valuable time and energy in sales efforts that will be successful.

- Of course, qualify *carefully*—if you don't qualify carefully or if you conclude incorrectly that an opportunity is not qualified, failing to pursue the opportunity could result in lost business.

The First Two Phases: A Role Play

01:00

Purpose: Provide role play practice in the "Earn the Right" and "Understand the Need" phases of the sales process.

> *Note: Materials required for this activity may be found in "The First Two Phases: A Role Play" learning activity beginning on page 293.*

TABLE GROUP ACTIVITY

BREAK *the workshop into table groups of three people each.*

DESCRIBE *the structure of role play.*

- There will be three rounds in this role play.

- Each of you will have the opportunity to play the role of salesperson, customer, and observer.

Instructions for Customer 1, 2, 3; Instructions for the Salesperson; Observer's Critique Sheet

DISTRIBUTE *these materials to each of the table groups: a set of "Instructions for Customer 1 (2, and 3)," (pages 299, 300, and 301) and three each of "Instructions for the Salesperson" (page 298) and "Observer's Critique Sheet" (page 297).*

PRESENT the basic instructions for the activity.

1. You will have 3 minutes to review your instructions and make notes prior to each round of the role play.

2. Once the role plays begin, the participant playing "observer" in each round will keep track of time.

3. Each round will be 5 minutes in length.

4. At the end of each round, 3 minutes will be allowed for discussion within the table group.

5. This procedure will be repeated until each participant in the table group has played each of the roles.

6. Finally, the full group will reconvene for a discussion of the role play experiences.

?

ASK this question.

- Are there any questions about the instructions, thus far?

ANSWER the questions, as appropriate.

REVIEW the instructions for customers, salespeople, and observers, either paraphrasing them or reading them aloud.

?

ASK this question.

- Are there any questions about the instructions before beginning?

ANSWER the questions, as appropriate.

ASK participants to move to their table groups.

MONITOR progress as the exercise moves forward, ensuring that the groups stay on schedule.

GROUP DISCUSSION

RECONVENE the full group.

MAKE this comment.

- Before we begin, please be sure that each of you has recorded on your "Instructions for the Salesperson" page the number of the "customer" with whom you played the role of salesperson.

- You will need to remember this for the next role play.

ALLOW a moment for participants to record this information.

MAKE this comment.

- Now, let's discuss your reactions to this role play.

ASK one or two participants to answer these questions as "salespeople."

- What did you hope to achieve during that sales situation?

- Why did you use the approach that you pursued during the role play?

- How effective was it from your point of view?

RECORD responses on a blank flipchart.

ENCOURAGE other participants to add comments, as appropriate.

ASK one or two participants to answer this question as "observers."

- As observers, what general reactions did you have about what was done well? Suggestions for improvement?

RECORD responses on another blank flipchart.

ENCOURAGE other participants to add comments, as appropriate.

ASK one or two participants to answer these questions as "customers."

- What was your perception of the overall sales interaction, from a sales point of view?

- How effective was the approach from your point of view as a customer?

RECORD responses on the blank flipchart.

ENCOURAGE other participants to make constructive comments regarding their impressions, alternatives, etc.

ASK each of the questions on the "Role Play Questions" flipcharts (page 412) as a means for summarizing the discussion of the role play.

- How effectively did the salesperson build rapport?

- What questioning techniques were effective from the salesperson's point of view? The customer's? The observer's?

- What alternate techniques might have been used?

- Did the salesperson learn about the customer's need?

- Did the salesperson earn the right to move ahead with the sale?

Role Play Questions

MAKE NOTES about responses on the "Role Play Questions" flipcharts.

LOOK FOR answers that allow you to reinforce the importance of key points on the "Observer's Critique Sheet."

- Made the customer comfortable, maintained good nonverbal contact

- Used general, specific, and leading questions effectively, organized them logically

- Listened to the customer

- Concentrated on the customer

- Verified understanding

- Qualified the opportunity

POST the "Role Play Questions" flipcharts in the "Sales Process" area.

ASK this question.

•   Are there any questions about this activity?

ANSWER the questions, as appropriate.

"Understand the Need" Assessment

00:10

Purpose: Provide an opportunity for participants to assess skills relevant to the "Understand the Need" phase.

INDIVIDUAL ASSESSMENT

INTRODUCE the assessment.

- You will now take a few minutes to complete a simple assessment of your skills relevant to the "Understand the Need" phase of the sales process.

"Understand the Need" Assessment

DISTRIBUTE the "'Understand the Need' Assessment" (page 351).

REVIEW the instructions on the assessment with participants.

ALLOW 3 minutes to complete the assessment.

GROUP DISCUSSION

ASK participants to volunteer steps in their personal action plans for improving skills relevant to the "Understand the Need" phase.

MAKE notes on a blank flipchart.

REINFORCE the value of the steps identified, referring to the "'Understand the Need' Assessment," as appropriate.

KEY POINTS

MAKE these key points as a summary.

- The importance of using a variety of questions, structured in a way that the salesperson gathers the required information about customer needs

- The importance of learning about both buying objectives and buying influences

- The importance of qualifying needs

Summary

00:05

Purpose: Review key points from the module, and provide a transition to the next module in the workshop.

FACILITATOR COMMENTARY

MAKE this comment.

- At this point, we have concluded Module 3 of our sales workshop.

- Let's review the key points that have been covered.

REVIEW the flipcharts that have been posted in the "Sales Process" area.

- Role Play Questions

- Understand the Need (Blank flipchart)

REVIEW other flipcharts that have been posted during the module, as appropriate.

Targeting Your Sales Efforts

REVIEW the flipchart that has been posted in the "Target" area.

- Approaches to Qualifying

MARK OFF the activity that has been completed on the "Targeting Your Sales Efforts" flipchart.

?

ASK this question.

- Are there any questions about this module?

ANSWER the questions, as appropriate.

Sales Workshop Agenda

MARK OFF the topics that have been covered on the "Sales Workshop Agenda" flipchart.

INDICATE the topics to be covered in the next module, using the "Sales Workshop Agenda" flipchart.

4. Make a Recommendation

Purpose

Stress the importance of the "Make a Recommendation" phase of the sales process; reinforce the role of communications skills in the "Make a Recommendation" phase of the sales process; introduce the topics of testing for readiness, describing benefits, and presenting recommendations, and establish their significance in the sales process.

Objectives

The participant will:
- Describe the role and importance of the "Make a Recommendation" phase of the sales process.
- Describe the role of key communications skills in this phase.
- Define the concept of testing for readiness.
- Describe techniques for testing for readiness during this phase of the sales process.
- Identify approaches for testing for readiness with his or her customers.
- Define the concept of benefits, and distinguish between features and benefits.
- Identify typical product/service benefits for use with his or her customers.
- Describe characteristics of effective recommendations.
- Develop an outline for an effective recommendation for use with his or her customers.

Agenda

(See next page)

Agenda

		Page	Timing[1]	Start	Stop
4	**Make a Recommendation**		**02:35**		
	Introduction	163	00:05		
	Testing for Readiness	165			
	• Group Discussion		00:10		
	• Individual "Target" Activity		00:15		
	Describing Benefits	169			
	• Group Discussion		00:20		
	• Individual "Target" Activity		00:15		
	• Individual Assessment		00:10		
	Presenting a Recommendation	175			
	• Group Discussion		00:15		
	• Table Group Exercise		00:30		
	• Individual "Target" Activity		00:20		
	"Make a Recommendation" Assessment	182	00:10		
	Summary	183	00:05		

---

[1] Suggested elapsed time.

Introduction

00:05

Make a Recommendation:
Overview

KEY POINTS

Purpose: Introduce the content of the module; overview key topics from the communications workshop; position the importance of this phase in the sales process.

FACILITATOR COMMENTARY

USE the "Make a Recommendation: Overview" overhead transparency (page 380) to describe the topics to be covered in the module.

MAKE these key points about the "Make a Recommendation" phase.

- Once you have a full understanding of what the customer needs and what will motivate him or her to buy, you are prepared to make a recommendation.

  - When you believe that you have reached that point, you will "test the water."

  - If the time seems to be right, you present your recommendation.

- Your recommendation must be a compelling case for buying, presented from the customer's point of view.

  - It must be presented logically.

  - It must be presented with enough conviction and forcefulness to convey your genuine belief in the recommendation that you are making.

KEY POINTS

MAKE these key points about communications skills in general.

- All five communications skills are important during this phase.

- As we will see, however, questioning, verifying, and explaining are of special importance.

KEY POINTS	***MAKE*** *these key points about the characteristics of a good explanation.*

- Simple language, no technical jargon

- Short, to the point

- Logical, clear transitions from one point to the next

- Credible—yet dynamic, vivid, exciting for the customer

- Focused on customer objectives

KEY POINT	***MAKE*** *this key point.*

- The skill with which you have completed the "Earn the Right" and "Understand the Need" phases has a direct impact on your success in the "Make a Recommendation" phase—which, in turn, is key to your success in completing the sale.

?

ASK *this question.*

- Are there any questions about making a recommendation before we move on to testing for readiness?

ANSWER *the questions, as appropriate.*

Testing for Readiness

00:25

Purpose: Discuss approaches to determining readiness for making a recommendation.

GROUP DISCUSSION

MAKE this comment.

- We are now ready to discuss the "Make a Recommendation" phase of the sales process.

- At this point, you believe that you understand the customer's need clearly, and now you must determine if you should make a recommendation to your customer.

ASK this question.

- How do you determine if it is time for a recommendation?

RECORD responses on a blank flipchart.

LOOK FOR answers that will allow you to reinforce these points.

- *Summarize* your understanding of the customer's need.

- *Verify* the accuracy and completeness of your understanding.

Notes regarding specific techniques for testing for readiness that are suitable in the participants' environment.

- _____

- _____

- _____

ASK this question as a quick review of approaches to verifying.

- What are the basic approaches that you can use to verify understanding?

LOOK FOR answers such as these—allowing you to lead the group to a conclusion about the discussion.

- Repeat what was said, *using different words.*

- Describe *what you think* the other person said.

KEY POINT   *MAKE* this key point.

- Don't forget to confirm the verification step by asking a question—an important part of the verifying skill.

Testing for Readiness

DISTRIBUTE the handout, "Testing for Readiness" (page 239).

ALLOW 2 minutes for participants to read the handout.

Notes regarding specific points that you wish to reinforce from the reading:

- _____

- _____

- _____

ASK this question.

- Are there any questions about testing for readiness?

ANSWER the questions, as appropriate.

INDIVIDUAL "TARGET" ACTIVITY

INTRODUCE a "Targeting Your Sales Efforts" activity focused on testing for readiness.

- In this "Targeting Your Sales Efforts" activity, you will identify approaches to testing for readiness with two of your typical customers.

Approaches to Testing for Readiness

DISTRIBUTE the learning activity, "Approaches to Testing for Readiness" (page 303).

REVIEW the instructions for the learning activity with participants.

SUGGEST that participants use the same customers as in the previous "Targeting Your Sales Efforts" activity on questioning, if appropriate.

ALLOW 5 minutes to complete the activity.

GROUP DISCUSSION

ASK a volunteer to describe one of his or her customers, and then approaches to testing for readiness for that customer.

Approaches to Testing for Readiness

MAKE notes on the "Approaches to Testing for Readiness" flipchart (page 414).

ASK one or two other volunteers to describe one of their customers, and their approaches to testing for readiness for that customer.

MAKE additional notes on the "Approaches to Testing for Readiness" flipchart.

REINFORCE the importance of summarizing and verifying in testing for readiness.

ASK other participants for comments and suggestions on the approaches identified—particularly those who were working with similar customers.

NOTE on the flipchart changes <u>to which the "owner" of the approach agrees</u>.

ALLOW 2 or 3 minutes at the conclusion of the discussion for participants to make notes and changes to their own work.

POST *the "Approaches to Testing for Readiness" flipchart in the "Target" area, while participants update their work.*

ASK *this question.*

• Are there any questions about the activity just completed?

ANSWER *the questions, as appropriate.*

Describing Benefits

00:45

Purpose: Define "benefit" and contrast benefits to "features"; provide practice in identifying benefits.

GROUP DISCUSSION

MAKE this comment.

- Your ability to describe benefits is key to making successful recommendations to your customers.

- Let's consider the terms "feature" and "benefit."

ASK this question.

- What does the term "feature" mean to you? What are some examples of features related to your product or service?

RECORD responses on the "Features and Benefits" flipchart (page 415).

Features and Benefits

LOOK FOR this answer, along with examples that are consistent with this definition.

- A characteristic of a product or service

Notes regarding typical features related to the participants' product or service:

- _____

- _____

- _____

ASK this question.

- What is a benefit? What are some examples of benefits related to the features you just identified?

RECORD responses on the "Features and Benefits" flipchart.

LOOK FOR answers that reinforce these points about a benefit, along with examples that are consistent with this definition.

- Something that promotes well-being or contributes to an improvement in condition

- A help, an advantage

Notes regarding typical benefits related to the features just identified:

- _____

- _____

- _____

ASK this question.

- What are the key characteristics of a well-stated benefit?

RECORD *responses on the "Features and Benefits" flipchart.*

LOOK FOR *answers that reinforce these points.*

- Clearly related to the customer's objective

- Perceived by the customers as *something of value to them*

ASK this question.

- How do the benefits you identified measure up to those characteristics? How might you improve them?

RECORD *responses on the "Features and Benefits" flipchart.*

LOOK FOR *answers that reinforce the characteristics just identified.*

Describing Benefits

DISTRIBUTE *the handout, "Describing Benefits" (pages 240 and 241).*

ALLOW *1 minute for participants to read the handout—asking them to ignore the exercise for the moment.*

Notes regarding specific points that you wish to reinforce from the reading:

- _____

- _____

- _____

POST *the "Features and Benefits" flipchart in the "Sales Skills" area.*

DIRECT *attention to the feature/benefit exercise in the handout.*

DIRECT attention to the feature/benefit exercise in the handout.

ALLOW 2 minutes to read the exercise.

ASK this question.

- What sort of benefit statement would you use for the first customer objective?

RECORD responses on a blank flipchart.

LOOK FOR an answer such as this (relevant features are listed in parentheses).

- You can store these cups easily and without worry (because they're lightweight, not easily broken, and pre-packed).

- They are ready to go when you need to transport them (because they're pre-packed).

REINFORCE the distinction between features and benefits, and the key characteristics of a benefit.

REPEAT the procedure for the second customer objective, looking for an answer such as this.

- These cups will go with any color of disposable serving items—plates, napkins, flatware, etc. (because they are white).

Describing Benefits

REINFORCE the definition and characteristics of benefits, using the "Describing Benefits" overhead transparency (page 381).

ASK this question.

- Are there any questions about the discussion of benefits?

ANSWER the questions, as appropriate.

INDIVIDUAL "TARGET" ACTIVITY

INTRODUCE a "Targeting Your Sales Efforts" activity focused on describing benefits.

- In this "Targeting Your Sales Efforts" activity, you will prepare benefit statements for products or services that will meet two typical customer objectives.

Benefit Statements

DISTRIBUTE the learning activity, "Benefit Statements" (page 306).

REVIEW the instructions for the learning activity with participants.

SUGGEST that participants use the product or service that they would anticipate recommending based on the previous "Targeting Your Sales Efforts" activity on testing for readiness, if appropriate.

ALLOW 5 minutes to complete the activity.

GROUP DISCUSSION

ASK a volunteer to describe one of his or her customer objectives, and then the benefit statement associated with that objective.

Benefit Statements

MAKE notes on the "Benefit Statements" flipchart (page 416).

ASK one or two other volunteers to describe one of their customer objectives, and then benefit statements for that objective.

MAKE additional notes on the "Benefit Statements" flipchart .

REINFORCE the distinction between features and benefits, and the characteristics of well-stated benefits.

- Feature—a characteristic of a product or service

- Benefit—something that promotes well-being or contributes to an improvement in condition; a help, advantage

- Characteristics of a well-stated benefit

  - Clearly related to the customer's objective

  - Perceived by customers as *something of value to them*

ASK *other participants for comments and suggestions on the benefit statements—particularly those who were working with similar customers.*

NOTE *on the flipchart changes <u>to which the "owner" of the approach agrees</u>.*

ALLOW *2 or 3 minutes at the conclusion of the discussion for participants to make notes and changes to their own work.*

POST *the "Benefit Statements" flipchart in the "Target" area, while participants update their work.*

ASK *this question.*

- Are there any questions about the activity just completed?

ANSWER *the questions, as appropriate.*

INDIVIDUAL ASSESSMENT

INTRODUCE the assessment.

- You will now take a few minutes to complete a simple assessment of your skills in describing benefits.

Describing Benefits Assessment

DISTRIBUTE the "Describing Benefits Assessment" (page 353).

REVIEW the instructions on the assessment with participants.

ALLOW 3 minutes to complete the assessment.

GROUP DISCUSSION

ASK participants to volunteer steps in their personal action plans for improving their skills in describing benefits.

MAKE notes on a blank flipchart.

REINFORCE the value of the steps identified, referring to the "Describing Benefits Assessment," as appropriate.

KEY POINTS

MAKE these key points as a summary.

- Be certain that the benefit is clearly related to the customer's objective.

- Additionally, be sure the benefit you describe is perceived by customers as *something of value to them.*

Sales Workshop Agenda

MARK OFF the topics that have been covered on the "Sales Workshop Agenda" flipchart.

Presenting a Recommendation

01:05

Recommendations

Purpose: Define the components of a good recommendation, and provide practice in developing recommendations.

GROUP DISCUSSION

MAKE this comment.

- Thus far, we've discussed several skills that are important to making successful recommendations.

ASK this question.

- Suppose you were a customer? What are the key things that you would look for in a successful recommendation?

RECORD responses on the "Recommendations" flipchart (page 417).

LOOK FOR answers that reinforce these points.

- Clear, logical explanation—starting with a clear opening statement

- Clear relationship of the recommendation to customer objectives

- Clear statement of benefits that are related to customer objectives

- A credible and compelling description of the competitive edge of the approach

KEY POINTS

MAKE these key points.

- "Competitive edge" is an element that we have not discussed thus far—and is an important element in a successful recommendation.

- A statement of competitive edge answers the questions, "Why buy from you? Why your product or service?"

- Such a statement shows how you can meet the customer's objectives in a superior fashion, and/or deliver superior benefits to the customer.

- Additionally, such a statement must be compelling and credible. It must *never* belittle or deride the competition— unless, of course, *you wish to risk throwing away a significant part of the credibility you have established.*

ASK this question.

- What is there about your product or service that contributes to your competitive edge with your customers?

- What other factors contribute to your competitive edge?

Competitive Edge

RECORD responses on the "Competitive Edge" flipchart (page 418)

LOOK FOR answers that suggest ways in which participants can demonstrate their ability to meet customer needs in a superior way, and/or deliver superior benefits.

Notes regarding elements that typically contribute to participants' competitive edge:

- _____

- _____

- _____

*Presenting
a Recommendation*

DISTRIBUTE the handout, "Presenting a Recommendation" (pages 242 through 245).

ALLOW 3 minutes for participants to read pages 242 and 243 of the handout—asking them to ignore the exercise for the moment.

MAKE this point from the "Tips for Successful Recommendations" section.

- Of course, all good recommendations end the same way— asking for the order.

- We will cover that topic in the module titled "Complete the Sale."

Notes regarding additional points that you wish to reinforce from the reading:

- _____

- _____

- _____

ASK this question.

- Are there any questions about recommendations, before we move to a "recommendation" demonstration?

ANSWER the questions, as appropriate.

POST the "Recommendations" and "Competitive Edge" flipcharts in the "Sales Process" area.

TABLE GROUP EXERCISE

BREAK the workshop into table groups of four to six people.

NAME the customer, buying objective, and product or service with which the table groups will work during this exercise.

Customer _____

Buying objective _____

Product or service _____

PRESENT the instructions for the exercise, contained in the handout "Making a Recommendation" (page 244).

ASK this question.

- Are there any questions about what you will be doing?

ANSWER the questions, as appropriate.

ALLOW 10 minutes for table groups to complete the activity.

GROUP DISCUSSION

RECONVENE the full group.

ASK one table group to describe the customer objective, and then the recommendation that would be used with that objective.

MAKE notes on a blank flipchart.

ASK other table groups for comments and suggestions on the recommendations developed.

MAKE additional notes on the flipchart.

REINFORCE these points about effective recommendations during the discussion.

- Clear, logical explanation

- Clear relationship of the recommendation to customer objectives

- Clear statement of benefits that are related to customer objectives

- A credible and compelling description of the competitive edge to be gained

ASK this question.

- Are there any questions about the results of the exercise?

ANSWER the questions, as appropriate.

INDIVIDUAL "TARGET" ACTIVITY

INTRODUCE a "Targeting Your Sales Efforts" activity focused on making recommendations.

- In this "Targeting Your Sales Efforts" activity, you will think about one of the customer objectives with which you have been working and develop an outline of a recommendation to address that objective.

Making a Recommendation

DISTRIBUTE the learning activity, "Making a Recommendation" (pages 309 and 310).

REVIEW the instructions for the learning activity with participants.

SUGGEST that participants use the product or service for which they identified benefits in the previous "Targeting Your Sales Efforts" activity benefits, if appropriate.

ALLOW 10 minutes to complete the activity.

GROUP DISCUSSION

ASK a volunteer to describe the customer objective, and then the recommendation that would be used with that objective.

MAKE notes on the "Making a Recommendation" flipchart (page 419).

Making a Recommendation

ASK one or two other volunteers to describe their objective, and the recommendation that they developed.

MAKE additional notes on the "Making a Recommendation" flipchart.

REINFORCE responses, based on the tips in the "Presenting a Recommendation" handout.

- Make the purpose of the recommendation clear.

- Organize the content logically, cover only relevant information, and include a clear statement of benefits.

- Provide a compelling description of your competitive edge— and make the entire recommendation enthusiastic.

- Make the recommendation *explicit*.

ASK other participants for comments and suggestions on the recommendations developed—particularly those who were working with similar objectives.

NOTE on the flipchart changes <u>to which the "owner" of the approach agrees</u>.

ALLOW 2 or 3 minutes at the conclusion of the discussion for participants to make notes and changes to their own work.

POST the "Making a Recommendation" flipchart in the "Target" area, while participants update their work.

ASK this question.

- Are there any questions about the activity just completed—or about the topic of recommendations?

ANSWER the questions, as appropriate.

"Make a Recommendation" Assessment

00:10   **Purpose:** Provide an opportunity for participants to assess skills relevant to the "Make a Recommendation" phase.

INDIVIDUAL ASSESSMENT

INTRODUCE the assessment.

• You will now take a few minutes to complete a simple assessment of skills relevant to the "Make a Recommendation" phase of the sales process.

"Make a Recommendation" Assessment

DISTRIBUTE the "'Make a Recommendation' Assessment" (page 355).

REVIEW the instructions on the assessment with participants.

ALLOW 3 minutes to complete the assessment.

GROUP DISCUSSION

ASK participants to volunteer steps in their personal action plans for improving skills relevant to the "Make a Recommendation" phase.

MAKE notes on a blank flipchart.

REINFORCE the value of the steps identified, referring to the "'Make a Recommendation' Assessment," as appropriate.

KEY POINTS   *MAKE these key points as a summary.*

• The importance of using good explaining skills

• The importance of well-stated benefits

• The importance of enthusiastic and explicit recommendations

Summary

00:05

Purpose: Review key points from the module, and provide a transition to the next module in the workshop.

FACILITATOR COMMENTARY

MAKE this comment.

- At this point, we have concluded Module 4 of our sales workshop.

- Let's review the key points that have been covered.

REVIEW the flipcharts that have been posted in the "Sales Process" area.

- Recommendations

- Competitive Edge

REVIEW the flipchart that has been posted in the "Sales Skills" area.

- Features and Benefits

REVIEW other flipcharts that have been posted during the module, as appropriate.

Targeting Your Sales Efforts

REVIEW the flipcharts that have been posted in the "Target" area.

- Approaches to Testing for Readiness

- Benefit Statements

- Making a Recommendation

MARK OFF activities that have been completed on the "Targeting Your Sales Efforts" flipchart.

ASK this question.

- Are there any questions about this module?

ANSWER the questions, as appropriate.

Sales Workshop Agenda

MARK OFF *the topics that have been covered on the "Sales Workshop Agenda" flipchart.*

INDICATE *the topics to be covered in the next module, using the "Sales Workshop Agenda" flipchart.*

5. Complete the Sale

Purpose
Stress the importance of the "Complete the Sale" phase of the sales process; reinforce the role of communications skills in the "Make a Recommendation" phase of the sales process; introduce the topics of asking for the order and handling obstacles, and establish their significance in the sales process.

Objectives
The participant will:
- Describe the role and importance of the "Complete the Sale" phase of the sales process.
- Describe the role of key communications skills in this phase.
- Describe approaches to asking for the order.
- Identify approaches for asking for the order from his or her customers.
- Define the concept of obstacle, including "special situation" obstacles.
- Describe approaches to handling obstacles.
- Identify common obstacles and approaches to handling them with his or her customers.

Agenda
(See next page)

Agenda

---

[1] Suggested elapsed time.

Introduction

00:05

Purpose: Introduce the content of the module; position the importance of this phase in the sales process.

*Complete the Sale:
Overview*

FACILITATOR COMMENTARY

USE the "Complete the Sale: Overview" overhead transparency (page 382) to describe the topics to be covered in the module, and their interrelationships.

KEY POINTS

MAKE these key points about the "Complete the Sale" phase.

- Once you recognize buying signals—indicating your customer's readiness—you need to ask for the order.

  – Because most of us don't like to hear the answer "No, I'm not . . . ," it is easy to avoid asking the key question.

  – In addition, we tend to think that we can avoid provoking obstacles if we don't ask for the order—when, in fact, obstacles are a great way to find out "where the customer is" and then progress toward completing the sale.

- As we will see, each of the five communications skills are important during this phase.

KEY POINTS

MAKE these key points.

- If you have moved through the sales process carefully and reached agreement with your customer at each step of the way, you have earned the right to ask for the order.

- And—if your recommendation reflects your understanding and the agreements you have reached with the customer, you have a very good chance of getting the answer you want!

ASK this question.

- Are there any questions about this module before we start?

ANSWER the questions, as appropriate.

Asking for the Order

01:00   **Purpose:** Discuss approaches to asking for the order.

                              GROUP DISCUSSION

MAKE this comment.

- Although it would be nice if customers "signed on the dotted line" all by themselves, sooner or later you need to ask for the order if you expect to make a sale.

- Although we did not discuss it in the previous module, asking for the order is actually the last step in presenting your recommendation.

ASK this question.

- What is the most difficult aspect of asking for the order, from your point of view?

RECORD responses on a blank flipchart.

LOOK FOR answers such as these.

- Determining the appropriate time

- Concern that the customer might raise an obstacle

- Concern—or fear—that the customer might say "No!"

KEY POINTS   *MAKE these key points.*

- As we will discuss shortly, a customer's obstacles actually can be your "friend"—because they are, in fact, an opportunity to find out what your customer is thinking and to address any problems that might exist.

- In a similar fashion, even when the customer says "No!" you have an opportunity to question and verify to find out why he or she said "No!"—and then address obstacles that surface.

- Bottom line—you must *ask for the order* if you expect to complete the sale.

- Of course, the timing of your request for the order is also an important issue.

ASK *this question.*

- What kinds of buying signals do you look for in order to determine if it is time to ask for the order?

Buying Signals

RECORD *responses on the "Buying Signals" flipchart (page 420).*

LOOK FOR *answers that are appropriate to the participants' situation—many of which will likely focus on nonverbal behaviors.*

Notes regarding buying signals that would be common in the participants' environment:

- _____

- _____

- _____

Asking for the Order

DESCRIBE *two basic approaches to asking for the order, using the "Asking for the Order" flipchart (page 421).*

ASK *this question.*

- What are some examples of each type of request, based on your sales situation?

RECORD *responses on the "Asking for the Order" flipchart (page 421).*

LOOK FOR *answers that fit each category.*

Notes regarding direct and assumptive requests that would be used by participants:

- _____

- _____

- _____

DISCUSS *variations on these techniques (e.g., impending event), if appropriate to the participants' environment.*

Note the variations you will discuss here, if any.

- _____

- _____

- _____

ASK *this question.*

- Which of the approaches—direct or assumptive—do you feel is preferable?

LOOK FOR *answers that allow you to reinforce these points.*

- A direct request is generally preferable when asking for the order.

- Unless other than direct approaches are used carefully, you run the risk of *appearing* to be manipulative—even if that is the farthest thing from your mind.

Asking for the Order

DISTRIBUTE *the handout, "Asking for the Order"* (pages 246 and 247).

ALLOW *2 minutes for participants to read the handout—asking them to ignore the exercise for the moment.*

Notes regarding specific points that you wish to reinforce from the reading:

- _____

- _____

- _____

POST *the "Buying Signals" and "Asking for the Order" flipcharts in the "Sales Process" area.*

ASK *this question.*

- Are there any questions about asking for the order, before we move on to a short table group activity?

ANSWER *the questions, as appropriate.*

TABLE GROUP EXERCISE

BREAK the workshop into table groups of four to six people.

NAME the customer, buying objective, and product or service with which the table groups will work during this exercise.

Customer _____

Buying objective _____

Product or service _____

PRESENT the instructions for the exercise, contained in the handout "Asking for the Order."

ASK this question.

- Are there any questions about what you will be doing?

ANSWER the questions, as appropriate.

ALLOW 10 minutes for table groups to complete the activity.

GROUP DISCUSSION

RECONVENE the full group.

ASK one table group to describe its approach to asking for the order, and the rationale for using it.

MAKE notes on a blank flipchart.

DISCUSS the rationale for the approach, especially if other than direct.

ASK other table groups for additional approaches, including the rationale for using them.

MAKE additional notes on the flipchart.

DISCUSS the approaches, including the rationale for the approach (especially if other than direct).

REINFORCE these points about asking for the order during the discussion.

- The direct approach is generally preferable.

- When approaches other than direct are used, they must not make the salesperson appear to be manipulative.

?

ASK this question.

- Are there any questions about the results of the exercise?

ANSWER the questions, as appropriate.

INDIVIDUAL "TARGET" ACTIVITY

INTRODUCE a "Targeting Your Sales Efforts" activity focused on asking for the order.

Approaches to Asking for the Order

- In this "Targeting Your Sales Efforts" activity, you will identify approaches for asking for the order, based on a recommendation you would present to one of your customers

DISTRIBUTE the learning activity, "Approaches to Asking for the Order" (pages 313 and 314).

REVIEW the instructions for the learning activity with participants.

SUGGEST that participants base this exercise on the recommendation developed in the previous "Targeting Your Sales Efforts" exercise, if appropriate.

ALLOW 10 minutes to complete the activity.

GROUP DISCUSSION

ASK a volunteer to describe his or her approach to asking for the order, after quickly reviewing the recommendation on which it is based.

Approaches to Asking for the Order

MAKE notes on the "Approaches to Asking for the Order" flipchart (page 422).

ASK one or two other volunteers to describe one of their approaches to asking for the order, after quickly reviewing the recommendation on which it is based.

MAKE additional notes on the "Approaches to Asking for the Order" flipchart.

REINFORCE responses, based on the "tips" in the "Asking for the Order" handout.

- Be sure the way in which you ask for the order projects confidence.

- Also, give your customer a chance to respond. *There is nothing wrong with silence.*

ASK other participants for comments and suggestions on the approaches to asking for the order—particularly those who were working with similar customers.

NOTE on the flipchart changes <u>to which the "owner" of the approach agrees</u>.

ALLOW 2 or 3 minutes at the conclusion of the discussion for participants to make notes and changes to their own work.

POST the "Approaches to Asking for the Order" flipchart in the "Target" area, while participants update their work.

ASK this question.

• Are there any questions about activity just completed?

ANSWER the questions, as appropriate.

Handling Obstacles

01:00

Purpose: Discuss obstacles and approaches to handling them.

GROUP DISCUSSION

MAKE this comment.

- Earlier in this module, we discussed a reason that often deters salespeople from asking for the order—the fear of raising an obstacle that will get in the way of completing the sale.

Obstacles

REVIEW the definition of obstacle, using the "Obstacles" overhead transparency (page 383).

ASK this question.

- What are some typical obstacles that you encounter in your sales situations?

Common Obstacles

RECORD responses on the "Common Obstacles" flipchart (page 423).

LOOK FOR answers that cover common obstacles in the participants' environment.

Notes regarding obstacles that are common in the participants' environment:

- _____

- _____

- _____

ASK this question.

- It is often suggested that you should view an obstacle presented by a customer as an opportunity. Why do you think that is the case?

Handling Obstacles

RECORD responses on the "Handling Obstacles" flipchart (page 424), under the heading "View Them as Opportunities."

LOOK FOR answers that allow you to reinforce these points.

- Obstacles provide an opportunity to learn about things that concern or bother the customer.

- The obstacle that is actually stated might be a "smokescreen" that is hiding other, perhaps more serious concerns.

- Obstacles are an opportunity to find out what the customer is thinking—and, having done that, they allow you to continue working with the customer and complete the sale.

ASK this question.

- What are the two basic steps you must take to handle an obstacle?

RECORD responses on the "Handling Obstacles" flipchart, under the heading "Steps."

LOOK FOR answers that allow you to reinforce these points.

- Understand clearly the obstacle being raised.

- Answer the question or address the issue.

ASK this question.

- What communications skills are important in handling obstacles?

LOOK FOR answers that allow you to reinforce the importance of using all five communications skills.

- Listening—to learn more about the obstacle

- Questioning—to clarify your understanding

- Verifying—to be sure you understand what the obstacle *really* is

- Observing—to pick up nonverbal clues that can contribute to your efforts to understand the obstacle as clearly as possible

- Explaining—to repeat, rephrase, or clarify your recommendation

REFER to the "Effective Selling" flipchart (page 387) during the discussion, as appropriate.

ASK this question.

- Are there any questions about this topic, thus far?

ANSWER the questions, as appropriate.

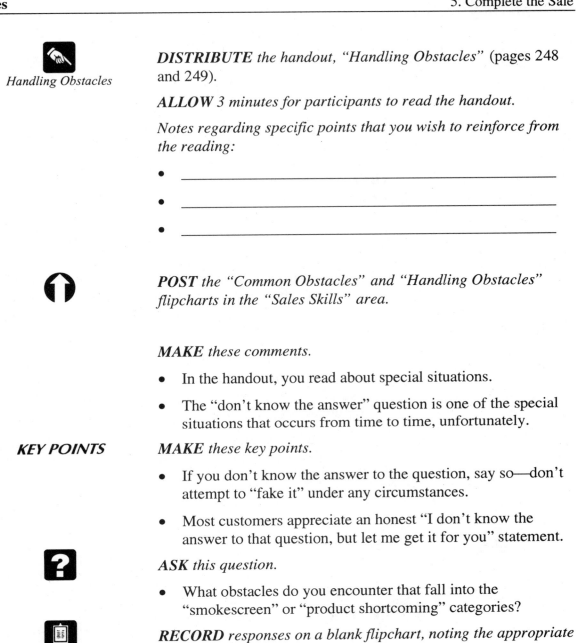

Handling Obstacles

DISTRIBUTE *the handout, "Handling Obstacles" (pages 248 and 249).*

ALLOW *3 minutes for participants to read the handout.*

Notes regarding specific points that you wish to reinforce from the reading:

- _____

- _____

- _____

POST *the "Common Obstacles" and "Handling Obstacles" flipcharts in the "Sales Skills" area.*

MAKE *these comments.*

- In the handout, you read about special situations.

- The "don't know the answer" question is one of the special situations that occurs from time to time, unfortunately.

KEY POINTS

MAKE *these key points.*

- If you don't know the answer to the question, say so—don't attempt to "fake it" under any circumstances.

- Most customers appreciate an honest "I don't know the answer to that question, but let me get it for you" statement.

ASK *this question.*

- What obstacles do you encounter that fall into the "smokescreen" or "product shortcoming" categories?

RECORD *responses on a blank flipchart, noting the appropriate category.*

Notes regarding typical "smokescreen" obstacles:

- _____

- _____

- _____

Notes regarding typical "product shortcoming" obstacles:

- _____

- _____

- _____

REFER *to the previously posted "Common Obstacles" flipchart for additional examples of these special situations.*

KEY POINTS   **MAKE** *these key points about "product shortcoming" obstacles.*

- When product shortcomings cannot be dealt with, recognize that you might need to terminate the sales effort—but do so gracefully, remembering the old adage about "not burning bridges behind you."

- Nobody has a "one size fits all" product or service that works with all customers or in all situations. If you determine that your product or service simply will not meet the customer's objectives, there is not a lot you can do about the situation.

- If you are unable to remove an obstacle to a sale, that does not mean you are a failure. If you know that you have given the sales situation your best effort, then that's all most people can ask.

ASK *this question.*

- Are there any questions about this topic before we move on to the next activity?

ANSWER *the questions, as appropriate.*

GROUP EXERCISE

SELECT one or two of the obstacles from the "Obstacles" flipchart.

ASK these questions of the group in order to determine how they would handle the obstacle.

- What do you think the obstacle really means?

- What question(s) would you ask to clarify your understanding?

- How would you verify that your understanding is correct?

- How would you then address the obstacle?

- What nonverbal clues might be of value in understanding and addressing the obstacle?

RECORD responses on a blank flipchart.

ENCOURAGE participants to make comments and suggestions that would improve the handling of the obstacle.

REINFORCE the key points in handling obstacles.

- Understand clearly the obstacle being raised.

- Answer the question or address the issue.

ASK this question.

- Are there any questions about the discussion of handling obstacles?

ANSWER the questions, as appropriate.

INDIVIDUAL "TARGET" ACTIVITY

INTRODUCE a "Targeting Your Sales Efforts" activity focused on handling obstacles.

- In this "Targeting Your Sales Efforts" activity, you will identify approaches for two or three obstacles that you encounter frequently.

Approaches to Handling Obstacles

DISTRIBUTE the learning activity, "Approaches to Handling Obstacles" (pages 317 and 318).

REVIEW the instructions for the learning activity with participants.

SUGGEST that participants use the same situation as in the "Targeting Your Sales Efforts" exercise on asking for the order, if appropriate.

ALLOW 10 minutes to complete the activity.

GROUP DISCUSSION

ASK a volunteer to describe one of his or her common obstacles, and then the approach to handling that obstacle.

Approaches to Handling Obstacles

MAKE notes on the "Approaches to Handling Obstacles" flipchart (page 425).

ASK one or two other volunteers to describe one of their common obstacles, and then their approaches to handling the obstacle.

MAKE additional notes on the "Approaches to Handling Obstacles" flipchart.

REINFORCE responses, based on the tips in the "Handling Obstacles" handout.

- Pause, take time to think—and analyze the obstacle.

- Clarify the obstacle as required, and verify your understanding.

- Handle the obstacle—and verify that you have addressed the issue to your customer's satisfaction.

ASK other participants for comments and suggestions on the approaches—particularly those who identified similar obstacles.

NOTE on the flipchart changes <u>to which the "owner" of the approach agrees</u>.

ALLOW 2 or 3 minutes at the conclusion of the discussion for participants to make notes and changes to their own work.

POST the "Approaches to Handling Obstacles" flipchart in the "Target" area, while participants update their work.

ASK this question.

• Are there any questions about the activity just completed?

ANSWER the questions, as appropriate.

INDIVIDUAL ASSESSMENT

INTRODUCE the assessment.

- You will now take a few minutes to complete a simple assessment of your skills in handling obstacles.

Handling Obstacles Assessment

DISTRIBUTE the "Handling Obstacles Assessment" (page 357).

REVIEW the instructions on the assessment with participants.

ALLOW 3 minutes to complete the assessment.

GROUP DISCUSSION

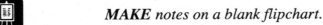

ASK participants to volunteer steps in their personal action plans for improving skills in handling obstacles.

MAKE notes on a blank flipchart.

REINFORCE the value of the steps identified, referring to the "Handling Obstacles Assessment," as appropriate.

KEY POINTS

MAKE these key points as a summary.

- Obstacles provide an excellent opportunity to learn about things that may be of concern to your customer.

- When you encounter an obstacle, be sure you understand accurately what it is—and then verify that you have handled it to your customer's satisfaction.

The Last Two Phases: A Role Play

01:00

Purpose: Provide role play practice in the "Make a Recommendation" and "Complete the Sale" phases of the sales process.

Note: Materials required for this activity may be found in "The Last Two Phases: A Role Play" learning activity beginning on page 319.

TABLE GROUP ACTIVITY

BREAK *the workshop into table groups of three people each.*

DESCRIBE *the structure of the role play.*

- This role play is a continuation of the previous role play, in which you practiced the "Earn the Right" and "Understand the Need" phases of the sales process.

- As before, there will be three rounds in this role play.

- Each of you will have the opportunity to play the role of salesperson, customer, and observer.

- You will play the same customer role as before—1, 2, or 3.

- Also, salespeople will role play with the *same* customer as before; if you role played with Customer 1 in the previous role play, you will play the role of Salesperson 1 in this role play, and so on.

*Instructions for
Customer 1, 2, 3;
Instructions for
Salesperson 1, 2, 3;
Observer's Critique Sheet*

DISTRIBUTE *handouts to each of the table groups; a set of* "Instructions for Customer" (pages 326, 328, and 330) *and* "Instructions for Salesperson" *handouts (pages 325, 327, and 329), and three each of the* "Observer's Critique Sheet" (page 324).

PRESENT *the basic instructions for the activity.*

1. You will have 3 minutes to review your instructions and make notes prior to each round of the role play.

2. Once the role plays begin, the participant playing "observer" in each round will keep track of time.

3. Each round will be 5 minutes in length.

4. At the end of each round, 3 minutes will be allowed for discussion within the table group.

5. This procedure will be repeated until each participant in the table group has played each of the roles.

6. Finally, the full group will reconvene for a discussion of the role play experiences.

ASK *this question.*

*   Are there any questions about the instructions, thus far?

ANSWER *the questions, as appropriate.*

REVIEW *the instructions in each of the three handouts, either paraphrasing them or reading them aloud.*

ASK *this question.*

*   Are there any questions about the instructions before beginning?

ANSWER *the questions, as appropriate.*

ASK *participants to move to their table groups.*

MONITOR *progress as the exercise moves forward, assuring that the groups stay on schedule.*

GROUP DISCUSSION

RECONVENE the full group.

MAKE this comment.

- Let's discuss your reactions to this role play.

ASK one or two participants to answer these questions as "salespeople."

- Why did you use the approach to making a recommendation and completing the sale that you pursued during the role play?

- How effective was it from your point of view?

RECORD responses on a blank flipchart.

ENCOURAGE other participants to add comments, as appropriate.

ASK one or two participants to answer this question as "observers."

- As observers, what general reactions did you have about what was done well? Suggestions for improvement?

RECORD responses on another blank flipchart.

ENCOURAGE other participants to add comments, as appropriate.

ASK one or two participants to answer these questions as "customers."

- What was your perception of the overall sales interaction?

- How effective was the approach from your point of view?

RECORD responses on the blank flipchart.

ENCOURAGE other participants to make constructive comments regarding their impressions, alternatives, etc.

***ASK** each of the questions on the "Role Play Questions" flipcharts* (pages 426 and 427, respectively) *as a means for summarizing the discussion of the role play.*

- Did the salesperson address the customer's buying objectives?
- How effectively was the explaining skill used?
- What might have been done more effectively?
- What technique was used to ask for the order?
- How effectively were obstacles handled?
- What might have been done more effectively?
- Did the salesperson *complete the sale*?

Role Play Questions

***MAKE NOTES** about responses on the "Role Play Questions" flipcharts.*

***LOOK FOR** answers that allow you to reinforce the importance of key points on the "Observer's Critique Sheet."*

- Presented a good recommendation.
- Used explaining skills effectively.
- Described benefits effectively.
- Handled obstacles effectively.

***ASK** this question.*

- Are there any questions about this activity?

***ANSWER** the questions, as appropriate.*

"Complete the Sale" Assessment

00:10

Purpose: Provide an opportunity for participants to assess skills relevant to the "Complete the Sale" phase.

INDIVIDUAL ASSESSMENT

INTRODUCE the assessment.

- You will now take a few minutes to complete a simple assessment of skills relevant to the "Complete the Sale" phase of the sales process.

"Complete the Sale" Assessment

DISTRIBUTE the "'Complete the Sale' Assessment" (page 359).

REVIEW the instructions on the assessment with participants.

ALLOW 3 minutes to complete the assessment.

GROUP DISCUSSION

ASK participants to volunteer steps in their personal action plans for improving skills relevant to the "Complete the Sale" phase.

MAKE notes on a blank flipchart.

REINFORCE the value of the steps identified, referring to the "'Complete the Sale' Assessment," as appropriate.

KEY POINTS

MAKE these key points as a summary.

- The importance of asking for the order—with confidence
- The importance of carefully and thoroughly handling obstacles
- The importance of *completing the sale!*

Summary

00:10

Purpose: Review key points from the module, and provide a summary of the one-day sales workshop.

FACILITATOR COMMENTARY

MAKE this comment.

- At this point, we have concluded Module 5 of our sales workshop—and the sales workshop itself.

- Let's review the key points that have been covered—both in this module and throughout this workshop.

Effective Selling

USE the "Effective Selling" flipchart to re-establish an overall context for the review and summary.

- The phases of the sales process

- Communications skills and their importance in the sales process

- Sales skills and their importance in the sales process

REVIEW the flipcharts that have been posted in the "Sales Process" area during this module, and highlight the others.

- Buying Signals

- Asking for the Order

REVIEW the flipcharts that have been posted in the "Sales Skills" area during this module, and highlight the others.

- Common Obstacles

- Handling Obstacles

REVIEW other flipcharts that have been posted during the module and/or throughout the workshop, as appropriate.

Targeting Your Sales Efforts

REVIEW the flipcharts that have been posted in the "Target" area during this module, and highlight the others.

- Approaches to Asking for the Order

- Approaches to Handling Obstacles

MARK OFF activities that have been completed on the "Targeting Your Sales Efforts" flipchart.

ASK this question.

- Are there any questions?

ANSWER the questions, as appropriate.

Sales Workshop Agenda

MARK OFF the topics that have been covered on the "Sales Workshop Agenda" flipchart.

MAKE these concluding comments.

- This brings the one-day sales workshop to a close.

- Thank you for your time and involvement in today's workshop.

- I am looking forward to working with you again in future sales training activities.

- Good luck as you apply the lessons learned in these sessions to your work!

Chapter Seven

Participant Handouts

In this section of *The ASTD Trainer's Sourcebook: Sales*, you will find participant handouts for use during your sales training sessions. You may use the handouts in two ways:

- Key them into your word processing system, either "as is" or customized to suit your specific needs.
- Copy the masters that you need from this book and make copies from them "as is."

Your Sales Experiences

Please do the following to complete this exercise.

- Think of recent sales experiences you have had—as a customer, a salesperson, and an observer.
- Think about the factors that were positive or good about these experiences and those that were unsatisfactory—even unpleasant.
- Make brief notes about these factors in the spaces below.

Your experiences as...	The Positive, the Good	The Unsatisfactory, the #@&
A Customer		
A Salesperson		
An Observer		

Effective Selling

Effective selling requires two things of you.

- A *way of thinking* about the sales situation that provides motivation and direction for your selling—a *mindset*
- A *way of doing* things during the sales situation that is based on techniques required for success in selling—a *skill set*

The *mindset* that will provide motivation and direction for you consists of two parts.

- *Key assumptions*—about the sales situation, and why both you and the customer are in a sales situation in the first place
- A *well-defined sales process*—a process that will help structure your actions and lead you efficiently from your first meeting with the customer to successfully completing the sale

Likewise, the *skill set* consists of two parts.

- *Communications skills*—skills that help you effectively gather information *from* your customer and present information *to* your customer throughout the sales process.
- *Sales skills*—skills that tend to be key to success in particular phases of the sales process.

In the illustration below, you see the phases of the sales process we recommend, along with five communications skills and four sales skills that we believe are key to effectively using this sales process.

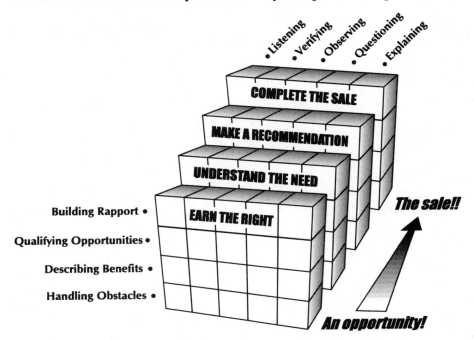

In the remaining pages, you will have the opportunity to read more about the mindset and skill set mentioned above.

Key Assumptions

There are a number of assumptions that are key to success as a salesperson. The first two are critical.

- From your point of view as a salesperson, the sale begins as *an opportunity*.
- Your challenge is to move from the opportunity to success—*completing the sale*.

Having made those assumptions, it is important that you make the following assumptions about the reasons that you and your customer find yourselves together in a sales situation. These assumptions are shown in the illustration below.

The customer...   **You...**

- Has a problem to solve or a need to satisfy

- Probably isn't convinced that he or she necessarily wishes to buy from you

- Wants help with the buying decision

- Is there to BUY!

opportunity

- Must earn the right to proceed in the sales effort with the customer

- Are there to understand the customer's need

- Are there to help the customer buy

- Are there to SELL!

The Sale!!!

The key message in this illustration can be summarized as follows.

- In a sales situation, your job is to *learn about the customer's need* and then *complete the sale*.

The sales process, along with application of key communications and sales skills, is designed to facilitate learning about the customer's needs and completing the sale.

The Sales Process

The sales process that we recommend is divided into four phases. As you read the definition of each of these phases, it is important to keep these points in mind. Depending on the nature of the situation in which you sell, . . .

- You might go through all four phases in one interaction with the customer—maybe two—and then complete the sale.
- You might be involved in several sales interactions—or sales calls—as you work through the phases and reach the point of completing the sale.

Earn the Right

This first phase is key to the success of your sales effort. This is the time at which you and your customer meet—the time at which you and your customer form your first impressions of one another, for better or for worse. Hopefully for the better, of course.

An important aspect of this phase is "building rapport"—one of the skills covered in the sales skills portion of these materials. A key result of successfully beginning to build rapport is *earning the right to proceed*—hence, the name of the phase.

- You must *build* that basic level of trust and confidence that encourages your customer to stay with you and, essentially, grant you the right to move forward with the sales effort.
- Such a level of trust and confidence is *not* something you can take for granted. *You must earn it.*

Understand the Need

Understanding the customer's need is the heart of the sales process. What you learn here influences what you do in the final two phases. It is here that you find out what is on your customer's mind—problems to be solved, needs to be satisfied, etc. The customer's buying objectives.

Additionally, you learn other things about the customer. What can he or she afford? What factors will influence the buying decision? Who will actually make the decision? Is the customer ready to make a decision? The customer's buying influences.

Make a Recommendation

Once you have a full understanding of what the customer needs and what will motivate him or her to buy, you are prepared to make a recommendation. When you believe that you have reached that point, you will "test the water" and—if the time seems to be right—you present your recommendation.

Your recommendation must be a compelling case for buying, presented from the customer's point of view. It must be presented logically—with conviction and forcefulness that conveys your genuine belief in the recommendation that you are making.

Complete the Sale

As you make your recommendation, there are many "buying signals" that indicate the customer's readiness to say "Yes! Where do I sign?"—gestures, smiles, questions, comments, etc. Your challenge is to recognize these signals—and ask for the order.

Often, asking for the order is not easy.

- Most of us don't like to hear the answer "No, I'm not . . . ," so it can be comfortable not to ask the question, to keep things moving along,—and avoid the perceived risk of asking that all-important question.
- Additionally, we don't like to provoke the objections or obstacles that might arise when asking for the order—because we must then understand them and address them successfully, or risk forfeiting the sale. On the other hand, obstacles are a great way of understanding just where the customer stands and, once you understand them and handle them effectively, the sale can be yours for the asking.

At this point in the sales process it is time to complete what you started and what you have worked toward—it is time to complete the sale. During this phase, it is important to keep these points in mind.

- If you have moved through the sales process carefully and reached agreement with your customer at each step of the way, you have earned the right to ask for the order.
- And—if your recommendation reflects your understanding and the agreements you have reached with the customer, you have a very good chance of getting the answer you want!

Now, let's look very briefly at the five communications skills that are important to the effective execution of the sales process.

Communications Skills

Five communications skills are important to the success of your sales efforts. These definitions are based on those in *Webster's New Collegiate Dictionary.*[*]

Listening

lis·ten·ing (from the old English "hlysnan") *1: making a conscious effort to hear 2: paying close attention*

Verifying

ver·i·fy·ing (from the Latin "make true") *1: proving to be true by evidence 2: testing or checking the accuracy or correctness of*

Questioning

ques·tion·ing (from the Latin "ask" or "inquire") *1: asking a question or questions of 2: putting queries to*

Observing

ob·serv·ing (from the Latin "guard" or "watch over") *1: noticing or perceiving something 2: paying special attention to*

Explaining

ex·plain·ing (from the Latin "make level") *1: making clear, plain, or understandable 2: giving the meaning or interpretation of*

Each of these communications skills is important to one degree or another in each of the phases of the sales process—and in executing certain sales skills that are important to the sales process.

---

[*] Based on definitions from *Webster's New World Dictionary of American English.* Simon & Schuster, Inc., New York, NY: 1994.

Sales Skills

The four key sales skills that we discuss in the workshop tend to be applicable at specific points in the sales process. In this section, we will briefly define and describe each of these skills. Once again, definitions are based on those in *Webster's New World Dictionary.*

Building Rapport

rap·port (from the Old French "to bring back") *1: relationship 2: agreement 3: harmony*

This skill is especially important in the first phase of the sales process—the time at which you begin earning the right to proceed. Of course, you must to continue to build on and develop rapport with your customer throughout the sales process.

Qualifying Opportunities

qual·i·fy (from the Latin "of what kind" and "make") *1: to make fit 2: to have the necessary or desirable qualities*

In sales, qualifying addresses the basic question, "Is this opportunity 'for real'?"

- Does the customer have a need? Is the customer interested in what you have to offer?
- Is the customer *ready* to buy?
- Is the customer *willing* to buy . . . from you?
- Is the customer *able* to buy?
- Are *you able to satisfy* the customer's need?

Positive answers—particularly early in the sales process—help to ensure you that you are spending your time on a sales effort that will pay off.

Describing Benefits

ben·e·fit (from the Latin "well" and "do") *1: anything contributing to an improvement in condition; help, advantage*

In sales, providing benefit goes beyond the simple ability to "contribute to an improvement in condition" and includes the even more important concept of demonstrating your ability to do so *from the perspective of the customer*. Describing benefits that are *important to your customer* is key to your ability to make recommendations successfully.

Handling Obstacles   **ob·sta·cle** (from the Latin "stand")   *1: anything that gets in the way or hinders*

Sooner or later—often later but, even better, sooner—your customer raises an obstacle. As we indicated earlier, it is important to remember that obstacles are a great way of understanding just where the customer stands. Once you understand the obstacles and handle them effectively, you can move forward and the sale can be yours for the asking.

In this sales workshop, you will explore the sales process, communications skills, and sales skills—as well as some other techniques that will help make your sales efforts as effective and successful as possible.

Active Listening: What and How

What Is Active Listening?

Active listening is the combination of two key communications skills, listening and verifying. [*]

lis·ten·ing (from the old English "hlysnan") *1: making a conscious effort to hear 2: paying close attention*

ver·i·fy·ing (from the Latin "make true") *1: proving to be true by evidence 2: testing or checking the accuracy or correctness of*

When you practice active listening, you are doing these things.

- Listening with a purpose
- Listening with undivided attention focused on the activity of listening—a conscious effort to hear
- Verifying as you listen, to ensure understanding

Tips on Active Listening

Here are seven tips that are helpful when you are attempting to make active listening one of your "second nature" behaviors.

❑ Listen attentively.
  - You must make the effort to concentrate on what the other person is saying, not what you're going to say next.
  - Be aware of your posture; the right posture enhances your ability to concentrate, eliminates distractions—and communicates that you are listening attentively.

❑ Verify your understanding.
  - Pause, think about what was said, and then think about what you will say.
  - Repeat what was said using different words—without adding anything new or your interpretation.
  - Describe what you *think* the other person said. This is a more complex approach because it requires you to add interpretation or inference—and it requires the other person to respond to those additions.

❑ Get confirmation that your verification was correct.
  - The actual statement you make is only half of verifying.
  - You must ask a question requesting the confirmation.

---

[*] The following definitions are based on *Webster's New World Dictionary of American English.* Simon & Schuster, Inc., New York, NY: 1994.

❑ Avoid appearing manipulative when seeking confirmation.
- Phrase your question in a neutral or positive way—for example, "Is that right?"

❑ Seek clarification if you do not understand something.
- Don't wait.
- Don't ignore your potential misunderstanding and risk letting it grow into an even larger misunderstanding.

❑ Assume responsibility when a misunderstanding occurs.
- Don't appear to blame the other person—for any reason, no matter how ineffectively he or she seems to be communicating with you.
- Remember that, as a salesperson, you want to build rapport. Making people feel foolish or at fault is not only rude but counterproductive.

❑ Take advantage of nonverbal clues.
- Maintain eye contact and an open posture, face the other person squarely.
- Be sensitive to the kind of nonverbal clues that you receive from the other person as you apply your active listening skills.
- Verify the nonverbal "messages" that you receive.

What clues are your customers giving you?

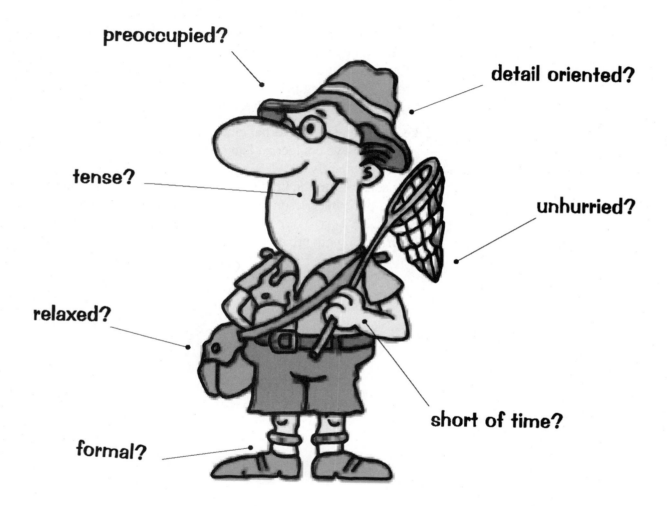

preoccupied?

detail oriented?

tense?

unhurried?

relaxed?

short of time?

formal?

Observing: What You Can Learn

Although the observing skill is valuable *throughout* the sales process, there are certain times when it is especially valuable—for example, at the beginning when you are attempting to build rapport.

- Observing your customer can tell you a great deal about his or her current state of mind—and his or her reaction to you.
- Your observations of the customer and his or her environment can also tell you a great deal about long-term behavior patterns—information that is especially important in longer-term sales relationships.

In sales situations, observing involves four steps.

- Look for a clue (or clues) that might suggest certain characteristics or traits in your customer.
- Interpret the clue—a particularly important step when you are drawing conclusions about the customer's longer-term behavior patterns.
- Verify the accuracy of your interpretation—and the presence of the characteristic that you think you detected.
- Use the clue and your interpretation of it—verified, of course—to help you relate to your customer and determine your next steps.

Observing Your Customer

In the first few seconds of a face-to-face meeting with a customer, the customer typically provides a lot of nonverbal clues—clues that can tell you a lot about the customer and his or her current state of mind, *if you observe them.*

Some common "states of mind" or characteristics are listed down the left side of the chart below.

- Write down clues that you might pick up from your customer that would point to each of those characteristics.
- Make notes about how you would interpret each clue.
- Then, make notes about ways in which you might verify your interpretation—a question, a statement, etc.
- Finally, indicate what you might do as a result of observing that clue.

Characteristic	Clues	Your Interpretation
Relaxed		
Tense		
Unhurried		
Short of time		
Preoccupied		
Formal		
Detail oriented		

Your Verification	Your Action

Observing Your Customer's Environment

If you meet on your customer's "territory," you can often observe things in his or her environment that tell you about longer-term behavior patterns.

Some common broadly-defined traits or characteristics that describe behavior are listed down the left side of the chart below.

- Write down some clues that you might pick up from your customer that would tell you something about each of these traits or characteristics.
- Make notes about how you would interpret each clue—for example, what might a clue tell you *specifically* about work habits.
- Then, make notes about ways in which you might verify your interpretation—a question, a statement, etc.
- Finally, indicate what you might do as a result of that observation.

Characteristic	Clues	Your Interpretation
Work habits		
Self-confidence		
Background		
Sphere of influence		
Thoroughness		
Interests (hobbies, family, etc.)		

Your Verification	Your Action

Why Customers Buy

When you work with customers to make a sale—and, therefore, help them to buy—there are two areas that you need to learn about and understand.

- Buying objectives—what your customer wishes to accomplish.
- Buying influences—factors that will influence your customer's buying decision.

Buying Objectives

When you meet a customer in a sales situation, the customer is typically there for one of two basic reasons.

- The customer is there because he or she has a *problem* to solve.
- The customer is there because he or she has a *need* to satisfy.

Consider these examples.

- A customer comes into a camera store to buy a new camera. She is leaving on vacation in a week—the old camera is broken and is not worth repairing. This customer has a *problem* to solve.
- Another customer comes into the camera store to by a new camera. However, this customer has last year's model; it is perfectly good but the new model has a number of advanced features that make it the year's leading-edge camera in its class. This customer has a *need* to satisfy.

The distinction between having a *problem* and having a *need* is not necessarily clear cut. However, as in these examples, *needs* that must be satisfied tend to have a strong emotional component to them—as with the person who must *have this year's camera.*

Of course, some people wish to buy a product or service for a combination of reasons. Consider a medical researcher who must travel to Paris to present the results of an important study.

- She goes to a travel agency to buy tickets to Paris. She has a *problem* to solve—getting to Paris.
- The study is so important that the presentation in Paris could "make" her career. Therefore, there is also a *need* to be satisfied—less objective and concrete, definitely more emotional in nature than simply getting to Paris.

Whatever motivates customers, they have reasons for buying—their buying objectives, which you must understand to be successful in your selling efforts.

Buying Influences

In addition to understanding buying objectives, it is also important to understand your customer's *buying influences*—those factors that will tip their buying decision toward you and your product or service.

Some of these influences are quite logical, straightforward, and objective in nature.

- Does your product or service meet the *requirements* that the customer has?
- Is the *price* acceptable? Does it fit within the customer's budget?
- Will the product or service be available *when the customer wants it*—at the right time?
- If *others are involved* in making the decision to buy your product or service, will they approve the purchase?
- Does the customer have *specific expectations* for your product or service that are longer term in nature—warranty, ongoing support, etc.?

Other buying influences are less objective, less easily explained—more emotional, more subjective in nature.

- Does the customer *like your product* or your service?
- Does the customer *like you*—or feel comfortable with you?
- Does the customer *believe in you* and your ability to meet his or her requirements, expectations, etc.?

Learning about buying objectives and buying influences is a major step in understanding the customer's needs—and ultimately, in completing the sale.

- You will understand the factors that *motivate the customer to buy from you.*
- You will determine whether the customer is *ready, willing, and able to buy.*
- By showing a real interest in your customer, you will continue to *build rapport.*
- With the rapport that you build, you will also *earn the right to continue your sales efforts.*

Types of Questions

You use questions to serve two broad functions as you work to understand your customer's need and ultimately complete the sale—to open the discussion up and to focus it.

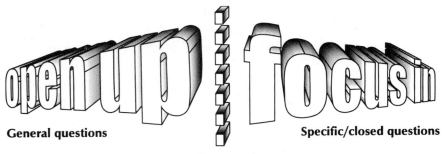

General questions   **Specific/closed questions**

Leading questions

As indicated above, there are three types of questions that are useful in this "open up, focus in" scheme.

- General questions are used to open up the discussion.
- Specific and closed questions are used to focus in.
- Leading questions can serve either purpose.

General Questions

General questions are useful throughout the sales process, whenever you need to probe and gather information from the customer.

- General questions typically begin with *what, how, who, why,* and *where*.
- Because such questions are difficult to answer in one or two words, they cause people to open up and talk with you.
- In addition, they allow you to expand the dialogue you are having with the customer by directing the discussion towards areas that are of interest to your sales efforts.

These questions are particularly useful early in a sales effort for one reason. In the very early stages, the last thing you wish to do is to give the customer the opportunity to answer a question with one or two words—in particular, the dread "No!"

Specific/Closed Questions

As you talk with your customer, there are times when you need brief, short, to-the-point answers.

- You need a specific piece of information.
- You need to verify and confirm your understanding.
- You need to focus the conversation and reach some sort of a conclusion.
- You need to refocus the conversation if it seems to be drifting away from the business at hand.

Questions that serve this purpose are referred to as *specific* questions. When a specific question requests a "yes" or "no" answer, it is often referred to as a *closed* question.

As with general questions, specific and closed questions are useful throughout the sales process—whenever you need to temporarily stop gathering new information and bring focus to the information you already have.

Leading Questions

Occasionally, you need to point your customer in a particular direction—a direction that will provide new information in areas of specific interest to you.

- You want to stimulate thinking in new directions ("What would happen if . . . ?").
- You want to cause the customer to evaluate the consequences of not acting ("What would happen if you didn't . . . ?").
- You want to force a reply that you wish to hear ("So, you think it would be wise to . . . ?").
- You want to force a choice in order to help you guide the discussion in the right direction ("Do you prefer . . . ?").

Questions that perform these functions for you are referred to as *leading* questions. Note that leading questions can either *open up* the discussion, or *focus in* the discussion—depending on your purpose at a specific point in time.

- Questions that fulfill the first two purposes above *open up* discussion.
- Questions that fulfill the last two *focus in* discussion.

Tips on Questioning

Here are some tips for questioning.

❑ Ask questions that will help you gather the types of information you need.
   - Use general questions when you want people to open up and talk.
   - Use specific questions when you need to focus the conversation, reach conclusions, etc.
   - Use leading questions when you need a specific answer or need to move the conversation in a specific direction.
   - Very early in a sales effort, avoid questions that can be answered with one or two words—especially "No!"

❑ Listen to the answers to your questions.
   - Focus on what the customer is saying.
   - Avoid formulating your next question while the customer is talking—particularly if that sort of activity easily distracts you from listening.

❑ Use a deliberate line of questioning that will take you and your customer where you need to go.
   - Determine what information you need in order to reach your goal of completing the sale.
   - Use a mix of general, specific/closed, and leading questions that will gather that information for you—and keep the discussion on track.
   - Constantly evaluate whether you are getting the information you need—and, if not, adjust your line of questioning accordingly.
   - Don't assume that a customer will always "open up" with general questions, "focus in" with specific questions, etc. Be ready to rephrase questions or adjust your approach if you are not getting the answers you need, or if you are not moving the discussion in the direction it needs to go.
   - Be sure that you don't give your customer the impression that he or she is being "grilled."

Explaining

ex·plain·ing (from the Latin "make level") * *1: making clear, plain, or understandable 2: giving the meaning or interpretation of*

Explaining is particularly important in two phases of the sales process.

- "Make a Recommendation," when you are presenting a recommendation
- "Complete the Sale," when you are handling any obstacles that might arise.

Here are some important points about the explaining skill.

- Keep in mind why you are using the explaining skill.
  - If you are presenting a recommendation, the reason you are using that skill is to put yourself in a position to ask for the order.
  - If you are handling an obstacle (or answering a question, in general), you are using the skill to clarify and address an issue or a concern (or to provide information that the customer has requested).

- Organize the content of your explanation—which you will likely be doing mentally, "on the fly."
  - Include *only* information that serves the purpose of the explanation.
  - Put the key points of the explanation in a logical order— logical from your point of view and, just as importantly, logical from the *customer's point of view*.
  - As you cover the key points of the explanation, add any supporting detail that is needed—but avoid the temptation to include detail that gets in the way or, worse yet, only confuses things.
  - Make the explanation clear and explicit—especially if you are presenting a recommendation, which is no time to "beat around the bush."

---

* Based on the definition from *Webster's New World Dictionary of American English*. Simon & Schuster, Inc., New York, NY: 1994.

- Present the explanation.
    - Follow the logic that you believe is appropriate.
    - If the explanation is, of necessity, long and/or complex, use an overview at the beginning and a summary at the end.
    - If it is *really* complex, consider "chunking" it and adding a few intermediate summaries so that you can be sure that your customer is following it—and that you're still on track.

Tips for Successful Explanations

Here are some tips for making successful explanations.

- ❑ Use simple language.
    - Avoid technical jargon that is—or easily could be—unknown to your customer.
    - Jargon is appropriate *only if* your customer uses and understands it, you understand it, *and* you use it appropriately.

- ❑ Keep the explanation short and to the point.

- ❑ Make sure the explanation is logical.

- ❑ Provide clear transitions from one point to the next.

- ❑ Be sure the explanation is credible and concrete.

- ❑ Make the explanation vivid and dynamic.

- ❑ Be sure you remain focused on the purpose of the explanation—and on the customer's objectives.

- ❑ If you don't know the answer to a question, *don't "fake it."*
    - Defer the question until you can get the information required—and then make your explanation.

Building Rapport

rap·port (from the Old French "to bring back") [*]
1: relationship 2: agreement 3: harmony

In contemporary use, "building rapport" refers to achieving a sense of relationship, agreement, and harmony. However, the word "rapport" actually derives from Old French and means "to bring back." In sales, the concept of "bringing back" is key to what we mean by "building rapport."

Building rapport is an ongoing process that is *only beginning* early in the sales effort. Therefore, you will have both *short-range* and *longer-range* objectives for building rapport.

Short-Range Objectives

These are some typical short-range objectives for building rapport.
- Make the customer comfortable in the sales situation.
- Begin to find out why the customer is there—gain a sense of the customer's need and how you can learn more about the need.
- Ensure that you will be able to continue the sales effort beyond its opening moments.

Objectives such as these must be met if you expect the customer to be around long enough for you to earn the right to proceed.

Longer-Range Objectives

Here are some typical longer-range objectives for building rapport.
- Gain attention so that you are able to begin a dialogue with the customer.
- *Begin* building a foundation of rapport between yourself and the customer—the sense of "harmony, affinity, and agreement" that is key to your success.
- *Earn the right* to proceed—ensuring that the customer will stay with you (and return if necessary), thus positioning yourself to learn about the customer's need and complete the sale.

A key point about building rapport is that it is *an ongoing process that is only <u>beginning</u> early in the sales effort*.

---

[*] Based on the definition from *Webster's New World Dictionary of American English*. Simon & Schuster, Inc., New York, NY: 1994.

Tips for Building Rapport

Here are some tips for building rapport.

❑ Act relaxed and at ease.
   –   Take a deep breath, smile, project a sense of "welcome."
   –   Shake hands, if that seems appropriate.

❑ Make the other person feel comfortable.
   –   Use an appropriate amount of "small talk" or other non-business conversation.
   –   For example, recall topics of personal interest from a previous conversation.

❑ Listen to the other person.
   –   Concentrate on the other person.
   –   Make a "conscious effort to hear."

❑ Take some time before moving into the "business" aspect of the discussion.
   –   Be sure to make the customer feel comfortable—don't put him or her on the defensive.
   –   Pay attention to clues from the customer that say to you "Okay, it's time to get down to business."

❑ Be aware of your own nonverbal behaviors—Make sure that they are positive.
   –   Face the customer—head on.
   –   Establish eye contact quickly—and then maintain it without seeming to stare.
   –   Be sure your posture is friendly and informal—not stiff or unnecessarily formal.
   –   Be receptive without seeming to smother or intimidate the customer.

❑ Project a positive image.
   –   Make sure that your attire and grooming are appropriate.
   –   If you are meeting the customer on "your territory," be sure your surroundings project the right image.

Qualifying Opportunities

qual·i·fy (from the Latin "of what kind" and "make") [*] *1: to make fit 2: to have the necessary or desirable qualities*

In sales, qualifying addresses the basic question, "Is this opportunity 'for real'?"

- Does the customer have a need? Is the customer interested in what you have to offer?
- Is the customer *ready* to buy?
- Is the customer *willing* to buy...from you?
- Is the customer *able* to buy?
- Are *you able to satisfy* the customer's need?

Positive answers to each of those questions qualify both the *customer* and the *opportunity*.

- The first four questions qualify the customer. Does the customer have a need and, if so, is he or she ready, willing, and able to buy?
- The fifth question qualifies the opportunity. Given that you have a qualified customer, are you able to satisfy that customer's need with your product or service?

Why Qualify?

Very simply, by qualifying opportunities, you increase the likelihood that you are investing your valuable time and energy in sales efforts that will succeed. Positive answers to those questions—particularly early in the sales process—help to ensure you that you are spending your time on a sales effort that will pay off.

How to Qualify

Basically, you must gather information that answers the qualifying questions and then evaluate the information to determine if you believe that the customer is qualified.

- You rely on questioning, listening, verifying, and observing to gather the information.
- You rely on your experience and judgment to evaluate the information.

More likely than not, you won't ask a customer—straight out—if he or she is "for real." Because you must infer that (or not infer it) based on the information that you collect, there is an element of

---

[*] Based on the definition from *Webster's New World Dictionary of American English.* Simon & Schuster, Inc., New York, NY: 1994.

risk involved in qualifying your customers—lost business if you don't qualify carefully or conclude incorrectly that an opportunity is not qualified. Your challenge is to reach as sound a conclusion about the opportunity as possible.

What If an Opportunity Isn't Qualified?

When an opportunity is not qualified, there are three basic alternatives.

- You can continue for a short period of time, hoping to build a bit more rapport with the customer and perhaps leave the door open for future sales activity. This is a good alternative in situations where the customer who is not qualified today— perhaps, simply not ready—might well be tomorrow. This option is also useful when your product or service doesn't meet the customer's needs—but it could be suitable when needs change.

- You can walk away at the earliest possible moment, thus saving your time. If it is a situation in which the opportunity is not qualified because your product or service doesn't meet the customer's needs, you're also saving the customer's time—a courtesy that might be remembered by the customer and, as a result, bring the customer back at a later date. Unless you've verified carefully and used good judgment, of course, the risk of losing a sale is higher with this alternative than with the first one.

- You can press on as far as possible, in the hope that you will eventually make a sale. Here, you certainly minimize the risk of losing business—but you increase the risk that you will be wasting your time and energy in a situation where the odds appear to be against winning.

Use the alternative that fits you and the situation, being mindful that there are times when you will be unable to make a sale no matter what you do.

Testing for Readiness

As you work to understand your customer's problem or need, you put together a line of questioning that helps you obtain the information you require about your customer's buying objectives and buying influences. At some point in the process, you will feel as if you have enough information.

How do you know you have enough information, and that it is time to make a recommendation? *Summarize* your understanding of the customer's situation and then *verify* that your understanding is accurate and complete.

- Summarizing and verifying the situation *as you perceive it* will tell you if you are as far along in the sales process as you think you are—or hope you are.
- You can also summarize and verify in a way that allows you to explore alternatives if appropriate—thus helping you to focus your recommendation more accurately.

Who knows! Your customer might be "chomping at the bit" and ready to buy on the spot. "Yes, I want that model right there!"

More likely, your customer will not be so accommodating—so you need to test to see if it is time to make a recommendation.

- Make a summary statement that rephrases what your customer has said. Than ask a question that will allow the customer to tell you if your understanding is accurate.
- Phrase your summary as a question—a question that also invites your customer to tell you if your understanding is complete and accurate.
- If you want to explore alternatives, you can combine the summary with a question that asks your customer to indicate which of two or more alternatives is most suitable.

Remember these points about testing for readiness.

- Whatever your approach to verifying, it is key that you ask the customer to confirm your understanding. "Is that correct?" "Yes . . ."
- However you test for readiness, you are inviting customers to provide important information to you. They agree that your understanding is complete. They provide information about preferable alternatives. They indicate areas where you need to probe further, learn more, etc.

Describing Benefits

ben·e·fit (from the Latin "well" and "do") [*] *1: anything contributing to an improvement in condition; help, advantage*

Benefits are key to the recommendation that you will present—key to showing your customer why the recommendation is good for him or her.

When you are presenting the benefits of your recommendation, it is important to keep the distinction between "feature" and "benefit" clear in your mind.

- *Features* address the question, "What are the characteristics of the product or service that are important to me, the customer?"
- *Benefits* address the questions, "So what? Why are the features important? What will they do for me?"

A well-stated benefit has these characteristics.

- The benefit is clearly related to the *customer's objective*.
- The benefit is perceived to be *something of value to the customer*.

If the customer does *not* perceive the benefit you describe as something of value to him or her, *it is not a benefit!*

---

[*] Based on the definition from *Webster's New World Dictionary of American English*. Simon & Schuster, Inc., New York, NY: 1994.

A Short Exercise

You will use the information below in a short exercise in identifying benefits.

Customer Objective 1	Characteristics of Styrofoam Cups	Benefit Statement
Looking for a type of coffee cup that can be easily stored and transported, that has minimal maintenance costs, and that is unbreakable and cheap	• Don't break easily • Lightweight • Packed in cartons • White	
Looking for a disposable cup that will go with any color of disposable dishes, napkins, and flatware	• Don't break easily • Lightweight • Packed in cartons • White	

Presenting a Recommendation

Two skills—explaining and describing benefits—are key to a successful recommendation. Your recommendations should have these characteristics.

- Clear, logical explanation—starting with a clear opening statement
- Clear relationship of the recommendation to customer objectives
- Clear statement of benefits that are related to customer objectives
- A credible and compelling description of the competitive edge of the approach

"Competitive edge" is an important element in a successful recommendation.

- A statement of competitive edge answers the questions, "Why buy from you? Why your product or service?"
- Such a statement shows how you can meet the customer's objectives in a superior fashion, and/or deliver superior benefits to the customer.
- Such a statement must be compelling and credible. It must *never* belittle or deride the competition—unless, of course, *you wish to throw away a significant part of the credibility you have established.*

Tips for Successful Recommendations

Here are some tips for presenting successful recommendations.

❑ Make the purpose clear—starting with a concise opening statement.

❑ Organize the content of the recommendation.
   – Put key points in a logical order—logical to you *and* your customer.
   – Include only relevant information—and only enough supporting details to ensure that the key points are clear.

❑ Use effective explaining skills.
   – Be sure the explanation is presented from the customer's point of view, with the customer's objectives as the focus.
   – Use overviews and summaries as appropriate.

❑ Include a clear statement of benefits, focused on the customer's objective.

❑ Provide a compelling description of your competitive edge.

❑ Communicate your enthusiasm for the recommendation not only through your choice of words, but also by gestures, expressions, posture, eye contact, and the pace of your speech.

❑ *Be certain that the recommendation itself is explicit.*

Finally, be certain that you...

❑ Ask for the order!

A Short Exercise

In this exercise, you will work in table groups to develop a short recommendation.

First, make notes of the customer, buying objective, and product or service described by your workshop facilitator.

The customer	
Buying objective	
Product or service	

Then, do the following.

- Identify the benefits you would include in the recommendation.
- Determine what you would include in the recommendation to describe your competitive edge.
- Write an opening statement for the recommendation.
- Outline the recommendation you would present, incorporating benefits and your competitive edge.

Benefits to be included	
Your competitive edge	

(Continued on the next page)

The opening statement	
Outline of the recommendation	

Asking for the Order

Once in a great while, your sales effort might be so dazzling that your customer just signs on the dotted line ☺—but not very often ☹. If you expect to complete the sale, you almost always have to *ask for the order*. Sigh ☺ !

Two Basic Approaches

There are two basic approaches to asking for the order—*direct* and *assumptive.*[*]

> **di·rect** (from the Latin "to lay straight") *1: by the shortest way, not roundabout 2: to the point; straightforward; frank*

You've presented your recommendation. You ask for the order. *Directly.* "Shall I book the cruise?" Frank. Straightforward.

> **as·sume** (from the Latin "to take up, claim") *1: take for granted, suppose something to be a fact*

Alternatively, you can assume that your customer has agreed—the *assumptive* approach. "Would you prefer to pay with a credit card or cash?" Not so frank, not so straightforward. A bit roundabout.

Occasionally, it might be easier for your customer to agree to this type of request—and for you to make such a request. However, a direct request is generally preferable when asking for the order. Unless other approaches are used carefully, you run the risk of *appearing* to be manipulative—even if that is the farthest thing from your mind.

Two Tips

Here are two simple tips worth keeping in mind when asking for the order.

❑ Be confident.
  – If you've worked to reach agreement with your customer throughout the sales process, you have "earned the right" to ask for the order.

❑ Let the customer respond.
  – Give your customer a chance to respond. Fight the temptation to jump in and break the silence. *There is nothing wrong with silence.* Just observe and listen—let silence be your ally.

---

[*] The following definitions based on *Webster's New World Dictionary of American English.* Simon & Schuster, Inc., New York, NY: 1994.

A Short Exercise

In this exercise, you will work in table groups to develop an approach to asking for the order.

First, make notes of the customer, buying objective, and product or service described by your workshop facilitator.

The customer	
Buying objective	
Product or service	

Then, do the following.
- Decide on the approach you will use.
- Indicate the reason you selected the approach.
- Develop the statement and/or question you will use to ask for the order.

The approach	
The reason for the approach	
The statement and/or question you will use	

Handling Obstacles

ob·sta·cle (from the Latin "stand") [*] *1: anything that gets in the way or hinders*

While it easy to think of obstacles as negative and unpleasant events, they are really opportunities.

- Obstacles provide an opportunity to learn about things that concern or bother the customer.
- The obstacle that is expressed by the customer might be a "smokescreen" that is hiding other, perhaps more serious concerns.
- Obstacles are an opportunity to find out what the customer is thinking—and, having done that, they allow you to continue working with your customer and complete the sale.

Techniques for Handling Obstacles

The key to successfully handling obstacles rests with the five basic communications skills that are important to selling.

- Listening—to learn more about the obstacle
- Questioning—to clarify your understanding
- Verifying—to be sure you understand what the obstacle *really* is
- Observing—to pick up nonverbal clues that can contribute to your efforts to understand the obstacle as clearly as possible
- Explaining—to address the obstacle and then to repeat, rephrase, or clarify your recommendation

"Special Situation" Obstacles

There are at three "special situation" obstacles that bear comment.

- "Don't Know the Answer"—Now and again, you will run across a situation where you simply do not have a reply for the obstacle or an answer to the question.
  - If you don't know the answer to the question, say so—don't attempt to "fake it" under any circumstances.
  - Most customers appreciate an honest, "I don't know the answer to that question, but let me get it for you" statement.

---

[*] Based on the definition from *Webster's New World Dictionary of American English.* Simon & Schuster, Inc., New York, NY: 1994.

- "Smokescreens"—Quite frequently, the obstacle raised by a customer might be masking other, more fundamental obstacles.
  - In these cases, you need to question and verify over and over, until you are at the fundamental obstacle—much like peeling the layers of an onion.
  - Having gotten to the "bottom of things," you can then deal with the obstacle—whether it was a genuine concern, a misunderstanding, etc.
- Product Shortcomings—Nobody has a "one size fits all" product or service that works with all customers.
  - If you determine that your product or service simply will not meet the customer's specifications or objectives, there is not a lot you can do about the situation.
  - When product shortcomings cannot be dealt with, recognize that you might need to terminate the sales effort—but do so gracefully, remembering the old adage about "not burning bridges behind you."

If you are unable to remove an obstacle to a sale, that does not mean you are a failure. If you know that you have given the sales situation your best effort, then that's all most people can ask.

Tips for Handling Obstacles

Here are some tips for handling obstacles.

❑ Pause. Take the time to think. Don't react immediately.

❑ Analyze the obstacle.
  - Is it an obstacle? A question?
  - What does it reflect? Disinterest? Misunderstanding? Something else, maybe not readily apparent?
  - Do you understand it?

❑ Clarify the obstacle, as necessary.

❑ Verify your understanding of the obstacle.
  - When verifying, be sure you don't accidentally sound as if you are agreeing with the obstacle.

❑ Handle the obstacle.

❑ Answer the question. Address the issue.
  - Verify that the customer feels you've handled it satisfactorily.
  - Move forward, and . . .

❑ Get the order!

Chapter Eight:

Learning Activities

In this section of *The ASTD Trainer's Sourcebook: Sales*, you will find learning activities for use during your sales training sessions. Each of the learning activities will have one or both of these components, depending on the nature of the activity and its use in the workshop.

- A set of instructions for your use during the activity. These instructions are in the same format as the training plans presented previously.
- Participant pages that need to be reproduced and provided to participants during the activity.

You may use the participant pages in two ways.

- Key them into your word processing system, either "as is" or customized to suit your specific needs.
- Copy the masters that you need from this book and make copies from them "as is."

Note: Several of the learning activities in this chapter are members of the "Targeting Your Sales Efforts" family. The learning activity titled "Typical Sales Situations and Customers" (page 256)—or equivalent participant thought activity to identify typical sales situations and customers—is prerequisite to completing the "Targeting Your Sales Efforts" activities.

What Did the Customer Say?[1]

00:15

Purpose: Stress the importance of effective communications skills by illustrating how easily communication can break down or be distorted.

TABLE GROUP ACTIVITY

BREAK the workshop into table groups of four to six people.

PRESENT the instructions for the learning activity.

1. I will ask one volunteer from each table group to go into the hall with me.

2. I will read to these volunteers a statement made by a customer. *They will not be allowed to take notes.*

3. Each volunteer will return to his or her table group and select one individual as a "listener." The volunteer will repeat the customer statement to the listener—out of hearing range of other team members or other teams. *The listener is not allowed to ask questions—just listen.*

4. That person, in turn, will select another listener and repeat what he or she heard. Once again—*no questions.*

5. That procedure will be repeated until there are no more listeners available in a table group.

6. The last listener in each group should make notes of what he or she heard.

ASK this question.

- Are there any questions about what you will be doing?

ANSWER the questions, as appropriate.

ASK participants to move into table groups and volunteers to come with you into the hall.

---

[1] Reprinted with permission of HRD Press, Inc., 22 Amherst Rd., Amherst, MA 01002, 1-800-822-2801 (U.S. and Canada) or (413) 253-3488.

READ the customer statement to the volunteers—either the one here or your own.

- We have a major problem with your company. We're launching a new product next month and our production schedule is in jeopardy because of the key component that you provide. We awarded you a contract a month ago for 10,000 components—the first shipment of which arrived on schedule two days ago. However, ten of the first 100 "out of the box" failed to meet our specifications. Our production manager, Fred Flemming, said "With a failure rate that high, it's pointless to test the rest—and another shipment's due in two days!" We need the components—on time and to specifications. You're in trouble! Your major competitor says they can have 5,000 up-to-spec components here in three days, and the rest within a week. So... can you replace that first shipment—and how fast? What confidence do we have that the remaining components will meet specifications?

Notes about your "customized" customer statement, if you elect to substitute your own:

ASK volunteers to return to their table groups.

GROUP DISCUSSION

RECONVENE the full group.

What You Believe the Customer Said

ASK one of the final listeners to report what he or she heard—making notes on the "What You Believe the Customer Said" flipchart (page 391).

ASK other final listeners to report on what they heard—making notes on the flipchart and noting additional points or differences, as well.

What the Customer Really Said

REVEAL the "What the Customer Really Said" flipchart (page 392).

COMPARE briefly the content of that flipchart with what the listeners reported hearing.

ASK this question.

- What was there about this exercise that interfered with successful communication?

LOOK FOR answers that allow you to lead the group to a conclusion such as this about the exercise.

- The exercise was somewhat artificial; people couldn't make notes, ask questions, or verify.

- Nonetheless, under the best of circumstances, it is difficult to concentrate and be a good listener.

- Effective communication is two-way and requires use of multiple skills—listening, questioning, verifying, observing, and explaining.

ASK this question.

- Are there any questions?

ANSWER the questions, as appropriate.

Typical Sales Situations and Customers

00:10

Purpose: Provide a foundation for a special series of activities, "Targeting Your Sales Efforts."

> *Note: This is not a stand-alone activity but, rather, is designed for use as a preparatory activity with the other "Targeting Your Sales Efforts" activities in this chapter.*

INDIVIDUAL "TARGET" ACTIVITY

INTRODUCE an initial activity that is the foundation for other "Targeting Your Sales Efforts" activities.

- In order to provide a basis for completing various "Targeting Your Sales Efforts" activities, you will now spend a short time identifying typical sales situations and typical customers whom you meet in those situations.

- Before you do that, let's review the typical sales situations that we discussed and to which we agreed during the one-hour seminar.

USE the "Typical Sales Situations" flipchart (pages 11 and 393) to review the nature of the sales interactions and sales process in which participants are typically involved.

Typical Sales Situations

Typical Sales Situations and Customers

DISTRIBUTE the learning activity, "Typical Sales Situations and Customers" (page 256).

REVIEW the instructions for the learning activity with participants.
ALLOW 5 minutes to complete the activity.

ASK this question.

- Are there any questions about the work you have just completed in this initial "Targeting Your Sales Efforts" activity?

ANSWER the questions, as appropriate.

Handout: Typical Sales Situations and Customers

In this "Targeting Your Sales Efforts" activity, you will identify typical situations under which you meet customers and then typical customers whom you meet in those situations. This work will form the foundation for other activities in this series.

- Identify a minimum of two *different* sales situations in which you meet customers. These could differ by location, the amount of time you spend, the degree of formality, etc.
- Then, identify the typical customers you meet in those situations. Of course, you might meet the same type of customer in more than one sales situation.

Write your answers in the spaces provided.

Sales Situations	Customers

Active Listening

00:35

Purpose: Provide practice in active listening skills.

Procedural notes: There are two things that you will need to do in preparation for this role play.

- *Select a topic on which each participant will be asked to speak when he or she plays the speaker role. A suggested topic is <u>participant expectations for the workshop</u>, based on the "Sales: A Quick Skills Assessment" and "Establishing Expectations" exercises (from the One-Hour Sales Seminar).*

- *Prepare handouts based on materials later in this section. Each individual will need copies of the instructions for <u>each</u> role—speaker, listener, and observer.*
  - *Speaker: page 260*
  - *Listener: pages 261 and 262*
  - *Observer: pages 263 and 264*

TABLE GROUP ACTIVITY

BREAK *the workshop into table groups of three people each.*

DESCRIBE *briefly the three roles and the topic of discussion for the "Active Listening" activity.*

- The *speaker* will talk about this topic.

  _____

  _____

  _____

- The *listener* will listen actively to what the speaker says, and employ verification techniques to assure accurate understanding.

- The *observer* will critique the role play, using a simple form to record his or her observations.

- There will be three rounds to the role play, so each of you will—in turn—play each of the three roles.

The Speaker Role;
The Listener Role;
The Observer Role

DISTRIBUTE *"The Speaker Role," "The Listener Role," and "The Observer Role" from the "Active Listening" learning activity (pages 260, 261 and 262, and 263 and 264 respectively).*

PRESENT *the basic instructions for the activity.*

1. Before the role plays begin, you will have 3 to 5 minutes to review your instructions and make notes about your topic on the handout called "The Speaker Role."

2. Once the role plays begin, the participant playing "observer" in each round will keep track of time.

3. Each role play discussion will be 3 minutes in length.

4. About 30 seconds before the end of the time period, the observer will ask the listener to summarize his or her understanding of the discussion.

5. At the end of each round, 3 minutes will be allowed for discussion within the table group.

6. This procedure will be repeated until each participant in the table group has played "speaker."

7. Finally, the full group will reconvene for a discussion of the active listening experiences.

ASK *this question.*

• Are there any questions about the instructions, thus far?

ANSWER *the questions, as appropriate.*

REVIEW *the instructions in each of the three handouts, either paraphrasing them or reading them aloud.*

ASK *this question.*

• Are there any questions about the instructions before beginning?

ANSWER *the questions, as appropriate.*

ASK *participants to move to their table groups.*

MONITOR *progress as the exercise moves forward, making sure that the groups stay on schedule.*

GROUP DISCUSSION

RECONVENE the full group.

ASK this question.

- As listeners, how did it feel to deliberately verify for understanding during the role play?

LOOK FOR answers such as these.

- Listening and verifying is work—it's not easy.

- Clearly, there is room for improvement in everyone's listening and verifying skills.

ASK this question.

- What verification techniques did you use? Which seemed most successful? Comfortable?

REINFORCE verification techniques covered in "Listener's Tips" and "Observer's Critique Sheet" during the discussion of techniques that were used, as appropriate.

- Confirms as a part of verification

- Seeks clarification when needed

- Assumes responsibility for misunderstanding

- Maintains eye contact

- Exhibits attentive body posture

ASK these questions.

- As speakers, how did it feel to have someone making a concerted effort to be sure they were understanding you?

- What effect do you think this type of listening has on your customers?

LOOK FOR answers such as these.

- It feels good to know the other person is really listening.

- It is surprising how often people don't understand what the other person really meant.

Active Listening

SUMMARIZE key points about active listening, using the "Active Listening" overhead transparency (page 368).

Handout: The Speaker Role

Preparing for the Role Play

1. Think about the topic on which the workshop facilitator has asked you to speak. Make notes in the space below.

2. Prepare an opening statement, so that the listener has a frame of reference for what you will be saying. Write this in the space below.

3. Review the instructions in the next section, "During the Role Play."

Your notes:

Your opening statement:

During the Role Play

1. Present your opening statement.

2. Then, begin to talk about your topic.

3. Respond to the questions posed by the listener.

4. Remember that you are leading the discussion—but the listener can redirect it as necessary to assure understanding.

After the Role Play

1. At the beginning of the table group discussion of your role play, briefly indicate to the listener whether you felt he or she really understood you.

2. During the discussion, add any comments you like to what the observer has to say about the role play.

3. During the group discussion after all the role plays have been completed, be sure to share your feelings.

Handout: The Listener Role

Preparing for the Role Play

1. Review the "Observer's Critique Sheet" (part of "The Observer's Role" handout) to remind yourself of the key things you should be doing as a listener.

2. Review "Listener's Tips" (the other page of this handout) for additional reminders of effective listening techniques.

3. You have 3 minutes to reach an understanding of what the speaker is discussing with you.

4. Review the instructions in the next section, "During the Role Play."

During the Role Play

Remembering that your objective is to learn about and reach a clear understanding of what the speaker is saying, ...

1. Look for places to stop the speaker and verify.

2. Be alert for areas that need clarification. If clarification is necessary, don't wait too long.

3. Remember that your task is to assure that *you understand* what is being said—the *speaker is leading* the discussion.

4. When the observer announces that time is nearly up, summarize your understanding of what the speaker has said.

After the Role Play

1. During the table group discussion, listen to the comments made by the observer and speaker in response to the role play. Add your thoughts, as appropriate.

2. During the group discussion after all the role plays have been completed, be sure to share your feelings.

Handout: Listener's Tips

Concentrate on the other person.

- Pay attention to *everything* that is said.
- Organize the information in your mind while you listen.
- Take notes of key words and phrases.
- Maintain eye contact.

Avoid planning your next comment, question, etc. while the other person is speaking.

- Use a pause to collect your thoughts before you make a statement or ask a question.

Ask for clarification when necessary.

- Be sure to ask for clarification in a way that puts the burden for not understanding on you, not the speaker.

Focus on what is not said as well as what is said.

- Be aware that there may be omissions and/or distortions in what you are hearing.
- When you detect omissions or distortions, ask questions and verify to fill the gaps.

Let the other person talk as long as the discussion is leading somewhere.

- If you feel there is a reason to limit the other person's speaking, avoid cutting the other person off in mid-sentence.

Handout: The Observer Role

Preparing for the Role Play

1. Review the critique sheet, included with this handout.

2. Note the two categories of listener behavior on the critique sheet—*behaviors that helped* and *behaviors that hindered* the listener's ability to listen.

3. Review the instructions in the next section, "During the Role Play."

During the Role Play

1. Time the speaker/listener discussion so that it does not run more than 2½ minutes.

2. Observe how the listener verified and the extent to which the listener allowed it to be the speaker's discussion.

3. Use the critique sheet during the discussion.

   - Each time the listener displays one of the various behaviors, make a check mark so you will have a count at the end of the role play.

   - If you are asked to be observer two times, use the "Situation 2" column for your second observation role.

4. At the 2½ minute mark, announce that it is time for the listener to summarize his or her understanding. Allocate 30 seconds for the summary.

After the Role Play

1. During the table group discussion, make comments based on your critique sheet.

2. During the group discussion after all the role plays have been completed, be sure to make general observations.

Handout: Observer's Critique Sheet

	Situation 1	Situation 2
Behaviors That Help		
• Verifies frequently	_____	_____
• Confirms as a part of verification	_____	_____
• Seeks clarification when needed	_____	_____
• Assumes responsibility for misunderstanding	_____	_____
• Maintains eye contact	_____	_____
• Exhibits attentive body posture	_____	_____
Behaviors That Hinder		
• Interrupts	_____	_____
• Leads the discussion	_____	_____
• Fails to seek clarification when needed	_____	_____
• Does not restate frequently	_____	_____
• Places burden for misunderstanding on the speaker	_____	_____
• Exhibits poor nonverbal contact	_____	_____

Questions for "Earn the Right"

00:15

Purpose: Provide an opportunity to develop general questions for use early in the "Earn the Right" phase.

INDIVIDUAL "TARGET" ACTIVITY

Questions for
"Earn the Right"

INTRODUCE a "Targeting Your Sales Efforts" activity focused on general questions.

- In this "Targeting Your Sales Efforts" activity, you will identify questions to use early in the "Earn the Right" phase, in two different situations.

DISTRIBUTE the learning activity, "Questions for 'Earn the Right'" (page 266).

REVIEW the instructions for the learning activity with participants.

ALLOW 5 minutes to complete the activity.

GROUP DISCUSSION

ASK a volunteer to describe one of his or her selling situations, the question(s) to be used, and the hoped-for result.

MAKE notes on a flipchart.

ASK one or two other volunteers with different situations to describe their question(s) and hoped-for results.

MAKE additional notes on the flipchart.

REINFORCE the use of general questions to open up discussion and get the customer talking.

ASK other participants for comments and suggestions on the questions—particularly those who were working with similar situations.

NOTE on the flipchart changes <u>to which the "owner" of the question(s) agrees</u>.

ALLOW 2 or 3 minutes at the conclusion of the discussion for participants to make notes and changes to their own work.

Handout: Questions for "Earn the Right"

In this "Targeting Your Sales Efforts" activity, you will identify questions to use at the beginning of a sale—questions that will encourage your customer to "open up" and help you begin to earn the right to proceed.

- Look at the sales situations that you have identified for this series of exercises.
- Select two situations where you believe your early questions might be different.
- Describe each situation briefly.
- Identify the question or questions that you would use.
- Describe the results that you hope to achieve with the question(s).

Write your answers in the spaces provided.

	Situation 1	**Situation 2**
Description of the situation		
The questions you would use		
Your hoped-for results		

Buying Objectives and Buying Influences

00:15

Purpose: Provide an opportunity to identify buying objectives and buying influences for typical customers.

INDIVIDUAL "TARGET" ACTIVITY

INTRODUCE a "Targeting Your Sales Efforts" activity focused on buying objectives and buying influences.

- In this "Targeting Your Sales Efforts" activity, you will identify buying objectives and buying influences for two of your typical customers.

Buying Objectives and Buying Influences

DISTRIBUTE the learning activity, "Buying Objectives and Buying Influences" (page 269).

REVIEW the instructions for the learning activity with participants.

ALLOW 5 minutes to complete the activity.

GROUP DISCUSSION

ASK a volunteer to first describe one of his or her customers, and then buying objectives and buying influences for that customer.

MAKE notes on a flipchart.

ASK one or two other volunteers to describe one of their customers, and then buying objectives and buying influences for that customer.

REINFORCE responses, based on the distinction between "buying objectives" and "buying influences."

- Buying objectives—what the customer wishes to accomplish.

- Buying influences—factors that will influence the customer's buying decision.

MAKE additional notes on the flipchart.

ASK other participants for comments and suggestions on the buying objectives and buying influences identified—particularly those who were working with similar customers.

NOTE on the flipchart changes <u>to which the "owner" of the approach agrees</u>.

ALLOW 2 or 3 minutes at the conclusion of the discussion for participants to make notes and changes to their own work.

Handout: Buying Objectives and Buying Influences

In this "Targeting Your Sales Efforts" activity, you will identify some buying objectives and buying influences for two of your typical customers.

- Look at the sales situations and typical customers that you have identified for this series of exercises.
- Select two typical customers from that list.
- Describe each customer briefly.
- Identify a typical buying objective for each customer.
- Identify typical buying influences that occur in connection with those customers and the buying objectives you have identified.

Write your answers in the spaces provided.

	Typical Customer 1	**Typical Customer 2**
Description of the customer		
A typical buying objective		
Typical buying influences		

A Questioning Demonstration

00:25

Purpose: Demonstrate questioning skills, using a simulated sales interaction.

Procedural note: In preparation for this demonstration, you need to prepare one copy of each of the following handouts, found later in this section.

- *Instructions for the Salesperson—page 274*
- *Instructions for the Customer—page 275*

Additionally, you will need copies of the "Observer's Critique Sheet" for each participant (page 273).

If you wish to customize this demonstration to your particular situation, you will need to rewrite the instructions for the salesperson and the customer—using the ones in this section as a model.

DEMONSTRATION ROLE PLAY

MAKE this comment.

- The purpose of this demonstration role play is to illustrate the use of questions in understanding a customer's need.

ASK for two volunteers—one to role play the "customer" and the other the "salesperson."

INDICATE that the remaining participants will function as observers during the role play.

Observer's Critique Sheet

DISTRIBUTE the "Observer's Critique Sheet" from the "A Questioning Demonstration" learning activity (page 273).

REVIEW the critique sheet with participants.

STRESS the points about using each of the question types and organizing the questions into a logical, productive sequence.

- Use general, specific/closed, and leading questions to open up and then focus the discussion, as needed.

Structure questioning logically so that your discussion produces the information that you need.

DISTRIBUTE the instruction sheets to the salesperson and customer (pages 274 and 275, respectively).

PRESENT the basic instructions for the activity.

1. We will take a short break during which the salesperson and customer will review their instructions and prepare themselves for the role play.

2. Following that, they will role play a sales situation for approximately 5 minutes.

3. I will signal the volunteers about 30 seconds before the role play is over, at which time the salesperson will summarize his or her understanding of the customer at that point in time.

4. The rest of you will then have 1 or 2 minutes to complete your critique sheets.

5. Then we will discuss the questioning demonstration as a group.

ALLOW 3 minutes for a break, during which the volunteers will prepare for their roles.

RECONVENE the group.

BEGIN the role play.

ANNOUNCE that it is time for the salesperson to summarize after about 4½ minutes.

ALLOW 30 seconds for the salesperson's summary.

GROUP DISCUSSION

MAKE this comment.

- Let's discuss the effectiveness of the questioning technique used in this demonstration role play.

ASK these questions of the salesperson.

- How did you make use of various question types during the demonstration?

- Why did you use that particular questioning approach?

- How effective was it from your point of view?

RECORD responses on a blank flipchart.

ASK this question.

- What general reactions do the observers have about what was done well? Suggestions for improvement?

REFER to each of the major categories on the critique sheet as you gather comments, in order to assure completeness of the discussion.
RECORD responses on another blank flipchart.

ASK these questions of the customer.

- What was your perception of the overall sales effort?

- How effective was the questioning technique from your point of view?

RECORD responses on a third blank flipchart.

ENCOURAGE observers to make additional constructive comments regarding their impressions, alternatives, etc.

Types of Questions

USE the "Types of Questions" overhead transparency (page 373) as a vehicle to summarize the demonstration and the discussion of question types.

ASK this question.

- Are there any questions about this demonstration?

ANSWER the questions, as appropriate.

Handout: Observer's Critique Sheet

Make notes about the effectiveness of the questioning demonstration in the spaces below.

Questioning Skill	Comment
Used questions effectively *Note examples of questions used here:* • General • Specific/closed • Leading	
Organized questions in a logical, productive sequence	
Verified understanding • Rephrased or interpreted; did not repeat verbatim • Confirmed understanding	
Observed the customer • Verified observations	
Concentrated on what the customer was saying	
Let the customer talk; did not monopolize the discussion	
Learned about the customer's . . . • Buying objectives • Buying influences	
General comments:	

Handout: Instructions for the Salesperson

You are a salesperson in a large home appliance outlet. This store sells several brands of large and small appliances, and typically offers a wide selection of models.

After greeting your customer and chatting briefly, you have begun to build rapport. In addition, you have just learned that your customer is interested in coffee makers.

Your mission is to learn as much as possible regarding your customer's interest in coffee makers.
- Buying objectives
- Buying influences

Make notes here about the questions that you plan to use. Use each of the question types as appropriate.

Handout: Instructions for the Customer

You have gone to a large home appliance outlet and have been approached by a salesperson. You have chatted briefly, and you feel reasonably comfortable with the salesperson.

The only thing the salesperson knows about you at this point is that you are interested in coffee makers.

The following are the characteristics of the coffee maker for which you are looking—which you may divulge as the salesperson asks the appropriate questions.

- Must be easy to use
- Must have a dripless design so that if someone removes the pot while coffee is still brewing, no mess is created
- Must be capable of holding up under steady use—four to five pots of coffee every day
- Must use a minimal amount of coffee—extracting the maximum flavor from every miserable little grain of coffee
- Should have a 12- to 15-cup capacity
- Should use either a permanent filter or disposable filters that are cheap, readily available, or ecologically correct
- Must cost less than $50
- Must be available in a color other than white

The following is additional information that may be divulged *only when the salesperson asks a question <u>specifically</u> requiring one or more of these facts as an answer.*

- You are looking for coffee makers to use in your offices.
- You will need 10 to 15 to place throughout the facility.
- You expect a quantity discount on the purchase.
- You are also considering a coffee service that provides all supplies, maintenance, etc.

Questions for "Understand the Need"

00:15

Purpose: Provide an opportunity to develop questions for use in understanding the customer's need.

INDIVIDUAL "TARGET" ACTIVITY

INTRODUCE a "Targeting Your Sales Efforts" activity focused on the use of questions in understanding the customer's need.

- In this "Targeting Your Sales Efforts" activity, you will think about two of your typical customers and their buying objectives, and then develop questions for each that could be used to understand their needs.

Questions for "Understand the Need"

DISTRIBUTE the learning activity, "Questions for 'Understand the Need'" (pages 278 and 279).

REVIEW the instructions for the learning activity with participants.

ALLOW 5 minutes to complete the activity.

GROUP DISCUSSION

ASK a volunteer to describe one of his or her customers and the typical buying objective, and then the questions of each type that could be used with the customer.

MAKE notes on a flipchart.

ASK one or two other volunteers to describe one of their customers and the buying objectives, and the questions that they developed.

MAKE additional notes on the flipchart.

REINFORCE responses, based on the tips in the "Types of Questions" handout.

- Ask questions that gather the types of information you need.

- Use a deliberate line of questioning to take you and your customer where you want to go.

ASK other participants for comments and suggestions on the questions developed—particularly those who were working with similar customers.

NOTE on the flipchart changes <u>to which the "owner" of the approach agrees</u>.

ALLOW 2 or 3 minutes at the conclusion of the discussion for participants to make notes and changes to their own work.

Handout: Questions for "Understand the Need"

In this "Targeting Your Sales Efforts" activity, you will develop sample questions that will help you gather the information you need from two typical customers.

- Look at the sales situations and typical customers that you have identified for this series of exercises.
- Select two typical customers from that list.
- Describe each customer briefly and identify a typical buying objective for each.
- Identify the information that you will need from each customer in order to prepare yourself to make a recommendation.
- Identify two or three general, specific/closed, and leading questions that you might use to gather this information.

Write your answers in the spaces provided.

	Customer 1	**Customer 2**
Description of the customer		
Typical buying objective		
Information that you will need		
General questions		

(Continued on the next page)

Handout: Questions for "Understand the Need"

Specific (and/or closed) questions		
Leading questions		

An Explaining Demonstration

00:25

Purpose: Demonstrate skills involved in explaining, using a simulated sales interaction.

> *Procedural note: In preparation for this demonstration, you need to prepare one copy of each of the following handouts, found later in this section.*
> - *Instructions for the Salesperson—page 284*
> - *Instructions for the Customer—page 285*
>
> *Additionally, you will need copies of the "Observer's Critique Sheet" for each participant (page 283).*
>
> *If you wish to customize this demonstration to your particular situation, you will need to rewrite the instructions for the salesperson and the customer—using the ones in this section as a model.*

DEMONSTRATION ROLE PLAY

MAKE *this comment.*

- The purpose of this demonstration role play is to illustrate the skill of explaining.

ASK *for two volunteers—one to role play the "customer" and the other the "salesperson."*

INDICATE *that the remaining participants will function as observers during the role play.*

Observer's Critique Sheet

DISTRIBUTE *the "Observer's Critique Sheet" from the "An Explaining Demonstration" learning activity (page 283).*

REVIEW *the critique sheet with participants.*

DISTRIBUTE *the instruction sheets to the salesperson and customer (pages 284 and 285, respectively).*

PRESENT *the basic instructions for the activity.*

1. We will take a short break during which the salesperson and customer will review their instructions and prepare themselves for the role play.

2. Following that, they will role play a sales situation for

3. I will signal the volunteers about 30 seconds before the role play is over, at which time the salesperson will bring his or her explanation to a close.

4. The rest of you will then have 1 or 2 minutes to complete your critique sheets.

5. Then, we will discuss the demonstration as a group.

ALLOW *3 minutes for a break, during which volunteers will prepare for their roles.*

RECONVENE *the group.*

BEGIN *the role play.*

ANNOUNCE *that it is time for the salesperson to bring the explanation to a close after about 4½ minutes.*

ALLOW *30 seconds for the salesperson to bring the explanation to a close.*

GROUP DISCUSSION

MAKE this comment.

- Let's discuss the effectiveness of the explaining technique that was used in this demonstration role play.

ASK these questions of the salesperson.

- How did you organize the content of your explanation?

- Why did you use that particular approach to explaining?

- How effective was it from your point of view?

RECORD responses on a blank flipchart.

ENCOURAGE observers to make additional constructive comments regarding their impressions, alternatives, etc.

ASK these questions of the customer—using the first question to probe into each of the major categories on the critique sheet.

- What was your perception of the explanation? Content organized? Clear transitions? Credible? Etc.?

- How effective was the overall approach from your point of view?

RECORD responses on another blank flipchart.

ENCOURAGE observers to make additional constructive comments regarding their impressions, alternatives, etc.

ASK this question.

- What general reactions do the observers have about what was done well? Suggestions for improvement?

RECORD responses on a third blank flipchart.

SUMMARIZE the discussion, referring to the flipcharts.

ASK this question.

- Are there any questions about this demonstration?

ANSWER the questions, as appropriate.

Handout: Observer's Critique Sheet

Make notes about the effectiveness of the explaining demonstration in the spaces below.

Questioning Skill	Comment
Used simple language, avoided jargon	
Kept the explanation short and to the point <ul><li>Key points in a logical order</li><li>Clear transitions between points</li></ul>	
Made the explanation credible and concrete	
Made the explanation vivid and dynamic	
Remained focused on the purpose of the explanation	
Acknowledged questions for which he or she did not know the answer; didn't attempt to "fake it"	
General comments:	

Handout: Instructions for the Salesperson

You are a salesperson in a large home appliance outlet. This store sells several brands of large and small appliances, and typically offers a wide selection of models.

You have been talking with a customer for several minutes and, at this point, feel you have learned the following about the customer's "coffee maker" buying objectives.

- Must be easy to use
- Must have a dripless design so that if someone removes the pot while coffee is still brewing, no mess is created
- Must be capable of holding up under steady use—four to five pots of coffee every day
- Must use a minimal amount of coffee—extracting the maximum flavor from every miserable little grain of coffee
- Should have a 12- to 15-cup capacity
- Should use either a permanent filter or disposable filters that are cheap, readily available, or ecologically correct
- Must cost less than $50
- Must be available in a color other than white

Examine the features of the *Sensa-Java Turbo 12* coffee maker.

- Up to 12-cup capacity
- Exclusive *Sensa-BooBoo* coffee basket—no spills when pot is removed
- 110-volt design, energy efficient
- Uses as much as 20% less coffee than competitors
- Automatic operation with built-in clock/timer
- Requires no special wiring, no plumbing
- *Sensa-Klutz* glass pot resists breakage

- *Sensa-Burn* automatic shut-off when pot is empty
- *Turbo-Jolt* control brews small quantities of coffee with full-pot flavor
- Long-lasting 14K gold-plated coffee filter
- Available in four decorator colors, two pedestrian colors
- Easy to operate, instructions in five languages
- Two-year full-replacement warranty for manufacturing defects

Based on those features and what you have learned from your customer, prepare an explanation of why your customer should buy the *Sensa-Java Turbo 12* coffee maker.

Handout: Instructions for the Customer

You have gone to a large home appliance outlet and have been speaking with a salesperson about your need for a new coffee maker.

At this point, you have described some (or all) of these characteristics of the coffee maker for which you are looking.

- Must be easy to use
- Must have a dripless design so that if someone removes the pot while coffee is still brewing, no mess is created
- Must be capable of holding up under steady use—four to five pots of coffee every day
- Must use a minimal amount of coffee—extracting the maximum flavor from every miserable little grain of coffee
- Should have a 12- to 15-cup capacity
- Should use either a permanent filter or disposable filters that are cheap, readily available, and ecologically correct.
- Must cost less than $50
- Must be available in a color other than white

The salesperson is now going to explain why he or she believes you should buy the **Sensa-Java Turbo 12** coffee maker—based on the information you have provided.

- Listen attentively.
- Make an occasional remark, ask an occasional question—if nothing other than, "Could you repeat that point?"

Beginning a Sale

00:15

Purpose: Provide an opportunity to identify approaches to beginning the sales effort with typical customers.

INDIVIDUAL "TARGET" ACTIVITY

INTRODUCE a "Targeting Your Sales Efforts" activity focused on beginning the sales effort.

- In this "Targeting Your Sales Efforts" activity, you will identify approaches for beginning sales efforts with your customers in two different situations.

*Beginning
a Sale*

DISTRIBUTE the learning activity, "Beginning a Sale" (pages 288 and 289).

REVIEW the instructions for the learning activity with participants.

ALLOW 5 minutes to complete the activity.

GROUP DISCUSSION

ASK a volunteer to describe one of his or her selling situations, the approach to be used, and the reason for the approach—with an emphasis on his or her proposed use of key skills.

- Questioning

- Observing

- Listening

- Building rapport

MAKE notes on a flipchart.

ASK one or two other volunteers with different situations to describe their selling situations, the approach to be used, and the reason for the approach.

MAKE additional notes on the flipchart.

REINFORCE responses, paying particular attention to the effective use of the skills listed above.

ASK other participants for comments and suggestions on the approaches—particularly those who were working with similar situations.

NOTE on the flipchart changes <u>to which the "owner" of the approach agrees</u>.

ALLOW 2 or 3 minutes at the conclusion of the discussion for participants to make notes and changes to their own work.

Handout: Beginning a Sale

In this "Targeting Your Sales Efforts" activity, you will develop approaches to beginning a sale.

- Look at the sales situations that you have identified for this series of exercises.
- Select two situations where the circumstances under which you meet the customers differ.
- Describe each situation briefly.
- State what you must do or accomplish in order to begin the sales interaction successfully.
- Describe your approach to beginning the interaction; that is, how will you use key skills to get off to a successful start.
    - Observing
    - Questioning
    - Listening
    - Rapport building
- Indicate your reason for selecting this approach—that is, why you feel that it suits the situation you have described.

Write your answers in the spaces provided.

	Situation 1	**Situation 2**
Description of the situation		
What you must do or accomplish		

(Continued on the next page)

Handout: Beginning a Sale

Your approach • Observing • Questioning • Listening • Rapport building		
The reasons for this approach		

Approaches to Qualifying

00:15

Purpose: Provide an opportunity to identify approaches to qualifying opportunities for typical customers.

INDIVIDUAL "TARGET" ACTIVITY

INTRODUCE a "Targeting Your Sales Efforts" activity focused on qualifying opportunities.

Approaches to Qualifying

- In this "Targeting Your Sales Efforts" activity, you will identify approaches for qualifying opportunities for two of your typical customers.

DISTRIBUTE the learning activity, "Approaches to Qualifying" (pages 291 and 292).

REVIEW the instructions for the learning activity with participants.
ALLOW 5 minutes to complete the activity.

GROUP DISCUSSION

ASK a volunteer to describe one of his or her customers, and then the approach to qualifying that customer.

MAKE notes on a flipchart.

ASK one or two other volunteers to describe one of their customers, and then the approach to qualifying for that customer.

MAKE additional notes on the flipchart.

REINFORCE responses that will allow participants to gather and evaluate the information needed to qualify an opportunity.

ASK other participants for comments and suggestions on the approaches to qualifying opportunities that have been identified—particularly those who were working with similar customers.

NOTE on the flipchart changes <u>to which the "owner" of the approach agrees</u>.

ALLOW 2 or 3 minutes at the conclusion of the discussion for participants to make notes and changes to their own work.

Handout: Approaches to Qualifying

In this "Targeting Your Sales Efforts" activity, you will develop approaches to qualifying opportunities with two typical customers.

- Look at the sales situations and typical customers that you have identified for this series of exercises.
- Select two typical customers from that list.
- Describe each customer briefly and identify a typical buying objective for each.
- Indicate what information you would need to qualify the opportunity.
- Then, indicate how you would gather the information—questions you would ask, things you might observe, etc.
- Finally, indicate how you would evaluate whether the opportunity is qualified, based on the information you gather.

Write your answers in the spaces provided.

	Customer 1	**Customer 2**
Description of the customer		
Typical buying objective		
Information that you will need		

(Continued on the next page)

Handout: Approaches to Qualifying

How you will gather the information		
How you will evaluate the information		

The First Two Phases: A Role Play

01:00

Purpose: Provide practice in the "Earn the Right" and "Understand the Need" phases of the sales process.

Procedural note: In preparation for this role play, you need to prepare copies of the following handouts for each participant, found later in this section.
- *Observer's Critique Sheet—page 297*
- *Instructions for the Salesperson—page 298*

Additionally, you will need <u>one set</u> of the following handouts per table group of three participants.
- *Instructions for Customer 1—page 299*
- *Instructions for Customer 2—page 300*
- *Instructions for Customer 3—page 301*

If you wish to customize this role play to your particular situation, you will need to rewrite the instructions for the salesperson and customers—using the ones in this section as a model.

TABLE GROUP ACTIVITY

BREAK *the workshop into table groups of three people each.*

DESCRIBE *the structure of role play.*

- There will be three rounds in this role play.

- Each of you will have the opportunity to play the role of salesperson, customer, and observer.

Instructions for Customer 1, 2, 3; Instructions for the Salesperson; Observer's Critique Sheet

DISTRIBUTE *these materials to each of the table groups: a set of "Instructions for Customer 1 (2, and 3)," (pages 299, 300, and 301) and three each of "Instructions for the Salesperson" (page 298) and "Observer's Critique Sheet" (page 297).*

PRESENT the basic instructions for the activity.

1. You will have 3 minutes to review your instructions and make notes prior to each round of the role play.

2. Once the role plays begin, the participant playing "observer" in each round will keep track of time.

3. Each round will be 5 minutes in length.

4. At the end of each round, 3 minutes will be allowed for discussion within the table group.

5. This procedure will be repeated until each participant in the table group has played each of the roles.

6. Finally, the full group will reconvene for a discussion of the role play experiences.

ASK *this question.*

- Are there any questions about the instructions, thus far?

ANSWER *the questions, as appropriate.*

REVIEW *the instructions for customers, salespeople, and observers, either paraphrasing them or reading them aloud.*

ASK *this question.*

- Are there any questions about the instructions before beginning?

ANSWER *the questions, as appropriate.*

ASK *participants to move to their table groups.*

MONITOR *progress as the exercise moves forward, making sure that the groups stay on schedule.*

GROUP DISCUSSION

RECONVENE the full group.

MAKE this comment, if you will be using the subsequent "The Last Two Phases: A Role Play" activity in conjunction with this activity.

- Before we begin, please be sure that each of you has recorded on your "Instructions for the Salesperson" page the number of the "customer" with whom you played the role of salesperson.

- You will need to remember this for the next role play.

ALLOW a moment for participants to record this information.

MAKE this comment.

- Now, let's discuss your reactions to this role play.

ASK one or two participants to answer these questions as "salespeople."

- What did you hope to achieve during that sales situation?

- Why did you use the approach that you pursued during the role play?

- How effective was it from your point of view?

RECORD responses on a blank flipchart.

ENCOURAGE other participants to add comments, as appropriate.

ASK one or two participants to answer this question as "observers."

- As observers, what general reactions did you have about what was done well? Suggestions for improvement?

RECORD responses on another blank flipchart.

ENCOURAGE other participants to add comments, as appropriate.

ASK one or two participants to answer these questions as "customers."

- What was your perception of the overall sales interaction, from a sales point of view?

- How effective was the approach from your point of view as a customer?

RECORD responses on the blank flipchart.

ENCOURAGE other participants to make constructive comments regarding their impressions, alternatives, etc.

ASK each of the questions on the "Role Play Questions" flipcharts (pages 412 and 413) as a means for summarizing the discussion of the role play.

- How effectively did the salesperson build rapport?

- What questioning techniques were effective from the salesperson's point of view? The customer's? The observer's?

- What alternate techniques might have been used?

- Did the salesperson learn about the customer's need?

- Did the salesperson earn the right to move ahead with the sale?

Role Play Questions

MAKE NOTES about responses on the "Role Play Questions" flipcharts.

LOOK FOR answers that allow you to summarize the discussion and reinforce the importance of key points on the "Observer's Critique Sheet."

- Made the customer comfortable, maintained good nonverbal contact

- Used general, specific, and leading questions effectively, organized them logically

- Listened to the customer

- Concentrated on the customer

- Verified understanding

- Qualified the opportunity

Handout: Observer's Critique Sheet

Follow these instructions for your role as observer.
- Review the critique sheet to familiarize yourself with it.
- When you are playing the role of observer, observe the role play *and* act as timekeeper.
  - Role play: 5 minutes, with a 30-second alert prior to the end of the role play
  - Discussion: 3 minutes
- Note the salesperson's behaviors by checking the appropriate lines in the column labeled "Situation 1." If you are observer a second time, use the column labeled "Situation 2."
- Record any general comments in the spaces provided below.

The Salesperson...	Situation 1	Situation 2
Made the customer comfortable	_____	_____
Maintained good nonverbal contact	_____	_____
Established and continued to build rapport	_____	_____
Observed carefully	_____	_____
Used questions effectively		
• General	_____	_____
• Specific and/or closed	_____	_____
• Leading	_____	_____
Organized questions in a logical, productive sequence	_____	_____
Verified understanding	_____	_____
Concentrated on the customer		
• Let the customer talk	_____	_____
• Listened to the answers to questions	_____	_____
Learned about the customer's objectives	_____	_____
Earned the right to continue the sale	_____	_____

General comments:

- Situation 1

- Situation 2

Handout: Instructions for the Salesperson

You are a salesperson in a large home appliance outlet. This store sells several brands of large and small appliances, and typically offers a wide selection of models.

You are about to begin a sales interaction with a customer, who is standing in the middle of a large display of automatic drip coffee makers—leading you to suspect that your customer might be looking for a coffee maker.

Your mission is to begin the sales interaction and learn as much as possible regarding your customer's need—that is, learn about your customer's...

- Buying objectives.
- Buying influences.

Make notes here about your approach:

Note: In preparation for a later role play, check the number of the "customer" with whom you played the role of salesperson.

❑ Customer 1   ❑ Customer 2   ❑ Customer 3

Handout: Instructions for Customer 1

You have gone to a large home appliance outlet and have been looking around the store as you head toward the small electric appliances department. As you stand in the middle of a large display of coffee makers, you notice you are being approached by a salesperson—neatly dressed and quite presentable in appearance.

You are here to buy a new automatic drip coffee maker for home. The coffee maker must have these characteristics—which you may divulge when the salesperson asks the appropriate questions.

- Must have a dripless design so that if someone removes the pot while coffee is still brewing, no mess is created
- Must use a minimal amount of coffee—extracting the maximum flavor from every miserable little grain of coffee
- Must make small quantities that are as flavorful as full pots
- Must have an automatic shut-off feature so that the carafe will not be ruined if it's left on the heating element when empty
- Should use either a permanent filter or disposable filters that are cheap, readily available, or ecologically correct
- Should have a good warranty, offering free replacement of defective units for at least one year
- Must cost less than $50

The salesperson should have the following understanding of your need by the end of the role play—but *only if he or she asks the questions that prompt you to provide the information.*

- Generally you make small quantities of coffee, but make full pots once or twice a week.
- The coffee maker must be more reliable and durable than the one you are replacing.
- You dislike paper filters—they're hard to get out of the box, hard to open, etc.

Remember, only divulge information when the salesperson asks a question seeking it.

Notes about how you might behave as a customer:

Handout: Instructions for Customer 2

You have gone to a large home appliance outlet and have been looking around the store as you head toward the small electric appliances department. As you stand in the middle of a large display of coffee makers, you notice you are being approached by a salesperson—neatly dressed and quite presentable in appearance.

You are here to buy a new automatic drip coffee maker for your office. In fact, if you find what you like, you will buy several. The coffee maker must have these characteristics—which you may divulge when the salesperson asks the appropriate questions.

- Must have a dripless design so that if someone removes the pot while coffee is still brewing, no mess is created
- Must be capable of holding up under steady use—a minimum of four to five pots of coffee every day
- Must have an automatic shut-off feature so that the carafe will not be ruined if it's left on the heating element when empty
- Should have a 12- to 15-cup capacity
- Should be energy efficient
- Should have a good warranty, offering free replacement of defective units for at least one year
- Must cost less than $50
- Must be available in a color other than white

The following is additional information that may be divulged *only when the salesperson asks a question <u>specifically</u> requiring one or more of these facts as an answer.*

- The coffee maker must be durable, with good warranty service.
- You will need to place 10 to 15 throughout the facility.
- Coffee makers are generally unattended, so they should be able to "behave themselves."
- Your coffee makers are scattered all over the office facility.

Remember, only divulge the above information when the salesperson asks a question seeking it.

Notes about how you might behave as a customer:

Handout: Instructions for Customer 3

You have gone to a large home appliance outlet and have been looking around the store as you head toward the small electric appliances department. As you stand in the middle of a large display of coffee makers, you notice you are being approached by a salesperson—neatly dressed and quite presentable in appearance.

You are here to buy a new automatic drip coffee maker for home. The coffee maker must have these characteristics—which you may divulge when the salesperson asks the appropriate questions.

- Must be easy to use
- Must have a dripless design so that if someone removes the pot while coffee is still brewing, no mess is created
- Must be capable of holding up under steady use—a minimum of four to five pots of coffee every day
- Must have an automatic shut-off feature so that the carafe will not be ruined if it's left on the heating element when empty
- Should have a 12- to 15-cup capacity
- Should use either a permanent filter or disposable filters that are cheap, readily available, or ecologically correct
- Must cost less than $50
- Must be available in a color other than white

The following is additional information that may be divulged *only when the salesperson asks a question* <u>*specifically*</u> *requiring one or more of these facts as an answer.*

- You make two or three pots per day.
- The coffee maker must fit the color scheme of your new kitchen.
- It must be easy to use, especially for your great-aunt, who is 80 years old and visiting from Tasmania.

Remember, only divulge the above information when the salesperson asks a question seeking it.

Notes about how you might behave as a customer:

Approaches to Testing for Readiness

00:15

Purpose: Provide an opportunity to identify approaches to testing for readiness with typical customers.

INDIVIDUAL "TARGET" ACTIVITY

INTRODUCE a "Targeting Your Sales Efforts" activity focused on testing for readiness.

Approaches to Testing for Readiness

- In this "Targeting Your Sales Efforts" activity, you will identify approaches to testing for readiness with two of your typical customers.

DISTRIBUTE the learning activity, "Approaches to Testing for Readiness" (page 303).

REVIEW the instructions for the learning activity with participants.

ALLOW 5 minutes to complete the activity.

GROUP DISCUSSION

ASK a volunteer to describe one of his or her customers, and then approaches to testing for readiness for that customer.

MAKE notes on a flipchart.

ASK one or two other volunteers to describe one of their customers, and their approaches to testing for readiness for that customer.

MAKE additional notes on the flipchart.

REINFORCE the importance of summarizing and verifying in testing for readiness.

ASK other participants for comments and suggestions on the approaches identified—particularly those who were working with similar customers.

NOTE on the flipchart changes <u>to which the "owner" of the approach agrees</u>.

ALLOW 2 or 3 minutes at the conclusion of the discussion for participants to make notes and changes to their own work.

Handout: Approaches to Testing for Readiness

In this "Targeting Your Sales Efforts" activity, you will develop approaches to testing for readiness to make a recommendation.

- Look at the sales situations and typical customers that you have identified for this series of exercises.
- Select two typical customers from that list.
- Describe each customer briefly and identify a typical buying objective for each.
- Think about the line of questioning that you would have pursued with each customer in order to understand the need.
- Then, indicate how you would test for readiness to make a recommendation to that customer.

Write your answers in the spaces provided.

	Customer 1	**Customer 2**
Description of the customer		
Typical buying objective		
Approach to testing for readiness		

Benefit Statements

00:15

Purpose: Provide an opportunity to prepare benefit statements that will meet typical customer objectives.

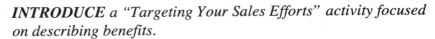

INDIVIDUAL "TARGET" ACTIVITY

INTRODUCE a "Targeting Your Sales Efforts" activity focused on describing benefits.

- In this "Targeting Your Sales Efforts" activity, you will prepare benefit statements for products or services that will meet two typical customer objectives.

Benefit Statements

DISTRIBUTE the learning activity, "Benefit Statements" (page 306).

REVIEW the instructions for the learning activity with participants.

ALLOW 5 minutes to complete the activity.

GROUP DISCUSSION

ASK a volunteer to describe one of his or her customer objectives, and then the benefit statement associated with that objective.

MAKE notes on a flipchart.

ASK one or two other volunteers to describe one of their customer objectives, and then benefit statements for that objective.

MAKE additional notes on the flipchart.

REINFORCE the distinction between features and benefits, and the characteristics of well-stated benefits.

- Feature—a characteristic of a product or service

- Benefit—something that promotes well-being or contributes to an improvement in condition; a help, advantage

- Characteristics of a well-stated benefit

  - Clearly related to the customer's objective

  - Perceived by customers as *something of value to them*

ASK other participants for comments and suggestions on the benefit statements—particularly those who were working with similar customers.

NOTE on the flipchart changes <u>to which the "owner" of the approach agrees</u>.

ALLOW 2 or 3 minutes at the conclusion of the discussion for participants to make notes and changes to their own work.

Handout: Benefit Statements

In this "Targeting Your Sales Efforts" activity, you will develop benefit statements for your product(s) or service(s).

- Look at the sales situations and typical customers that you have identified for this series of exercises.
- Select two typical customers from that list.
- Identify a typical buying objective for each customer.
- Identify the product or service that you would recommend to meet that objective.
- Then, write a statement of the benefits that the customer will realize.

Write your answers in the spaces provided.

	Customer 1	**Customer 2**
Customer buying objective		
The product or service		
Statement of benefits		

Making a Recommendation

00:20

Purpose: Provide an opportunity to develop an outline for a recommendation that addresses a typical customer objective.

INDIVIDUAL "TARGET" ACTIVITY

INTRODUCE a "Targeting Your Sales Efforts" activity focused on making recommendations.

- In this "Targeting Your Sales Efforts" activity, you will think about one of the customer objectives with which you have been working and develop an outline of a recommendation to address that objective.

Making a Recommendation

DISTRIBUTE the learning activity, "Making a Recommendation" (pages 309 and 310).

REVIEW the instructions for the learning activity with participants.

ALLOW 10 minutes to complete the activity.

GROUP DISCUSSION

ASK a volunteer to describe the customer objective, and then the recommendation that would be used with that objective.

MAKE notes on a flipchart.

ASK one or two other volunteers to describe their objective, and the recommendation that they developed.

MAKE additional notes on the flipchart.

REINFORCE responses, based on these tips.

- Make the purpose of the recommendation clear.

- Organize the content logically, make sure that you cover only relevant information, and include a clear statement of benefits.

- Provide a compelling description of your competitive edge—and make the entire recommendation enthusiastic.

- Make the recommendation *explicit.*

ASK other participants for comments and suggestions on the recommendations developed—particularly those who were working with similar objectives.

NOTE on the flipchart changes <u>to which the "owner" of the approach agrees</u>.

ALLOW 2 or 3 minutes at the conclusion of the discussion for participants to make notes and changes to their own work.

Handout: Making a Recommendation

In this "Targeting Your Sales Efforts" activity, you will develop the structure of a recommendation that you might present to a customer.

- Look at the sales situations and typical customers that you have identified for this series of exercises.
- Select one typical customer from that list.
- Describe the customer briefly, identify a typical buying objective, and identify the product or service you would recommend.
- Identify the benefits you would include in the recommendation.
- Determine what you would include in the recommendation that would give you a competitive edge.
- Write an opening statement for your recommendation.
- Outline the recommendation you would present, incorporating benefits and your competitive edge.

Write your answers in the spaces provided.

Description of the customer	
Typical buying objective	
Product or service	
Benefits to be included	
Your competitive edge	

(Continued on the next page)

Handout: Making a Recommendation

Your opening statement	
Outline of the recommendation	

Approaches to Asking for the Order

00:20

Purpose: Provide an opportunity to identify approaches to asking for the order.

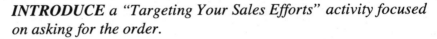

INDIVIDUAL "TARGET" ACTIVITY

INTRODUCE a "Targeting Your Sales Efforts" activity focused on asking for the order.

- In this "Targeting Your Sales Efforts" activity, you will identify approaches for asking for the order, based on a recommendation you would present to one of your customers

Approaches to Asking for the Order

DISTRIBUTE the learning activity, "Approaches to Asking for the Order" (pages 313 and 314).

REVIEW the instructions for the learning activity with participants.

ALLOW 10 minutes to complete the activity.

GROUP DISCUSSION

ASK a volunteer to describe his or her approach to asking for the order, after quickly reviewing the recommendation on which it is based.

MAKE notes on a flipchart.

ASK one or two other volunteers to describe one of their approaches to asking for the order, after quickly reviewing the recommendation on which it is based.

MAKE additional notes on the flipchart.

REINFORCE responses, based on these tips.

- Be sure the way in which you ask for the order projects confidence.

- Also, give your customer a chance to respond. *There is nothing wrong with silence.*

ASK other participants for comments and suggestions on the approaches to asking for the order—particularly those who were working with similar customers.

NOTE *on the flipchart changes* <u>*to which the "owner" of the*</u> <u>*approach agrees.*</u>

ALLOW *2 or 3 minutes at the conclusion of the discussion for participants to make notes and changes to their own work.*

Handout: Approaches to Asking for the Order

In this "Targeting Your Sales Efforts" activity, you will identify a sales situation and then develop different approaches to asking for the order.

- Look at the sales situations and typical customers that you have identified for this series of exercises.
- Select one typical customer from that list.
- Describe the customer briefly, identify a typical buying objective, and summarize *very briefly* your recommendation to that customer.
- For that situation, identify three approaches to asking for the order.
- Then, indicate the circumstances under which you would use each approach, and why you would use it.

Write your answers in the spaces provided.

Description of the customer	
Typical buying objective	
Brief summary of recommendation	
First approach to "asking for the order" Circumstances Why?	

(Continued on the next page)

Handout: Approaches to Asking for the Order

Second approach to "asking for the order" Circumstances Why?	
Third approach to "asking for the order" Circumstances Why?	

Approaches to Handling Obstacles

00:20

Purpose: Provide an opportunity to identify approaches to handling typical obstacles.

INDIVIDUAL "TARGET" ACTIVITY

INTRODUCE a "Targeting Your Sales Efforts" activity focused on handling obstacles.

- In this "Targeting Your Sales Efforts" activity, you will identify approaches for two or three obstacles that you encounter frequently.

Approaches to Handling Obstacles

DISTRIBUTE the learning activity, "Approaches to Handling Obstacles" (pages 317 and 318).

REVIEW the instructions for the learning activity with participants.

ALLOW 10 minutes to complete the activity.

GROUP DISCUSSION

ASK a volunteer to describe one of his or her common obstacles, and then the approach to handling that obstacle.

MAKE notes on a flipchart.

ASK one or two other volunteers to describe one of their common obstacles, and then their approaches to handling the obstacle.

MAKE additional notes on flipchart.

REINFORCE responses, based on these tips.

- Pause, take time to think—and analyze the obstacle.

- Clarify the obstacle as required, and verify your understanding.

- Handle the obstacle—and verify that you have addressed the issue to your customer's satisfaction.

ASK other participants for comments and suggestions on the approaches—particularly those who identified similar obstacles.

NOTE on the flipchart changes <u>to which the "owner" of the</u> <u>approach agrees</u>.

ALLOW 2 or 3 minutes at the conclusion of the discussion for participants to make notes and changes to their own work.

Handout: Approaches to Handling Obstacles

In this "Targeting Your Sales Efforts" activity, you will identify a sales situation and then develop approaches to handling two different obstacles.

- Look at the sales situations and typical customers that you have identified for this series of exercises.
- Select one typical customer from that list.
- Describe the customer briefly, identify a typical buying objective, and summarize *very briefly* your recommendation to that customer.
- For that situation, identify two common obstacles that might arise when you ask for the order.
- Then, write down what the obstacle means, how you would handle it, and how you would verify that you have successfully handled the obstacle.

Write your answers in the spaces provided.

Description of the customer	
Typical buying objective	
Brief summary of recommendation	
Obstacle 1	
Its meaning	
How you would handle it	
How you would verify successful handling	

(Continued on next page)

Handout: Approaches to Handling Obstacles

Obstacle 2	
Its meaning	
How you would handle it	
How you would verify successful handling	

The Last Two Phases: A Role Play

01:00

Purpose: Provide practice in the "Make a Recommendation" and "Complete the Sale" phases of the sales process.

Procedural note: In preparation for this role play, you need to prepare copies of the following handout for each participant, found later in this section.

- *Observer's Critique Sheet—page 324*

Additionally, you will need <u>one set</u> of the following handouts per table group of three participants.

- *Instructions for Salesperson 1—page 325*
- *Instructions for Customer 1—page 326*
- *Instructions for Salesperson 2—page 327*
- *Instructions for Customer 2—page 328*
- *Instructions for Salesperson 3—page 329*
- *Instructions for Customer 3—page 330*

If you wish to customize this role play to your particular situation, you will need to rewrite the instructions for the salespeople and customers—using the ones in this section as a model.

TABLE GROUP ACTIVITY

BREAK *the workshop into table groups of three people each.*

DESCRIBE *the structure of the role play, adapting the description as appropriate if this activity is not being used in conjunction with "The First Two Phases: A Role Play."*

- This role play is a continuation of the previous role play, in which you practiced the "Earn the Right" and "Understand the Need" phases of the sales process.

- As before, there will be three rounds in this role play.

- Each of you will have the opportunity to play the role of salesperson, customer, and observer.

- You will play the same customer role as before—1, 2, or 3.

- Also, salespeople will role play with the *same* customer as before; if you role played with Customer 1 in the previous role play, you will play the role of Salesperson 1 in this role play, and so on.

Instructions for Customer 1, 2, 3; Instructions for Salesperson 1, 2, 3; Observer's Critique Sheet

***DISTRIBUTE** handouts to each of the table groups; a set of "Instructions for Customer" (pages 326, 328, and 330) and "Instructions for Salesperson" handouts (pages 325, 327, and 329), and three each of the "Observer's Critique Sheet" (page 324).*

***PRESENT** the basic instructions for the activity.*

1. You will have 3 minutes to review your instructions and make notes prior to each round of the role play.

2. Once the role plays begin, the participant playing "observer" in each round will keep track of time.

3. Each round will be 5 minutes in length.

4. At the end of each round, 3 minutes will be allowed for discussion within the table group.

5. This procedure will be repeated until each participant in the table group has played each of the roles.

6. Finally, the full group will reconvene for a discussion of the role play experiences.

***ASK** this question.*

- Are there any questions about the instructions, thus far?

***ANSWER** the questions, as appropriate.*

***REVIEW** the instructions in each of the three handouts, either paraphrasing them or reading them aloud.*

ASK this question.

- Are there any questions about the instructions before beginning?

ANSWER the questions, as appropriate.

ASK participants to move to their table groups.

MONITOR progress as the exercise moves forward, making sure that the groups stay on schedule.

GROUP DISCUSSION

RECONVENE the full group.

MAKE this comment.

- Let's discuss your reactions to this role play.

ASK one or two participants to answer these questions as "salespeople."

- Why did you use the approach to making a recommendation and completing the sale that you pursued during the role play?

- How effective was it from your point of view?

RECORD responses on a blank flipchart.

ENCOURAGE other participants to add comments, as appropriate.

ASK one or two participants to answer this question as "observers."

- As observers, what general reactions did you have about what was done well? Suggestions for improvement?

RECORD responses on another blank flipchart.

ENCOURAGE other participants to add comments, as appropriate.

ASK one or two participants to answer these questions as "customers."

- What was your perception of the overall sales interaction?

- How effective was the approach from your point of view?

RECORD responses on the blank flipchart.

ENCOURAGE other participants to make constructive comments regarding their impressions, alternatives, etc.

ASK each of the questions on the "Role Play Questions" flipcharts (pages 426 and 427) as a means for summarizing the discussion of the role play.

- Did the salesperson address the customer's buying objectives?

- How effectively was the explaining skill used?

- What might have been done more effectively?

- What technique was used to ask for the order?

- How effectively were obstacles handled?

- What might have been done more effectively?

- Did the salesperson *complete the sale*?

Role Play Questions

MAKE NOTES *about responses on the "Role Play Questions" flipcharts.*

LOOK FOR *answers that allow you to summarize the discussions and reinforce the importance of key points on the "Observer's Critique Sheet."*

- Presented a good recommendation.

- Used explaining skills effectively.

- Described benefits effectively.

- Handled obstacles effectively.

ASK *this question.*

- Are there any questions about this activity?

ANSWER *the questions, as appropriate.*

Handout: Observer's Critique Sheet

Follow these instructions for your role as observer.
- Review the critique sheet to familiarize yourself with it.
- When you are playing the role of observer, observe the role play *and* act as timekeeper.
  - Role play: 5 minutes, with a 30-second alert prior to the end of the role play
  - Discussion: 3 minutes
- Note the salesperson's behaviors by checking the appropriate lines in the column labeled "Situation 1." If you are observer a second time, use the column labeled "Situation 2."

The Salesperson . . .	Situation 1	Situation 2
Presented a good recommendation		
• Made purpose clear	_____	_____
• Made content relevant, logically organized	_____	_____
• Included a clear statement of benefits	_____	_____
• Included a statement of competitive edge	_____	_____
• Communicated enthusiasm	_____	_____
Used explaining skills effectively		
• Simple language	_____	_____
• Short and to the point	_____	_____
• Credible, concrete, vivid, dynamic	_____	_____
• Remained focused on customer objectives	_____	_____
Described benefits effectively		
• Related to the customer's objective	_____	_____
• Perceived to be something of value by the customer	_____	_____
Handled obstacles effectively		
• Analyzed and clarified the obstacle, as necessary	_____	_____
• Verified understanding of the obstacle	_____	_____
• Handled the obstacle and verified that it was addressed effectively	_____	_____
Completed the sale!	_____	_____

Handout: Instructions for Salesperson 1

Based on discussions with your customer, you are going to recommend the *Sensa-Java Turbo 12* coffee maker. It has the following features.

- Up to 12-cup capacity
- Exclusive *Sensa-BooBoo* coffee basket—no spills when pot is removed
- 110-volt design, energy efficient
- Uses as much as 20% less coffee than competitors
- Automatic operation with built-in clock/timer
- Requires no special wiring, no plumbing
- *Sensa-Klutz* glass pot resists breakage

- *Sensa-Burn* automatic shut-off when pot is empty
- *Turbo-Jolt* control brews small quantities of coffee with full-pot flavor
- Long-lasting 14K gold-plated coffee filter
- Available in four decorator colors, two pedestrian colors
- Easy to operate, instructions in five languages
- Two-year full-replacement warranty for manufacturing defects

You understand that your customer wants a coffee maker fitting these requirements.

- Your customer generally makes small quantities of coffee, but makes full pots once or twice a week.
- The coffee maker must be more reliable and durable than the one being replaced.
- Your customer dislikes paper filters—they are hard to get out of the box and hard to open.

Make notes here about your approach.

Opening statement

The recommendation

Asking for the order

Handout: Instructions for Customer 1

You have discussed your requirements for a coffee maker with the salesperson, and you have provided this basic information.

- Generally you make small quantities of coffee, but make full pots once or twice a week.
- The coffee maker must be more reliable and durable than the one you are replacing.
- You dislike paper filters—they're hard to get out of the box, hard to open, etc.

To cause the salesperson to respond, here are some questions or comments you might make during the recommendation.

- How much coffee does it use to make a pot?
- My nephew can never wait till the coffee is done brewing—he pulls the pot out and gets coffee all over!
- An 18K gold-plated filter?! Why do I need that? It must be expensive.

Notes about how you might behave as a customer:

Handout: Instructions for Salesperson 2

Based on discussions with your customer, you are going to recommend the *Sensa-Java Turbo 12* coffee maker. It has the following features.

- Up to 12-cup capacity
- Exclusive *Sensa-BooBoo* coffee basket—no spills when pot is removed
- 110-volt design, energy efficient
- Uses as much as 20% less coffee than competitors
- Automatic operation with built-in clock/timer
- Requires no special wiring, no plumbing
- *Sensa-Klutz* glass pot resists breakage

- *Sensa-Burn* automatic shut-off when pot is empty
- *Turbo-Jolt* control brews small quantities of coffee with full-pot flavor
- Long-lasting 14K gold-plated coffee filter
- Available in four decorator colors, two pedestrian colors
- Easy to operate, instructions in five languages
- Two-year full-replacement warranty for manufacturing defects

You understand that your customer wants a coffee maker fitting these requirements.

- It must be durable, with good warranty service.
- Your customer needs to place 10 to 15 throughout the facility.
- Their coffee makers are generally left unattended, so they should be able to "behave themselves."
- Coffee makers are scattered all over the office facility.

Make notes here about your approach.

Opening statement

The recommendation

Asking for the order

Handout: Instructions for Customer 2

You have discussed your requirements for a coffee maker with the salesperson, and you have provided this basic information.

- The coffee maker must be durable, with good warranty service.
- You will need to place 10 to 15 throughout the facility.
- Your coffee makers are generally left unattended, so they should be able to "behave themselves."
- Your coffee makers are scattered all over the office facility.

To cause the salesperson to respond, here are some questions or comments you might make during the recommendation.

- Is it energy efficient?
- Are you sure that my people won't make a mess with this machine?
- Tell me one more time about the warranty, please.

Notes about how you might behave as a customer:

Handout: Instructions for Salesperson 3

Based on discussions with your customer, you are going to recommend the *Sensa-Java Turbo 12* coffee maker. It has the following features:

- Up to 12-cup capacity
- Exclusive *Sensa-BooBoo* coffee basket—no spills when pot is removed
- 110-volt design, energy efficient
- Uses as much as 20% less coffee than competitors
- Automatic operation with built-in clock/timer
- Requires no special wiring, no plumbing
- *Sensa-Klutz* glass pot resists breakage
- *Sensa-Burn* automatic shut-off when pot is empty
- *Turbo-Jolt* control brews small quantities of coffee with full-pot flavor
- Long-lasting 14K gold-plated coffee filter
- Available in four decorator colors, two pedestrian colors
- Easy to operate, instructions in five languages
- Two-year full-replacement warranty for manufacturing defects

You understand that your customer wants a coffee maker fitting these requirements.

- Your customer makes two or three pots per day.
- The coffee maker must fit the color scheme of the customer's new kitchen.
- It must be easy to use, especially for the customer's great-aunt who is 80 years old and visiting from Tasmania.

Make notes here about your approach.

Opening statement

The recommendation

Asking for the order

Handout: Instructions for Customer 3

You have discussed your requirements for a coffee maker with the salesperson, and you have provided this basic information.

- You make two or three pots per day.
- The coffee maker must fit the color scheme of your new kitchen.
- It must be easy to use, especially for your great-aunt who is 80 years old and visiting from Tasmania.

To cause the salesperson to respond, here are some questions or comments you might make during the recommendation.

- What kind of filters does it use?
- Hmmmm. My great-aunt only makes two or three cups at a time.
- What happens if we forget to shut the thing off? Old folks can be forgetful you know—but, then, who am I to talk.

Notes about how you might behave as a customer:

Chapter Nine:

Assessments

In this section of *The ASTD Trainer's Sourcebook: Sales*, you will find assessments and other tools for use during your sales training sessions. As with the learning activities in the previous chapter, each of the assessments will have these components.

- A set of instructions for your use during the assessment. These instructions are in the same format as the training plans presented previously.
- A participant page that needs to be reproduced and provided to participants for the assessment.

You may use the assessments and other tools in two ways.

- Key them into your word processing system, either "as is" or customized to suit your specific needs.
- Copy the masters that you need from this book and make copies from them "as is."

After the workshop . . .

This collection of simple assessments helps set the stage for training—and more importantly, for ongoing self-improvement activities that participants can undertake once they leave the session.

Encourage managers to use these assessments as coaching tools. Additionally, encourage workshop participants to use these assessments over and over again as they confront real-life sales situations. Their growth as salespersons will benefit from maintaining a sharp awareness of these necessary skills.

Sales: A Quick Skills Assessment

00:10

Purpose: Provide an opportunity for participants to assess their sales skills at a broad level, in conjunction with establishing expectations for the half-day communications and full-day sales workshops.

Note: This assessment can be used for a variety of purposes, one of which is establishing participant expectations for sales training. That is the purpose for which instructions are provided here.

INDIVIDUAL ASSESSMENT

INTRODUCE the assessment, adapting the description as appropriate if this activity is not being used in the half-day communications workshop or the one-day sales workshop.

- You will now take a few minutes to complete a simple assessment of your skills in sales—an assessment based on three of the topic areas important to effective selling.

- You will then use the desired areas of improvement that you identify in this assessment to stimulate thinking about your expectations for the half-day communications and full-day sales workshops.

Sales: A Quick Skills Assessment

DISTRIBUTE the "Sales: A Quick Skills Assessment" (page 335).

REVIEW the instructions on the assessment with participants.

ALLOW 3 minutes to complete the assessment.

> **Procedural note:** *During the discussion that follows, you will ask participants to volunteer desired improvements <u>with the highest priority</u>—their expectations for the workshop(s).*
>
> - *You should note these on a flipchart, and attempt to group similar expectations together.*
>
> - *However, do not concern yourself with separating communications- and sales-related expectations.*
>
> *Indicate the following at the conclusion of the discussion:*
>
> - *Those expectations that <u>will</u> be met during your workshop(s)*
>
> - *Those that <u>will not</u> be met—along with an indication of ways in which participants will be able to satisfy those expectations through other workshops, personal growth activities, independent study, etc.*
>
> *To facilitate this discussion, consider writing expectations that <u>will</u> be met on the left side of the flipchart, and those that <u>will not</u> be met on the right side.*

GROUP DISCUSSION

ASK *participants to volunteer the highest priority improvements to be made as a result of your workshops.*

RECORD *expectations on a flipchart, grouping similar expectations together.*

INDICATE *the following at the conclusion of the discussion:*

- Those expectations that <u>will</u> be met during the two workshops

- Those that <u>will not</u> be met—along with an indication of ways in which participants will be able to satisfy them

Sales: A Quick Skills Assessment

This assessment is based on the descriptions and definitions of the sales process, communications skills, and sales skills contained in *Effective Selling*.

- Refer to the descriptions and definitions in that document to refresh your memories, as required.
- Rate yourself in each of the areas—sales process phases, communications, and sales.
  - 7 is "comfortable, little need for improvement."
  - 4 is "so-so, need improvement."
  - 1 is "uncomfortable, major need for improvement."
- Note specific areas of improvement related to each that you would like to address in a workshop such as this.
- Mark three to five improvements that are your highest priority.

Skill Areas	Rating	Specific Improvements
Sales Process		
• Earn the Right	1 2 3 4 5 6 7	
• Understand the Need	1 2 3 4 5 6 7	
• Make a Recommendation	1 2 3 4 5 6 7	
• Complete the Sale	1 2 3 4 5 6 7	
Communications		
• Listening	1 2 3 4 5 6 7	
• Verifying	1 2 3 4 5 6 7	
• Questioning	1 2 3 4 5 6 7	
• Observing	1 2 3 4 5 6 7	
• Explaining	1 2 3 4 5 6 7	
Sales		
• Building Rapport	1 2 3 4 5 6 7	
• Qualifying Opportunities	1 2 3 4 5 6 7	
• Describing Benefits	1 2 3 4 5 6 7	
• Handling Obstacles	1 2 3 4 5 6 7	

Active Listening Assessment

00:10

Purpose: Provide an opportunity for participants to assess skills relevant to active listening.

INDIVIDUAL ASSESSMENT

INTRODUCE the assessment, adapting the description as appropriate, if this activity is not being used in the half-day communications workshop or the one-day sales workshop.

- You will now take a few minutes to complete a simple assessment of your skills in active listening.

*Active Listening
Assessment*

DISTRIBUTE the "Active Listening Assessment" (page 337).

REVIEW the instructions on the assessment with participants.

ALLOW 3 minutes to complete the assessment.

GROUP DISCUSSION

ASK participants to volunteer steps in their personal action plans for improving active listening skills.

MAKE notes on a blank flipchart.

REINFORCE the value of the steps identified, referring to the "Active Listening Assessment" as appropriate.

KEY POINTS

MAKE these key points as a summary.

- Listening is an excellent technique for building a good relationship with your customers.

- It is a way to express a genuine interest in the other person and what he or she has to say.

Active Listening Assessment

This assessment covers key techniques in active listening.
- Rate yourself on each of the techniques.
  - 7 is "comfortable, little need for improvement."
  - 4 is "so-so, need improvement."
  - 1 is "uncomfortable, major need for improvement."
- Note specific areas of improvement related to each that you would like to address.
- As a personal action plan, identify two or three steps you will take to improve your skills in this area and write them in the space provided below the assessment.

I . . .	Rating	Specific Improvements
• Verify frequently.	1 2 3 4 5 6 7	
• Do not interrupt.	1 2 3 4 5 6 7	
• Restate frequently.	1 2 3 4 5 6 7	
• Confirm as a part of verification.	1 2 3 4 5 6 7	
• Avoid leading the discussion.	1 2 3 4 5 6 7	
• Seek clarification when needed.	1 2 3 4 5 6 7	
• Assume responsibility for misunderstanding.	1 2 3 4 5 6 7	
• Maintain eye contact.	1 2 3 4 5 6 7	
• Exhibit attentive body posture.	1 2 3 4 5 6 7	

Personal action plan for improvement:

1. _____

2. _____

3. _____

What Impressions Do You Make?

00:10

Purpose: Provide an opportunity for participants to assess the impressions they make on others.

INDIVIDUAL ASSESSMENT

INTRODUCE the assessment.

- In any situation, including sales, observing is a two-way street.

- Now that you've thought about the clues you can get about your customers, it's time to think about the clues you reveal to them—*the impressions you make* on your customers.

What Impressions Do You Make?

DISTRIBUTE the assessment, "What Impressions Do You Make?" (page 339).

REVIEW the instructions on the assessment with participants.

ALLOW 3 minutes to complete the assessment.

GROUP DISCUSSION

ASK participants to volunteer steps in their personal action plans for improving the impressions they make on others.

MAKE notes on a blank flipchart.

REINFORCE the value of the steps identified, referring to key points such as these.

- Awareness of nonverbal behaviors
    - Facing customer
    - Eye contact
    - Friendly posture
    - Receptiveness

- Positive image, including grooming and environment

KEY POINTS

MAKE these key points as a summary.

- Properly used, observing is a very powerful skill.

- By observing, you are able to learn a great deal about your customers—*and they learn about you, too.*

What Impressions Do You Make?

In any situation, observing is a two-way street. In sales, you form impressions of your customers *and* they form impressions of you.

This assessment looks at the impression that you make.

- Rate yourself on each aspect of the impression you make.
  - 7 represents "good, little need for improvement."
  - 4 represents "average, need improvement."
  - 1 represents "poor, major need for improvement."
- Note specific areas of improvement related to each that you would like to address.
- As a personal action plan, identify two or three steps you will take to improve the impression you make and write them in the space provided below the assessment.

My . . .	Rating	Specific Improvements
• Clothing	1 2 3 4 5 6 7	
• Personal grooming	1 2 3 4 5 6 7	
• Speech patterns	1 2 3 4 5 6 7	
• Posture	1 2 3 4 5 6 7	
• Gestures	1 2 3 4 5 6 7	
• Eye contact	1 2 3 4 5 6 7	
• Surroundings	1 2 3 4 5 6 7	

Personal action plan for improvement:

1. _____
2. _____
3. _____

Questioning Assessment

00:10

Purpose: Provide an opportunity for participants to assess skills relevant to questioning.

INDIVIDUAL ASSESSMENT

INTRODUCE the assessment.

- You will now take a few minutes to complete a simple assessment of your skills in questioning.

Questioning Assessment

DISTRIBUTE the "Questioning Assessment" (page 341).

REVIEW the instructions on the assessment with participants.

ALLOW 3 minutes to complete the assessment.

GROUP DISCUSSION

ASK participants to volunteer steps in their personal action plans for improving questioning skills.

MAKE notes on a blank flipchart.

REINFORCE the value of the steps identified, referring to the "Questioning Assessment," as appropriate.

KEY POINTS

MAKE these key points as a summary.

- The skillful use of logically organized general, specific, and leading questions is important to success in the "Understand the Need" phase of the sales process—and throughout the sales process.

- Key to your success in questioning, of course, is careful use of the listening and verifying skills.

Questioning Assessment

This assessment covers key techniques in questioning.

- Rate yourself on each of the techniques.
  - 7 is "comfortable, little need for improvement."
  - 4 is "so-so, need improvement."
  - 1 is "uncomfortable, major need for improvement."
- Note specific areas of improvement related to each that you would like to address.

- As a personal action plan, identify two or three steps you will take to improve your skills in this area and write them in the space provided below the assessment.

I . . .	Rating	Specific Improvements
• Use general questions to "open up" my customer.	1 2 3 4 5 6 7	
• Use specific/closed questions to "focus in."	1 2 3 4 5 6 7	
• Use leading questions to direct a customer's thinking and comments.	1 2 3 4 5 6 7	
• Listen to the answers to my questions.	1 2 3 4 5 6 7	
• Verify my understanding.	1 2 3 4 5 6 7	
• Organize questions into a productive sequence.	1 2 3 4 5 6 7	
• Successfully gather the information I need.	1 2 3 4 5 6 7	

Personal action plan for improvement:

1. _____

2. _____

3. _____

Explaining Assessment

00:10

Purpose: Provide an opportunity for participants to assess skills relevant to explaining.

INDIVIDUAL ASSESSMENT

INTRODUCE the assessment.

- You will now take a few minutes to complete a simple assessment of your skills in explaining.

Explaining Assessment

DISTRIBUTE the "Explaining Assessment" (page 343).

REVIEW the instructions on the assessment with participants.

ALLOW 3 minutes to complete the assessment.

GROUP DISCUSSION

ASK participants to volunteer steps in their personal action plans for improving explaining skills.

MAKE notes on a blank flipchart.

REINFORCE the value of the steps identified, referring to the "Explaining Assessment," as appropriate.

KEY POINTS

MAKE these key points as a summary.

- The explaining skill is key to your success in making recommendations and handling obstacles.

- In addition, it is important at any time you have to answer a question.

Explaining Assessment

This assessment covers key techniques in explaining.

- Rate yourself on each of the techniques.
  - 7 is "comfortable, little need for improvement."
  - 4 is "so-so, need improvement."
  - 1 is "uncomfortable, major need for improvement."
- Note specific areas of improvement related to each that you would like to address.

- As a personal action plan, identify two or three steps you will take to improve your skills in this area and write them in the space provided below the assessment.

I . . .	Rating	Specific Improvements
• Use simple language.	1 2 3 4 5 6 7	
• Avoid jargon, unless appropriate.	1 2 3 4 5 6 7	
• Keep the explanation short and to the point.	1 2 3 4 5 6 7	
• Make the explanation logical.	1 2 3 4 5 6 7	
• Provide clear transitions.	1 2 3 4 5 6 7	
• Make it credible, concrete.	1 2 3 4 5 6 7	
• Make it vivid and dynamic.	1 2 3 4 5 6 7	
• Stay focused on the purpose of the explanation.	1 2 3 4 5 6 7	
• Stay focused on the customer's objectives.	1 2 3 4 5 6 7	
• Don't "fake" answers.	1 2 3 4 5 6 7	

Personal action plan for improvement:

1. _____

2. _____

3. _____

Building Rapport Assessment

00:10

Purpose: Provide an opportunity for participants to assess skills relevant to building rapport.

INDIVIDUAL ASSESSMENT

INTRODUCE the assessment.

- You will now take a few minutes to complete a simple assessment of your skills in building rapport.

Building Rapport Assessment

DISTRIBUTE the "Building Rapport Assessment" (page 345).

REVIEW the instructions on the assessment with participants.

ALLOW 3 minutes to complete the assessment.

GROUP DISCUSSION

ASK participants to volunteer steps in their personal action plans for improving skills in building rapport.

MAKE notes on a blank flipchart.

REINFORCE the value of the steps identified, referring to the "Building Rapport Assessment," as appropriate.

KEY POINTS

MAKE these key points as a summary.

- Building rapport is an ongoing process, with short- and longer-range objectives.

- In the short range, your focus is on making the customer comfortable, getting a sense of why the customer is there, and ensuring that your interaction with the customer will continue beyond its opening moments.

- In the longer range, your focus is beginning a dialogue with the customer, building a solid foundation of rapport, and ensuring that you earn—and maintain—the right to proceed.

Building Rapport Assessment

This assessment covers key techniques in building rapport.

- Rate yourself on each of the techniques.
  - 7 is "comfortable, little need for improvement."
  - 4 is "so-so, need improvement."
  - 1 is "uncomfortable, major need for improvement."
- Note specific areas of improvement related to each that you would like to address.
- As a personal action plan, identify two or three steps you will take to improve your skills in this area and write them in the space provided below the assessment.

I . . .	Rating	Specific Improvements
• Act relaxed and at ease.	1 2 3 4 5 6 7	
• Make the other person feel comfortable.	1 2 3 4 5 6 7	
• Take time before moving into "business."		
– Customer comfort	1 2 3 4 5 6 7	
– Sensitivity to clues	1 2 3 4 5 6 7	
• Listen!	1 2 3 4 5 6 7	
• Am aware of my nonverbal behaviors.		
– Facing customer	1 2 3 4 5 6 7	
– Eye contact	1 2 3 4 5 6 7	
– Friendly posture	1 2 3 4 5 6 7	
– Receptiveness	1 2 3 4 5 6 7	
• Project a positive image.		
– My grooming	1 2 3 4 5 6 7	
– My environment	1 2 3 4 5 6 7	

Personal action plan for improvement:

1. _____

2. _____

3. _____

"Earn the Right" Assessment

00:10

Purpose: Provide an opportunity for participants to assess skills relevant to the "Earn the Right" phase.

INDIVIDUAL ASSESSMENT

INTRODUCE the assessment.

- You will now take a few minutes to complete a simple assessment of skills relevant to the "Earn the Right" phase of the sales process.

"Earn the Right" Assessment

DISTRIBUTE the "'Earn the Right' Assessment" (page 347).

REVIEW the instructions on the assessment with participants.

ALLOW 3 minutes to complete the assessment.

GROUP DISCUSSION

ASK participants to volunteer steps in their personal action plans for improving skills relevant to the "Earn the Right" phase.

MAKE notes on a blank flipchart.

REINFORCE the value of the steps identified, referring to the "'Earn the Right' Assessment," as appropriate.

KEY POINTS

MAKE these key points as a summary.

- The importance of making the customer feel comfortable
- The importance of observing to begin to learn about the customer
- The use of general questions to "open up" the customer
- The importance of listening

"Earn the Right" Assessment

This assessment covers key techniques in the "Earn the Right" phase of the sales process.

- Rate yourself on each of the techniques.
    - 7 is "comfortable, little need for improvement."
    - 4 is "so-so, need improvement."
    - 1 is "uncomfortable, major need for improvement."
- Note specific areas of improvement related to each that you would like to address.
- As a personal action plan, identify two or three steps you will take to improve your skills in this phase and write them in the space provided below the assessment.

I . . .	Rating	Specific Improvements
• Act relaxed and at ease.	1 2 3 4 5 6 7	
• Make the other person feel comfortable.	1 2 3 4 5 6 7	
• Take time before moving into "business."	1 2 3 4 5 6 7	
• Am aware of my nonverbal behaviors.	1 2 3 4 5 6 7	
• Project a positive image.	1 2 3 4 5 6 7	
• Look for clues that tell me about my customer.	1 2 3 4 5 6 7	
• Interpret the clues and verify my interpretations.	1 2 3 4 5 6 7	
• Use general questions early in the sales effort.	1 2 3 4 5 6 7	
• Avoid questions that can be answered with one word.	1 2 3 4 5 6 7	
• Listen!	1 2 3 4 5 6 7	

Personal action plan for improvement:

1. _____

2. _____

3. _____

Qualifying Skills Assessment

00:10

Purpose: Provide an opportunity for participants to assess skills relevant to qualifying opportunities.

INDIVIDUAL ASSESSMENT

INTRODUCE the assessment.

- You will now take a few minutes to complete a simple assessment of your skills in qualifying opportunities.

Qualifying Skills Assessment

DISTRIBUTE the assessment, "Qualifying Skills Assessment" (page 349).

REVIEW the instructions on the assessment with participants.

ALLOW 3 minutes to complete the assessment.

GROUP DISCUSSION

ASK participants to volunteer steps in their personal action plans for improving qualifying skills.

MAKE notes on a blank flipchart.

REINFORCE the value of the steps identified, referring to the "Qualifying Skills Assessment," as appropriate.

KEY POINTS

MAKE these key points as a summary.

- By qualifying opportunities, you increase the likelihood that you are investing your valuable time and energy in sales efforts that will be successful.

- Of course, qualify *carefully*—if you don't qualify carefully or if you conclude incorrectly that an opportunity is not qualified, failing to pursue the opportunity could result in lost business.

Qualifying Skills Assessment

This assessment covers key techniques in qualifying skills.

- Rate yourself on each of the techniques.
  - 7 is "comfortable, little need for improvement."
  - 4 is "so-so, need improvement."
  - 1 is "uncomfortable, major need for improvement."
- Note specific areas of improvement related to each that you would like to address.

- As a personal action plan, identify two or three steps you will take to improve your skills in this area and write them in the space provided below the assessment.

I . . .	Rating	Specific Improvements
• Use questioning, listening, and verifying skills to qualify opportunities.	1 2 3 4 5 6 7	
• Use the observing skill as an additional tool in qualifying.	1 2 3 4 5 6 7	
• Successfully assess the information I gather.	1 2 3 4 5 6 7	
• Qualify opportunities as quickly as possible.	1 2 3 4 5 6 7	
• Recognize situations where my product or service will not meet customer needs.	1 2 3 4 5 6 7	
• Let go of opportunities that are not qualified.	1 2 3 4 5 6 7	
• Use qualifying as a tool to help make most effective use of my selling time.	1 2 3 4 5 6 7	

Personal action plan for improvement:

1. _____

2. _____

3. _____

"Understand the Need" Assessment

00:10

Purpose: Provide an opportunity for participants to assess skills relevant to the "Understand the Need" phase.

INDIVIDUAL ASSESSMENT

INTRODUCE the assessment.

- You will now take a few minutes to complete a simple assessment of your skills relevant to the "Understand the Need" phase of the sales process.

"Understand the Need" Assessment

DISTRIBUTE the "'Understand the Need' Assessment" (page 351).

REVIEW the instructions on the assessment with participants.

ALLOW 3 minutes to complete the assessment.

GROUP DISCUSSION

ASK participants to volunteer steps in their personal action plans for improving skills relevant to the "Understand the Need" phase.

MAKE notes on a blank flipchart.

REINFORCE the value of the steps identified, referring to the "'Understand the Need' Assessment," as appropriate.

KEY POINTS

MAKE these key points as a summary.

- The importance of using a variety of questions, structured in a way that the salesperson gathers the required information about customer needs

- The importance of learning about both buying objectives and buying influences

- The importance of qualifying opportunities

"Understand the Need" Assessment

This assessment covers key techniques in the "Understand the Need" phase of the sales process.

- Rate yourself on each of the techniques.
  - 7 is "comfortable, little need for improvement."
  - 4 is "so-so, need improvement."
  - 1 is "uncomfortable, major need for improvement."
- Note specific areas of improvement related to each that you would like to address.

- As a personal action plan, identify two or three steps you will take to improve your skills in this phase and write them in the space provided below the assessment.

I . . .	Rating	Specific Improvements
• Quickly focus in on customer's problem/need.	1 2 3 4 5 6 7	
• Use a variety of question types to gather information about buying objectives.	1 2 3 4 5 6 7	
• Organize questions in a logical, productive sequence.	1 2 3 4 5 6 7	
• Listen to the answers to my questions.	1 2 3 4 5 6 7	
• Determine factors that will influence the buying decision.	1 2 3 4 5 6 7	
• Use qualifying as a tool to make effective use of time.	1 2 3 4 5 6 7	
• Gain a full understanding of the problem/need.	1 2 3 4 5 6 7	

Personal action plan for improvement:

1. _____

2. _____

3. _____

Describing Benefits Assessment

00:10

Purpose: Provide an opportunity for participants to assess skills relevant to describing benefits.

INDIVIDUAL ASSESSMENT

INTRODUCE the assessment.

- You will now take a few minutes to complete a simple assessment of your skills in describing benefits.

Describing Benefits Assessment

DISTRIBUTE the "Describing Benefits Assessment" (page 353).

REVIEW the instructions on the assessment with participants.

ALLOW 3 minutes to complete the assessment.

GROUP DISCUSSION

ASK participants to volunteer steps in their personal action plans for improving their skills in describing benefits.

MAKE notes on a blank flipchart.

REINFORCE the value of the steps identified, referring to the "Describing Benefits Assessment," as appropriate.

KEY POINTS

MAKE these key points as a summary.

- Be certain that the benefit is clearly related to the customer's objective.

- Additionally, be sure the benefit you describe is perceived by customers as *something of value to them.*

Describing Benefits Assessment

This assessment covers key techniques involved in describing benefits.

- Rate yourself on each of the techniques.
  - 7 is "comfortable, little need for improvement."
  - 4 is "so-so, need improvement."
  - 1 is "uncomfortable, major need for improvement."
- Note specific areas of improvement related to each that you would like to address.

- As a personal action plan, identify two or three steps you will take to improve your skills in this area and write them in the space provided below the assessment.

I . . .	Rating	Specific Improvements
• Identify product/service features that are relevant to customer objectives.	1 2 3 4 5 6 7	
• Identify benefits related to those features.	1 2 3 4 5 6 7	
• Make the benefit statement interesting, exciting, dynamic.	1 2 3 4 5 6 7	
• Relate the benefit statement to customer objectives.	1 2 3 4 5 6 7	
• Make sure that the benefit is perceived to be of value to the customer.	1 2 3 4 5 6 7	

Personal action plan for improvement:

1. _____

2. _____

3. _____

"Make a Recommendation" Assessment

00:10

Purpose: Provide an opportunity for participants to assess skills relevant to the "Make a Recommendation" phase.

INDIVIDUAL ASSESSMENT

INTRODUCE the assessment.

- You will now take a few minutes to complete a simple assessment of skills relevant to the "Make a Recommendation" phase of the sales process.

"Make a Recommendation"
Assessment

DISTRIBUTE the "'Make a Recommendation' Assessment" *(page 355).*

REVIEW the instructions on the assessment with participants.

ALLOW 3 minutes to complete the assessment.

GROUP DISCUSSION

ASK participants to volunteer steps in their personal action plans for improving skills relevant to the "Make a Recommendation" phase.

MAKE notes on a blank flipchart.

REINFORCE the value of the steps identified, referring to the "'Make a Recommendation' Assessment," as appropriate.

KEY POINTS

MAKE these key points as a summary.

- The importance of using good explaining skills

- The importance of well-stated benefits

- The importance of enthusiastic and explicit recommendations

"Make a Recommendation" Assessment

This assessment covers key techniques in the "Make a Recommendation" phase of the sales process.

- Rate yourself on each of the techniques.
  - 7 is "comfortable, little need for improvement."
  - 4 is "so-so, need improvement."
  - 1 is "uncomfortable, major need for improvement."
- Note specific areas of improvement related to each that you would like to address.

- As a personal action plan, identify two or three steps you will take to improve your skills in this phase and write them in the space provided below the assessment.

I . . .	Rating	Specific Improvements
• Provide a clear statement of purpose.	1 2 3 4 5 6 7	
• Organize content logically, for myself *and* customer.	1 2 3 4 5 6 7	
• Include only relevant information.	1 2 3 4 5 6 7	
• Present explanation from customer's point of view.	1 2 3 4 5 6 7	
• Use overviews and summaries, when necessary.	1 2 3 4 5 6 7	
• Include a clear statement of benefits.	1 2 3 4 5 6 7	
• Describe my competitive edge.	1 2 3 4 5 6 7	
• Communicate enthusiasm.	1 2 3 4 5 6 7	
• Make the recommendation *explicit*.	1 2 3 4 5 6 7	

Personal action plan for improvement:

1. _____

2. _____

3. _____

Handling Obstacles Assessment

00:10

Purpose: Provide an opportunity for participants to assess skills relevant to handling obstacles.

INDIVIDUAL ASSESSMENT

INTRODUCE the assessment.

- You will now take a few minutes to complete a simple assessment of your skills in handling obstacles.

*Handling Obstacles
Assessment*

*DISTRIBUTE the "Handling Obstacles Assessment"
(page 357).*

REVIEW the instructions on the assessment with participants.

ALLOW 3 minutes to complete the assessment.

GROUP DISCUSSION

ASK participants to volunteer steps in their personal action plans for improving skills in handling obstacles.

MAKE notes on a blank flipchart.

REINFORCE the value of the steps identified, referring to the "Handling Obstacles Assessment," as appropriate.

KEY POINTS

MAKE these key points as a summary.

- Obstacles provide an excellent opportunity to learn about things that may be of concern to your customer.

- When you encounter an obstacle, be sure you understand accurately what it is—and then verify that you have handled it to your customer's satisfaction.

Handling Obstacles Assessment

This assessment covers key techniques in handling obstacles.

- Rate yourself on each of the techniques.
  - 7 is "comfortable, little need for improvement."
  - 4 is "so-so, need improvement."
  - 1 is "uncomfortable, major need for improvement."
- Note specific areas of improvement related to each that you would like to address.

- As a personal action plan, identify two or three steps you will take to improve your skills in this area and write them in the space provided below the assessment.

I . . .	Rating	Specific Improvements
• Pause, think, avoid reacting immediately.	1 2 3 4 5 6 7	
• Analyze the obstacle, determine what it means.	1 2 3 4 5 6 7	
• Clarify the obstacle.	1 2 3 4 5 6 7	
• Verify my understanding.	1 2 3 4 5 6 7	
• Handle the obstacle.	1 2 3 4 5 6 7	
• Verify that the customer feels the obstacle has been handled satisfactorily.	1 2 3 4 5 6 7	

Personal action plan for improvement:

1. _____
2. _____
3. _____

"Complete the Sale" Assessment

00:10

Purpose: Provide an opportunity for participants to assess skills relevant to the "Complete the Sale" phase.

INDIVIDUAL ASSESSMENT

INTRODUCE the assessment.

- You will now take a few minutes to complete a simple assessment of skills relevant to the "Complete the Sale" phase of the sales process.

"Complete the Sale" Assessment

DISTRIBUTE the "'Complete the Sale' Assessment" (page 359).

REVIEW the instructions on the assessment with participants.

ALLOW 3 minutes to complete the assessment.

GROUP DISCUSSION

ASK participants to volunteer steps in their personal action plans for improving skills relevant to the "Complete the Sale" phase.

MAKE notes on a blank flipchart.

REINFORCE the value of the steps identified, referring to the "'Complete the Sale' Assessment," as appropriate.

KEY POINTS

MAKE these key points as a summary.

- The importance of asking for the order—with confidence

- The importance of carefully and thoroughly handling obstacles

- The importance of *completing the sale!*

"Complete the Sale" Assessment

This assessment covers key techniques in the "Complete the Sale" phase of the sales process.

- Rate yourself on each of the techniques.
    - 7 is "comfortable, little need for improvement."
    - 4 is "so-so, need improvement."
    - 1 is "uncomfortable, major need for improvement."
- Note specific areas of improvement related to each that you would like to address.

- As a personal action plan, identify two or three steps you will take to improve your skills in this phase and write them in the space provided below the assessment.

I . . .	Rating	Specific Improvements
• Select the best approach to asking for the order.	1 2 3 4 5 6 7	
• Ask for the order with confidence.	1 2 3 4 5 6 7	
• Let the customer respond.	1 2 3 4 5 6 7	
• Use silence to advantage.	1 2 3 4 5 6 7	
• Pause, avoid reacting immediately to obstacles.	1 2 3 4 5 6 7	
• Analyze obstacles.	1 2 3 4 5 6 7	
• Clarify obstacles, verify my understanding.	1 2 3 4 5 6 7	
• Handle obstacles.	1 2 3 4 5 6 7	
• Verify they have been handled satisfactorily.	1 2 3 4 5 6 7	
• Complete the sale!	1 2 3 4 5 6 7	

Personal action plan for improvement:

1. _____

2. _____

3. _____

Chapter Ten:

Overhead Transparencies

In this section of *The ASTD Trainer's Sourcebook: Sales*, you will find overhead transparency masters for use during your sales training sessions. You may use these in two ways.

- Key them into your word processing system, either "as is" or customized to suit your specific needs.
- Copy the masters that you need from this book and make transparencies from them "as is."

Our Purpose

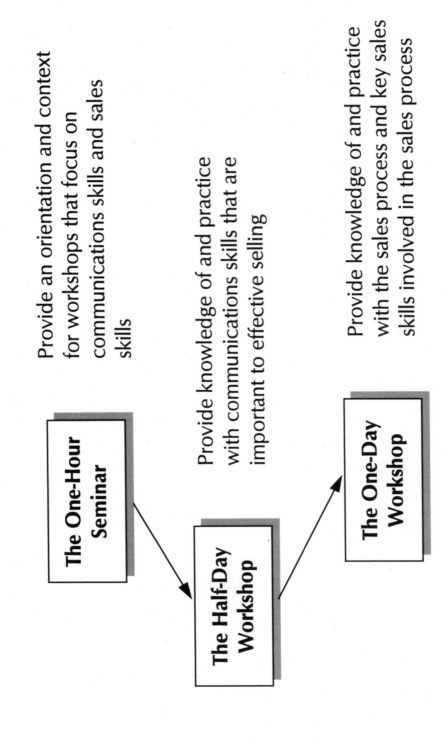

The One-Hour Seminar

Provide an orientation and context for workshops that focus on communications skills and sales skills

The Half-Day Workshop

Provide knowledge of and practice with communications skills that are important to effective selling

The One-Day Workshop

Provide knowledge of and practice with the sales process and key sales skills involved in the sales process

Key Assumptions

The customer...

- Has a problem to solve or a need to satisfy

- Probably isn't convinced that he or she necessarily wishes to buy from you

- Wants help with the buying decision

- Is there to BUY!

You...

- Must earn the right to proceed in the sales effort with the customer

- Are there to understand the customer's need

- Are there to help the customer buy

- Are there to SELL!

Opportunity

The Sale!!!

Effective Selling

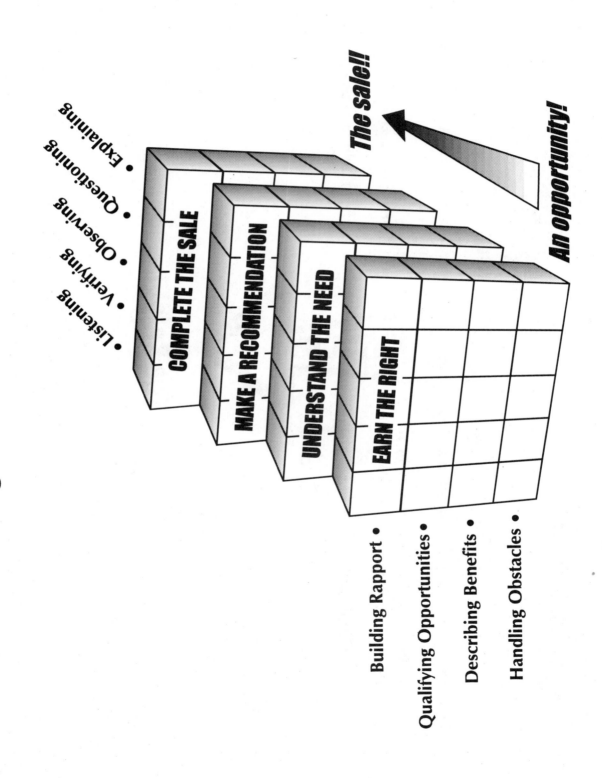

An opportunity!

The sale!

- Listening
- Verifying
- Observing
- Questioning
- Explaining

COMPLETE THE SALE

MAKE A RECOMMENDATION

UNDERSTAND THE NEED

EARN THE RIGHT

- Building Rapport
- Qualifying Opportunities
- Describing Benefits
- Handling Obstacles

Workshop Roles

Your Roles

- Participate actively in all workshop activities

- Contribute your insights and experience to group discussions

- Work toward achieving workshop goals

- Observe conventions of "common politeness"

Facilitator's Role

- Encourage discussion and provide help, as needed

- Stimulate your thinking

- Help synthesize group discussions

- Guide the group toward achievement of workshop goals

- Maintain the pace of the workshop

365

Workshop Guidelines

Common politeness
- One conversation at a time
- Everyone has an equal voice
- No "put downs" or emotional words

Efficiency
- Help control our time
- Try to make your comments brief and to the point

Responsibility
- Accept your share of responsibility for outcomes
- Accept challenges
- Assure that comments recorded on flipcharts are accurate, reflecting your intent and meaning
- Listen!

Listening and Verifying: Overview

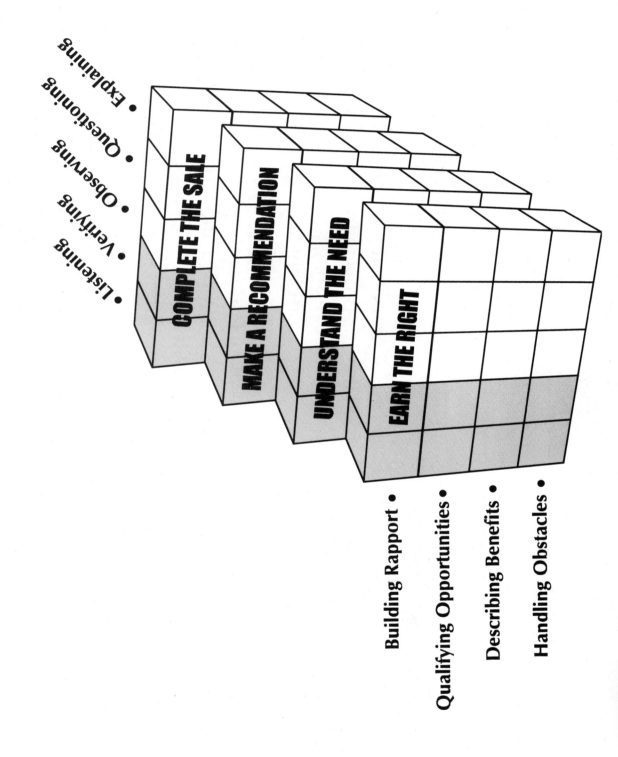

Listening • Verifying • Observing • Questioning • Explaining

COMPLETE THE SALE

MAKE A RECOMMENDATION

UNDERSTAND THE NEED

EARN THE RIGHT

Building Rapport •
Qualifying Opportunities •
Describing Benefits •
Handling Obstacles •

367

Active Listening

The integration of *listening* and *verifying*

lis·ten·ing (from the old English) *

1: making a conscious effort to hear

2: paying close attention

ver·i·fy·ing (from the Latin "make true")

1: proving to be true by evidence

2: testing or checking the accuracy or correctness of

- Listening with a purpose
- Listening with undivided attention focused on the listening activity
- Verifying as you listen, to ensure understanding

---

* Based on definitions from *Webster's New World Dictionary of American English.* Simon & Schuster, Inc., New York, NY: 1994.

Observing and Questioning: Overview

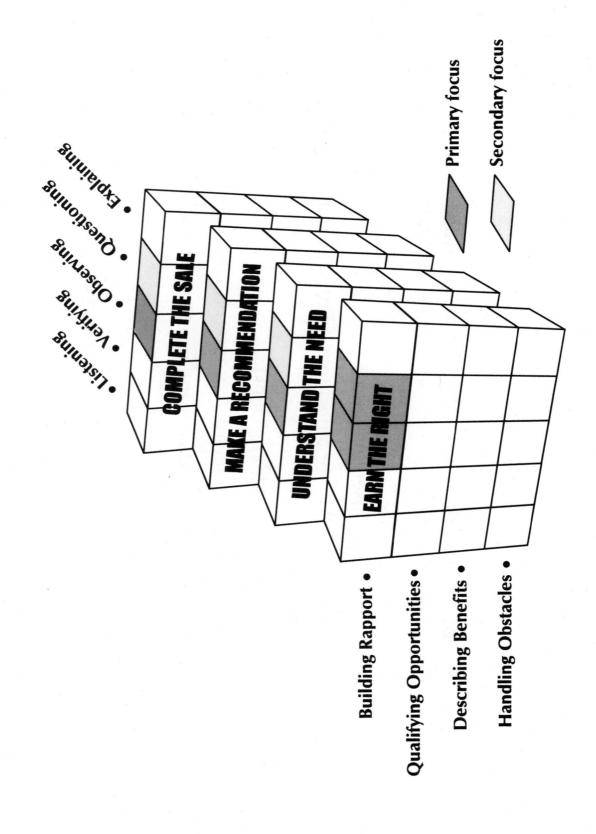

Listening •

Verifying •

Observing •

Questioning •

Explaining •

COMPLETE THE SALE

MAKE A RECOMMENDATION

UNDERSTAND THE NEED

EARN THE RIGHT

• Building Rapport

• Qualifying Opportunities

• Describing Benefits

• Handling Obstacles

Primary focus

Secondary focus

Observing

ob·serv·ing (from the Latin "guard" or "watch over")*
1: noticing or perceiving something 2: paying special attention to

Four steps in observing

- Look for a clue (or clues) that point to certain characteristics or traits

- Interpret the clue (or clues)

- Verify the accuracy of your interpretation

- Use your clue and your interpretation to help relate to customer, determine next steps

* Based on definitions from *Webster's New World Dictionary of American English*. Simon & Schuster, Inc., New York, NY: 1994.

Early Questions

General questions

- Begin with *what, who, how, why,* and *where*

- Cause people to open up and talk

More on Questions: Overview

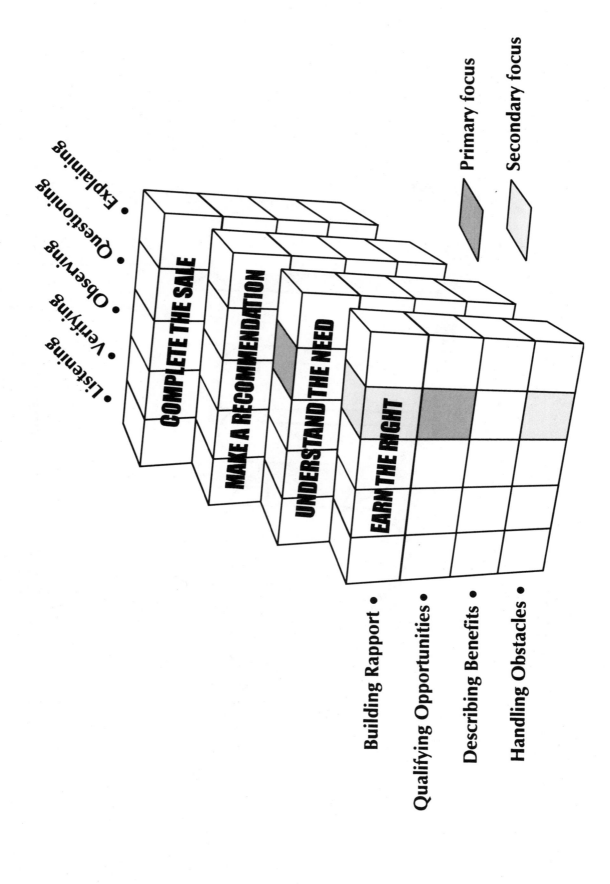

Types of Questions

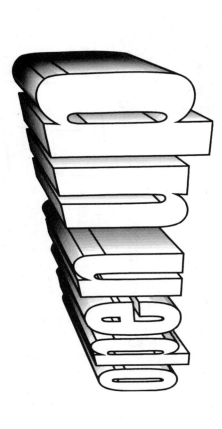

General questions

- Begin with *what, who, how, why,* and *where*
- Cause people to open up and talk

Leading questions

- Cause people to "open up" by . . .
  - stimulating thinking in new directions
  - Causing customer to evaluate consequences of not acting
- Cause people to "focus in" by . . .
  - Forcing a reply you wish to hear
  - Forcing a choice

Specific/closed questions

- With specific, to get a specific piece of information
- With closed, to get a "Yes" or "No" answer
- Use to . . . .
  - Verify and confirm understanding
  - Focus conversation to reach a conclusion
  - Refocus conversation that has strayed

Explaining: Overview

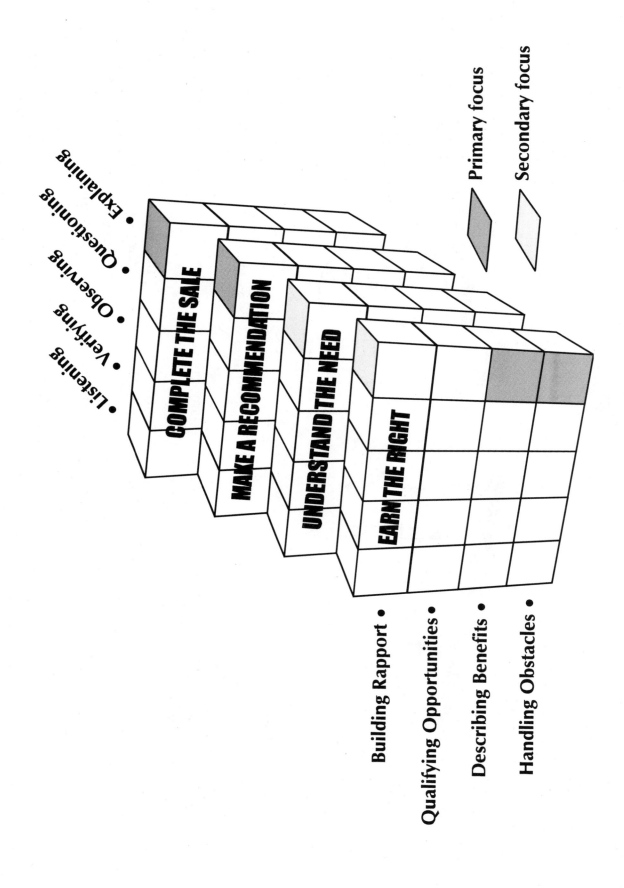

Explaining

ex·plain·ing (from the Latin "make level")*
1: making clear, plain, or understandable
2: giving the meaning or interpretation of

* Based on definitions from *Webster's New World Dictionary of American English.* Simon & Schuster, Inc., New York, NY: 1994.

Earn the Right: Overview

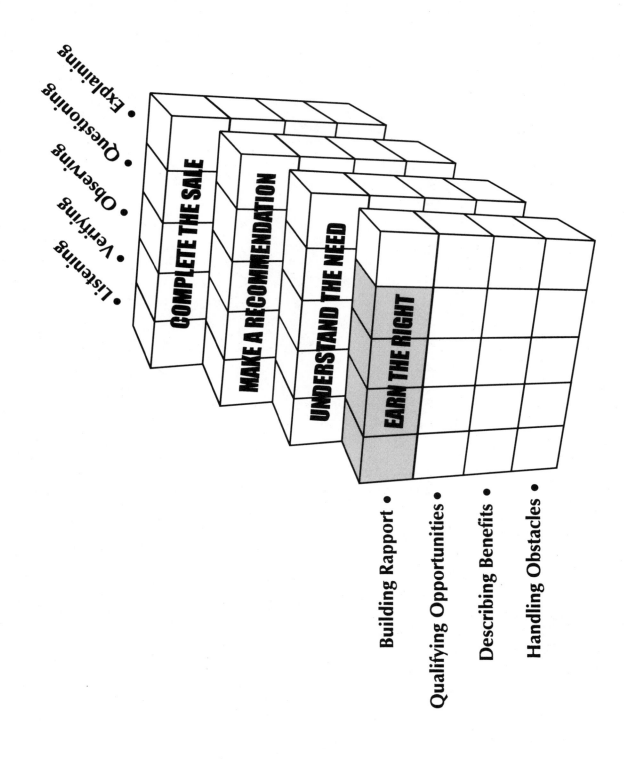

- Listening
- Verifying
- Observing
- Questioning
- Explaining

COMPLETE THE SALE

MAKE A RECOMMENDATION

UNDERSTAND THE NEED

EARN THE RIGHT

- Building Rapport
- Qualifying Opportunities
- Describing Benefits
- Handling Obstacles

Building Rapport

rap·port (from the French "to bring back") *
1: relationship 2: agreement 3: harmony

Two categories of objectives in establishing rapport

- Short range
- Longer range

Building rapport is an ongoing process that
only begins early in the sales effort.

---

* Based on definitions from *Webster's New World Dictionary of American English.* Simon & Schuster, Inc., New York, NY: 1994.

Understand the Need: Overview

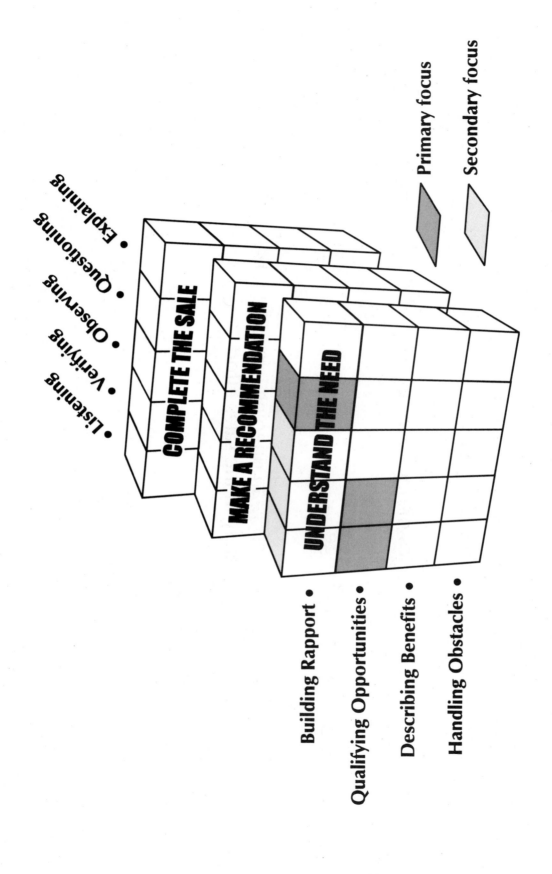

Qualifying Opportunities

qual·i·fy (from the Latin "of what kind" and "make") *
1: to make fit 2: to have the necessary or desirable qualities

Does the customer have a need?

Is the customer *ready* to buy?

Is the customer *willing* to buy . . . from you?

Is the customer *able* to buy?

Are *you able to satisfy* the customer's need?

* Based on definitions from *Webster's New World Dictionary of American English.* Simon & Schuster, Inc., New York, NY: 1994.

Make a Recommendation: Overview

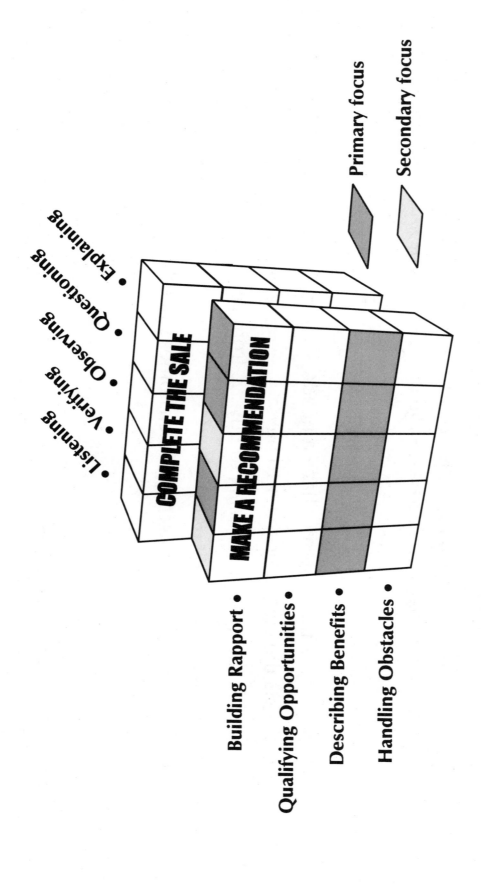

- Listening
- Verifying
- Observing
- Questioning
- Explaining

- Building Rapport
- Qualifying Opportunities
- Describing Benefits
- Handling Obstacles

COMPLETE THE SALE

MAKE A RECOMMENDATION

Primary focus

Secondary focus

Describing Benefits

ben·e·fit (from the Latin "well" and "do")* 1: *anything contributing to an improvement in condition; help, advantage*

Characteristics of a well-stated benefit

- Clearly related to the customer's objective
- Perceived by the customer as something of value

---

* Based on definitions from *Webster's New World Dictionary of American English*. Simon & Schuster, Inc., New York, NY: 1994.

Complete the Sale: Overview

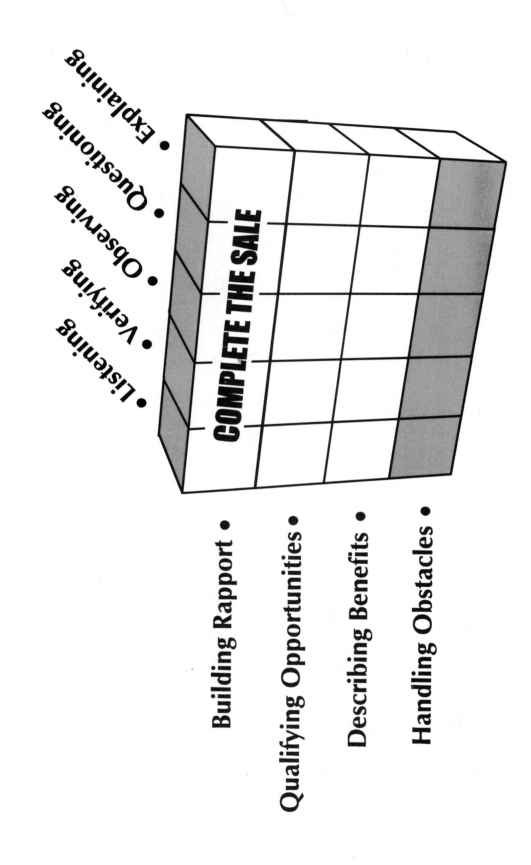

- Listening
- Verifying
- Observing
- Questioning
- Explaining

- Building Rapport
- Qualifying Opportunities
- Describing Benefits
- Handling Obstacles

COMPLETE THE SALE

Obstacles

ob·sta·cle (from the Latin "stand")* *1: anything that gets in the way or hinders*

---
[1]* Based on definitions from *Webster's New World Dictionary of American English*. Simon & Schuster, Inc., New York, NY: 1994.

Chapter Eleven:

Prepared Flipcharts

As indicated in the Introduction, we recommend that you prepare many of the flipcharts that you will use in advance.

- With prepared flipcharts, you have one less task to perform during the workshop itself.
- Prepared flipcharts, ready for your use on flipchart stands, are a reminder of the structure and flow of the workshop.
- Your overall facilitation of the workshop will be smoother and more professional.

This chapter includes "masters" for each of the prepared flipcharts that we recommend. You can turn these masters into prepared flipcharts in one of two ways.

- Copy the text by hand onto flipcharts.
- Use the pages as masters in a flipchart or poster making device.

Here are some suggestions for preparing these flipcharts.

- *Use two flipchart pads, as indicated in "Getting Everything Ready" (page 38).* This gives you greater flexibility, especially on those occasions when you need to work with or refer to two flipcharts at once.
- *Leave a blank page between each prepared flipchart.* In that way, the copy on the next flipchart in the pad will not be visible through the one you are currently using. Additionally, the blank pages might come in handy if you suddenly need a blank.
- *Be certain that the flip charts are legible.*

In the training plans we suggest posting these prepared flipcharts in specific "areas" after use in order to simplify subsequent reference. Here are the areas, with approximate numbers of flipcharts in parentheses (prepared and otherwise).

Area	One-Hour Seminar	Half-Day Workshop	One-Day Workshop
Workshop Overview	✓ (6)	✓ (4)	✓ (6)
Communications Skills	✓ (2)	✓ (10)	✓ (4)
Sales Skills			✓ (10)
Sales Process		✓ (4)	✓ (14)
Targeting Your Sales Efforts		✓ (5)	✓ (8)

SALES EXPERIENCES

	The Positive	The Unsatisfactory
Customer		
Salesperson		
Observer		

EFFECTIVE SELLING

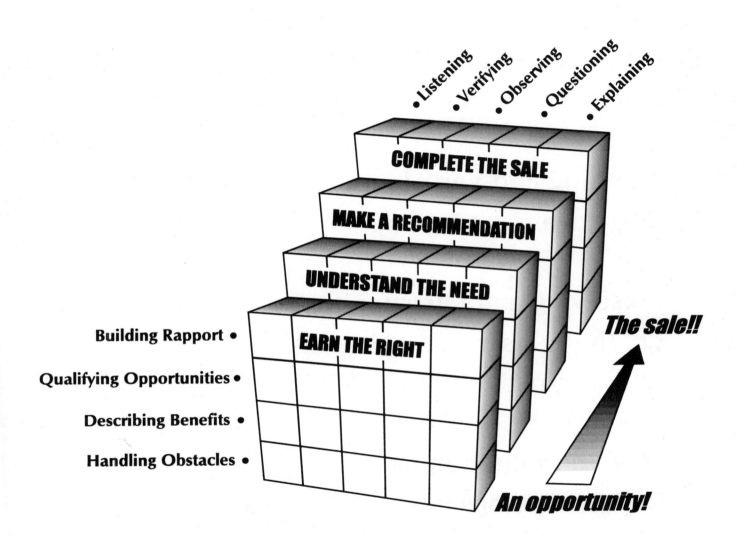

COMMUNICATIONS WORKSHOP AGENDA

Introduction to the Workshop

❑ Overview and Orientation

❑ Targeting Your Sales Efforts

Listening and Verifying

❑ Active Listening

Observing and Questioning

❑ The "Observing" Skill

❑ Introduction to Questioning

More on Questioning

❑ Buying Objectives and Influences

❑ Additional Question Types

Explaining

❑ The Explaining Skill

❑ Summary

SALES WORKSHOP AGENDA

Introduction to the Workshop
- ❑ Overview and Orientation

Earn the Right
- ❑ Building Rapport
- ❑ "Earn the Right" Assessment

Understand the Need
- ❑ Qualifying Opportunities
- ❑ The First Two Phases: A Role Play
- ❑ "Understand the Need" Assessment

Make a Recommendation
- ❑ Testing for Readiness
- ❑ Describing Benefits
- ❑ Presenting a Recommendation
- ❑ "Make a Recommendation" Assessment

Complete the Sale
- ❑ Asking for the Order
- ❑ Handling Obstacles
- ❑ "Complete the Sale" Assessment
- ❑ Summary

WORKSHOP EXPECTATIONS

WHAT YOU BELIEVE THE CUSTOMER SAID

-
-
-
-

WHAT THE CUSTOMER REALLY SAID

We have a major problem with your company

- Launching a new product next month; our production schedule is in jeopardy because of a component you provide

- Awarded you a contract for 10,000 components a month ago; first shipment arrived on schedule

- Ten of first 100 components failed to meet specs

We need components!

- Your major competitor can have 5,000 up-to-spec components here in three days

- Remainder here within a week

Can you replace the first shipment?

- How fast?

- What confidence can we have that these components will meet spec?

TYPICAL SALES SITUATIONS

Sales interaction

Sales process

COMMUNICATIONS WORKSHOP: LOGISTICS

Day and Date:

Time:

Location:

Dress:

COMMUNICATIONS WORKSHOP: PURPOSE AND GOALS

Purpose

- Provide knowledge of and practice with communications skills important to effective selling

Goals

- Relate effective selling to the importance of effective communications skills

- Describe and apply active listening and verifying skills throughout sales process

- Describe and apply observing and questioning skills, especially as used during "Earn the Right"

- Describe buying objectives and buying influences; describe and apply additional questioning skills, especially during "Understand the Need"

- Describe and apply explaining skill throughout the sales process

TARGETING YOUR SALES EFFORTS

❑ Typical Sales Situations and Customers

❑ Questions for "Earn the Right"

❑ Buying Objectives and Buying Influences

❑ Questions for "Understand the Need"

❑ Beginning a Sale

❑ Approaches to Qualifying

❑ Approaches to Testing for Readiness

❑ Benefit Statements

❑ Making a Recommendation

❑ Approaches to Asking for the Order

❑ Approaches to Handling Obstacles

OBSERVING

Your customer | **Your customer's environment**

QUESTIONS FOR "EARN THE RIGHT"

BUYING OBJECTIVES

What the customer wants to accomplish

BUYING INFLUENCES

Factors that will influence the customer's buying decision

WHY CUSTOMERS BUY

SPECIFIC/CLOSED QUESTIONS

Specific

Closed

LEADING QUESTIONS

Open up

Focus in

Questions for "Understand the Need"

EXPLAINING SKILL

SALES WORKSHOP: LOGISTICS

Day and Date:

Time:

Location:

Dress:

SALES WORKSHOP: PURPOSE AND GOALS

Purpose

- Provide knowledge of and practice with sales process and key sales skills important to effective selling; reinforce role of communications skills

Goals

- Relate effective communications and sales skills to effective selling
- Describe "Earn the Right," apply communications skills, begin to build rapport
- Describe "Understand the Need," apply communications skills, qualify opportunities
- Describe "Make a Recommendation," apply communications skills, test for readiness, present recommendations, describe benefits
- Describe "Complete the Sale," apply communications skills, ask for the order, handle obstacles
- Integrate knowledge and skills into successful selling approaches

WHAT DO YOU WANT TO ACCOMPLISH?

Short range

Longer range

BUILDING RAPPORT

BEGINNING A SALE

Approaches to Qualifying

ROLE PLAY QUESTIONS

- How effectively did the salesperson build rapport?

- What questioning techniques were effective from the salesperson's point of view? The customer's? The observer's?

- What alternate techniques might have been used?

ROLE PLAY QUESTIONS, CONTINUED

- Did the salesperson learn about the customer's need?

- Did the salesperson earn the right to move ahead with the sale?

Approaches to
Testing for Readiness

FEATURES AND BENEFITS

Feature

Benefit

BENEFIT STATEMENTS

RECOMMENDATIONS

COMPETITIVE EDGE

Making a Recommendation

BUYING SIGNALS

ASKING FOR THE ORDER

Direct—a direct request

- Shall I book the cruise?

Assumptive—you assume the customer has agreed, and ask for concurrence

- Would you like to pay with cash or a credit card?

APPROACHES TO
ASKING FOR THE ORDER

COMMON OBSTACLES

HANDLING OBSTACLES

View them as opportunities

Steps

APPROACHES TO HANDLING OBSTACLES

ROLE PLAY QUESTIONS

- Did the salesperson address the customer's buying objectives?

- How effectively was the explaining skill used?

- What might have been done more effectively?

ROLE PLAY QUESTIONS, CONTINUED

- What technique was used to ask for the order?

- How effectively were obstacles handled?

- What might have been done more effectively?

- Did the salesperson *complete the sale?*

Appendix: Recommended Resources

In this section of *The ASTD Trainer's Sourcebook: Sales*, you will find notes on a few key books that can be used to support your training effort.

Allesandra, Ph.D., Tony, Jim Cathcart, and John Monoky, Ph.D. *Be Your Own Sales Manager.* New York: Prentice Hall Press, 1990.

This book might be considered a primer on tactics for managing one's own accounts, territory, and time. It encourages a goal-oriented approach to one's own career, and provides numerous formulas and organizational tools to manage it. This book is good for the new salesperson who does not have access to account management software.

Blake, Jane Srygley, and Robert R. Blake. *The Grid of Sales Excellence: New Insights into a Proven System of Effective Sales,* 2nd edition. New York: McGraw-Hill, Inc., 1980.

This book, aimed at salespeople, provides a nine-by-nine grid as a context for explaining orientation and behaviors of salespeople and customers. For the analytical salesperson, this book may provide insight into one's own preferences and pitfalls.

Carew, Jack. *You'll Never Get No for an Answer.* New York: Simon and Schuster, 1987.

Carew is a salesperson's salesperson. The text is laced with lots of personal examples of key lessons he has learned over a lifetime of selling. The anecdotes describe personal "mistakes" and the realizations they fostered. It's easy to read. New salespeople seem to like this book.

Craig, Robert L., and Leslie Kelly, Eds. *Sales Training Handbook: A Guide to Developing Sales Performance.* Englewood Cliffs, New Jersey: Prentice Hall, 1990.

Sponsored by the American Society for Training and Development (ASTD) this handbook is a must for sales trainers. It offers practical advice from seasoned and respected professionals covering the entire range of sales training activities.

Fetterman, Roger L., and H. Richard Byrne. *Interactive Selling in the '90s: Applying Information Technology, Multimedia & Electronic Communications to the Sales Process.* San Diego, CA: Ellipsys International Publications, Inc., 1995

This book proposes a vision for the successful implementation of interactive selling systems—based on extensive research of existing technology, knowledge of the sales and buying processes, and interviews with industry professionals who use interactive selling to their competitive advantage.

Hopkins, Tom. *How to Master the Art of Selling.* New York: Warner Books, 1982.

Hopkins combines the many traditional selling techniques with self-motivational advice, both designed to help people become "sales champions." The book is short and easy to read.

Johnson, MD, Spencer, with Larry Wilson. *The One Minute Sales Person.* New York: William Morrow and Company, Inc., 1984.

A short book that focuses on the critical moments before, during and after a sales call—and sales assignment—that heighten the likelihood of success. A good reinforcer for the salesperson who knows the skills.

Karrass, Gary. *Negotiate to Close.* New York: Simon and Schuster, 1985.

Negotiating is not for the timid or for those who need instant gratification. Karrass deals with the psychological and tactical requirements needed to "unlock your negotiating strength." This could be a handbook for the sales trainer, as well as an introduction or reinforcer for experienced salespeople.

Mandino, Og. *The Greatest Salesman in the World.* New York: Bantam Books, 1985

This little motivational gem was first published in 1968 and is still as relevant to today's salespeople. Told in the form of a parable, the book speaks to basic fears, motivations, and disciplines each salesperson must deal with in himself or herself.

Miller, Robert B., and Stephen E Heiman, with Tad Tuleja. *Conceptual Selling.* Berkeley, CA: Miller-Heiman, Inc. 1987.

Conceptual Selling is a guide to customer-focused selling. It covers the basics of win-win sales calls and the personal disciplines and attitudes that improve one's chance of success.

Rackham, Neil. *SPIN Selling.* New York: McGraw-Hill, 1988.

A highly credible resource (based on observation and analysis of thousands of sales calls) which emphasizes selling in a larger, more complex sales environment. The book provides solid reinforcement for focusing on the customer, asking questions and listening. Valuable to the sales trainer and to experienced salespeople.

Wilson, Larry, with Hersch Wilson. *Changing the Game: The New Way to Sell.* New York: Simon & Schuster, 1988.

The book looks at fundamental questions about success in a dynamically evolving field—from the perspective of a number of top performers whose words form the basis for the argument of each chapter. Through them, Wilson describes how customers and successful salespeople are changing the rules of the selling game. Experienced salespeople, particularly those whose markets are changing, will find much of interest in this book.

Wenschlag, Roger. *The Versatile Salesperson.* New York: John Wiley & Sons, Inc., 1987.

People buy from people, and those who can recognize the buyer's social style and can adapt to that style will build more buying relationships. For salespeople who have mastered the basics of conducting calls and managing time and territory, this book can help them identify buyer types, type preferences in making decisions, and how to modify one's own behavior to make the buyer more comfortable in reaching a decision to buy.

Index